ALSO BY I. M. DESTLER:

Presidents, Bureaucrats, Foreign Policy: The Politics of Organizational Reform

ALSO BY LESLIE GELB:

The Irony of Vietnam: The System Worked (with Richard Betts)

ALSO BY ANTHONY LAKE:

The "Tar Baby" Option: American Policy Toward Southern Rhodesia

I.M. Destler, Leslie H. Gelb
and Anthony Lake

OUR OWN WORST ENEMY

The Unmaking of American Foreign Policy

REVISED AND UPDATED EDITION

A TOUCHSTONE BOOK
Published by Simon & Schuster, Inc.
NEW YORK

First Touchstone Edition, 1985

Published by Simon & Schuster, Inc.
Simon & Schuster Building
Rockefeller Center
1230 Avenue of the Americas
New York, New York 10020
TOUCHSTONE and colophon are registered trademarks
of Simon & Schuster, Inc.

Designed by Eve Kirch

Manufactured in the United States of America

10 9 8 7 6 5 4 Pbk.

Library of Congress Cataloging in Publication Data

Destler, I. M.
Our own worst enemy.
(A Touchstone book)
Bibliography: p.
Includes index.
1. United States—Foreign relations—1945-
2. United States—Foreign relations administration.
I. Gelb, Leslie H. II. Lake, Anthony. III. Title.
E840.D45 1985 327.73 85-18376
ISBN 978-1-4767-9187-6

Contents

Preface

This book grows out of a concern each of us has come to feel, more and more intensely, about the way we Americans make foreign policy. In its initial conception, the book was to focus mainly on the damage done to our national interests by conflict within the U.S. executive branch, and specifically between the State Department and the White House staff. But the more we thought and talked about our problems, the more we found ourselves looking beyond the damaging battles within our bureaucracy to changes in Congress, in the press, in our elites and, above all, in the interplay between national politics and foreign policy.

As we sought to dissect these separate changes and then put the overall picture back together, we found ourselves looking at a larger process of coming apart, an unmaking of American foreign policy, a disintegration of our capacity to operate sensibly and persistently within a difficult world. This unmaking began with Vietnam. But it also had important roots beyond Vietnam, in the broader opening up of American society and institutions in the sixties and seventies. It has been going on for most of our adult lives. But it was not until we stepped back from our individual preoccupations that we began to see the picture whole.

We cannot claim to be above the battles we recount, or blameless in the broader coming apart this book seeks to analyze, for each of us has been a participant in some of the developments we describe. When we write about the new professional elite, for example, we must include ourselves in that group. When we argue in our conclusion that our problems are beyond bureaucratic reform, even beyond changes that can be undertaken in Washington, it is a recognition of our own limits and those of the "insider" community we inhabit. Readers may thus see this book as the functional equivalent of a public complaint by members of an orchestra that its playing has become discordant. We have tried, however, to be as objective as possible in describing the decline and apportioning blame. And we believe very deeply that until we start looking beyond the bureaucracy, beyond Washington, remedies will continue to elude us. In this book we seek to explain why.

Between the conception of this book and its completion, we have accumulated many obligations. We owe particular thanks to our legal adviser and agent, Ronald Goldfarb, who encouraged us to undertake this venture and persist in it, and who helped work out some problems along the way. We are grateful also to Alice Mayhew, our editor at Simon and Schuster, who has combined enthusiasm for the project with helpful advice on how to broaden our audience. And we benefited greatly from conversations with former officials who were generous in sharing their recollections, and their insights.

Amalia Honick, Jane Gilman, and David Kaplan provided useful research assistance. Samuel Berger, David Kaplan, Eleanor Hard Lake, Gordon Levin, Nelson Polsby, and Peter Szanton read the entire manuscript in draft and offered suggestions both critical and valuable. Alease Vaughn, Wendy Berg, Hiroko Jolley, Midge Bowser, and Lurleen Dowell typed successive draft chapters.

In addition, each of us accumulated his own separate debts as he sought to reconcile this venture with his obligations to his primary employer. Destler wishes to thank Thomas L. Hughes, President of the Carnegie Endowment for International Peace, for granting him leave time to work on the book, and C. Fred Bergsten, Director of the Institute for International Economics, to which he moved during the book's final stages. Gelb wishes to acknowledge the many editors of *The New York Times* who have labored to teach him how to write. Lake wishes to express special appreciation to Amherst College and the Frost Library for their support. But none of the above, helpful though they were, bear responsibility for any defects in the final product. For those, we can only blame one another.

Introduction: Foreign Policy Breakdown

In Washington, daily news stories and cocktail-party confessionals; in editorials and classrooms across the country; in the banalities and profundities of officials, diplomats, columnists and scholars—we hear the same lament: Something is wrong with American foreign policy. Debates rage over the reasons for our inability to come to terms with the world, or bring the world to terms with us. Who now argues that nothing is wrong?

There is no doubt that the world has changed. It has become more complicated, more dangerous, less susceptible to American influence. This is well known. It is time that Americans also recognize the ways in which we ourselves have changed when it comes to making our foreign policies.

It is the contention of this book that for two decades now, not only our government but our whole society has been undergoing a systemic breakdown when attempting to fashion a coherent and consistent approach to the world. The signs of the breakdown can be found in public attitudes and politicians' promises; in the behavior of the Congress, the press, and the foreign policy establishment; and within the offices of the White House, the State and Defense Departments, and other foreign policy agencies. And the breakdown has produced policies with a peculiar blend of self-righteousness and self-doubt.

At home, policy makers devour one another in a game that approaches a national blood sport, as White House aides and Cabinet officers do daily battle behind the scenes and through the press. Congress and the President play pin-the-tail-on-the-donkey (or -elephant) over who has the responsibility for foreign policy and who gets the blame for foreign failure. Political play acting is better rewarded than hard work; political speechmaking passes as serious policy making. Our debates give more weight to ideological "certainties" than to the ambiguities of reality. Tolerance and trust, the essential ingredients of a healthy democratic system, are always sought for oneself but rarely given to others.

The result is policies that speak more for the vagaries of our own politics than to the conditions of the world in which we must live. In January 1977, Jimmy Carter proclaimed a new American foreign policy that would set right the sins of his predecessors. Four years later, Ronald Reagan said he would reject and reverse the international course of Jimmy Carter. To a foreigner unversed in our ways, such erratic behavior by so powerful a nation can only seem bizarre, if not dangerous. But to most Americans, it seems perfectly understandable, for we have become all too accustomed to giving our own partisan struggles priority over consistency or coherence in our foreign policies.

By most measures, the United States is still the strongest power in the world and will remain so for many years to come. And our foreign-policy problems are by no means unmanageable. But we are taken less and less seriously by our friends as well as our adversaries. World problems and conflicts that could be tempered by competent and consistent American leadership are left to fester. We seem unable either to flow with change in the developing world or prevent change contrary to our interests. Our relations with the Soviet Union have been torn into shreds, and together with Moscow we have put ourselves in deadly straits—a situation in which peace hinges on the mutual terror of nuclear war, with little else to create restraint and moderation.

We have lost a coherent sense of United States national interests, the enduring purposes of policy that flow from values, geography, and our place in the hierarchy of world power. In almost all other nations, it takes a revolution to redefine these basic purposes. For the last two decades in the United States, it has required only a Presidential election or the prospect of one. In May 1983, former West German Chancellor Helmut Schmidt went public with a widely shared lament:

> As Chancellor I worked under four presidents, and it's quite an experience, I can tell you. . . . First Carter sent his vice-president to tell us almost everything done by his predecessors was wrong and implied that our cooperation was in vain and something different had to start. Then, along comes Reagan and tells us the same thing.

"The alliance needs continuity," Schmidt tells us. "We've put all our eggs in your basket."

But the American basket is badly frayed. The political bodies of Presidents and Secretaries of State are strewn all over the place. Ronald Reagan's four immediate predecessors all were felled, and foreign policy played a major role. Each, save Richard M. Nixon in 1972 and Ronald Reagan in 1984, faced a serious renomination challenge in the primaries, and each challenge exposed deep ideological cleavages on foreign affairs. And at Cabinet level and below, the foreign-policy stage has come to resemble the final gory scene of *Hamlet*, played in gray flannel and pinstripes.

Why do we act this way? The heart of the problem, it seems to us, is this:

> For two decades, the making of American foreign policy has been growing far more political—or more precisely, far more partisan and ideological. The White House has succumbed, as former Secretary of State Alexander Haig recently put it, to "the impulse to view the presidency as a public relations opportunity and to regard Government as a campaign for reelection." And in less exalted locations, we Americans—politicians and experts alike—have been spending more time, energy and passion in fighting ourselves than we have in trying, as a nation, to understand and deal with a rapidly changing world.

Some Americans have come to live with our condition by seeing it as readily curable; others by dismissing it as hopeless; and many by adjusting to it and believing that it is no worse than it has been before.

The easy cure is usually sought in an attractive fantasy: We need only find a Prince Charming whose kiss can awaken the Sleeping Beauty of an effective foreign policy. The problem can be put in order simply by putting the right man or woman in the right job. Thus, the sighs of satisfaction could be heard throughout most of Washington in the summer of 1982, when President Reagan replaced Secretary of State Alexander Haig with George P. Shultz. "Let George do it!" became a rallying cry in the White House and among the capitol's *congnoscenti.* But in Washington, even the most powerful fairy tale has a short half-life. And when Sleeping Beauty fails to stir after repeated embraces, many of those who were first to proclaim Prince Charming come to condemn him as the frog. Still, many hope that another Prince, perhaps a Henry Kissinger, could perform the necessary feats of magic.

For others, there is hope in bureaucratic engineering, in a search for organizational means to restore the Secretary of State to his "rightful place" and put the national-security adviser back in his. Such schemes have risen to prominence in the first and last months of every administration for the last dozen years. But in between they are mostly forgotten, for such schemes are neither as easy nor as crucial as they are portrayed. Bureaucratic fixes can help, but they will not produce grand results. Foreign policy is not merely the product of bureaucratic maneuver; it flows from our larger political system. Ideas and ideology are as important as the organization tables of the government. Yet often in academic circles, students of foreign policy are taught to think about the federal bureaucracy first and national politics second.

Then, there are those—often scholars—who conclude that the maladies are beyond correction. To them, the problem lies not so much in ourselves as in our stars, beyond our reach. It is in the malaise and bureaucratization of postindustrial societies, or in the inevitable fragmentation of power attendant on modern government and the collapse of traditional values. The world is simply too complex to be managed much better than it is. Certainly, there is some truth to all of this, and there is wisdom in understanding the limits imposed by forces larger than ourselves. Yet, hope and effort are too easily abandoned in the sweep of such analyses.

Finally, some take solace in the belief that the way we make our foreign policy today is not really so different from what it was in the first two decades after World War II. There have always been a left and a right, rivalries between White House courtiers and departmental barons, abrupt shifts in policy, deception, and people playing politics with the national interest. Today's vices may be proportioned somewhat differently, but the net result, so this argument goes, is the same.

It is our contention that this last judgment is profoundly wrong; that the ways in which we have made our foreign policy in the last twenty years are worse, even far worse in many respects, than in the two decades following World War II. And still more important is the fact that to whatever degree things are worse, we can far less afford such policy disarray. We no longer have the cushion of military and economic preponderance that we had in the 1950s and 1960s. We are no longer so strong; others are not so weak. The mistakes hurt more, and the wounds are not so easily healed. And in a nuclear age, the risks are ever more immense.

That we are failing badly and needlessly must be understood before we have a chance to set matters right, before it is clear what can and must be remedied. The problems are at once deeper than seeking salvation in a Prince Charming or some rearrangement of the bureaucratic puzzle palace—yet not so hopeless that we are past saving.

How *is* American foreign-policy making different from the way it was in the first twenty years after World War II? What was there about policy and politics that served us well then—and does not now?

There was certainly much to deplore about our behavior during that period. We succumbed to the redbaiting and McCarthyism that not only destroyed the careers of honorable and talented men, but postponed the day when more than a handful of politicians could dare to suggest moves to improve relations with Moscow. We failed in the late 1950s and early 1960s to exploit the emerging deep split between China and Russia. We did not see that Ho Chi Minh might be a nationalist as well as a Communist. And there was the awful case of President Kennedy's fearing to call off the Bay of Pigs invasion that had been planned under his predecessor. One should not view this period through rose-tinted glasses. Nor do we argue that

Americans can—or should—go back to the days of almost unchallenged Presidential supremacy, Congressional passivity, and a press as well as a public who, for the most part, took the President's pronouncements on trust.

Still, the years after 1945 were years of considerable policy creativity. The policies and programs put together under President Truman, virtually all of them continued under President Eisenhower, were a creative triumph—the Marshall Plan to rebuild the shattered European economies and stabilize their political systems; the North Atlantic Treaty Organization to defend the West; successful programs to bring our former blood enemies, Germany and Japan, into the democratic community; a substantial military-aid effort to bolster friends abroad under attack; encouragement of our European allies to grant independence to their colonies in Asia and Africa. These efforts had coherence and purposefulness. A central goal was to contain the spread of Soviet influence. At the same time, there was willingness to develop non-American centers of strength in Europe. Whatever the shortcomings of these programs in understanding or level of effort, they represented the most generous and far-reaching of any great power in history. To be sure, the United States benefited. But it also sacrificed, and others benefited as well.

Truman and Eisenhower, and Kennedy to a lesser extent, were also prepared to make politically unpopular decisions, often the hallmark of a keen sense of the national interest. Conservatives put a great deal of heat on Mr. Truman to do something to prevent a Communist victory in China prior to 1949. But almost without exception, those who knew the situation in China believed that providing more aid to the Nationalist anti-Communist forces would be throwing good money after bad and that the Nationalists were corrupt and divided beyond hope. For the former Senator from Missouri it would have been far easier to ask Congress for additional funds than to step aside from the civil war in China as he did. And Truman was to pay a high political price for accepting the advice of almost all his military and political experts in limiting the use of American force in the Korean War.

Eisenhower also took leadership stands that were probably unwise on political grounds. This was so in 1956, when he opposed the British, French, and Israeli invasion of Egypt under Gamal Abdel

Nasser. Nasser was ranked high on the hit list of the American public. But Eisenhower believed strongly that the United States had to uphold the principle that attacks by sovereign states against other sovereign states could not be condoned. And like his predecessor, the former World War II military hero kept in check enormous pressures for vast increases in military spending. Both Truman and Eisenhower understood the national-security value of a sound American economy, and neither was panicked into seeing the Soviet military machine as ten feet tall.

There is a strong tendency to attribute the successes of these first fifteen years after the war to "politics stopping at the water's edge." These were said to be the halcyon days of bipartisanship or nonpartisanship, of Democrats and Republicans putting national interests above party interests. But such a description has always been more myth than reality. Conservatives and liberals were at one another's throat constantly. There was never a time when Truman was not besieged. The Korean War and rolling back Soviet influence in Europe were major campaign themes for Eisenhower in 1952 against Adlai E. Stevenson, the Democratic candidate. Stevenson tried to make foreign policy a key issue in the 1956 campaign, and Mr. Kennedy succeeded in doing so in 1960.

But while politics was never in short supply, it was moderated by a near-consensus in elite and general public opinion. The leadership in the Executive Branch and the Congress each knew where the other stood, and both were ready to make deals that fit both the national interest and party interests. The prevailing anti-Communist ideology, though thoroughly ingrained in what was commonly called a consensus, did not preclude the practical. The doctrinaire quality of the consensus was finally to produce disaster in Vietnam and the destruction of the consensus itself. But it was also true, paradoxically, that the existence of the consensus created room for maneuver and doing sensible things. Support for generous aid levels and anticolonialism, while necessarily justified in terms of meeting the Communist threat, was generally considered to be politically acceptable and even statesmanlike.

Take the case of Senator Arthur H. Vandenberg, Republican of Michigan. As chairman of the Senate Foreign Relations Committee from 1947 to 1949, the former isolationist joined hands with the administration and brought the country into a new and unprecedented era of internationalism. But this wily old politician had his own reasons for reaching out. Despite his subsequent canonization as the patron saint of bipartisanship, Vandenberg was as much a partisan as a statesman.

Reflecting on the limits of cooperation, he wrote that "When and where it is possible, in clearly channeled and clearly defined projects, for the legislature, the executive and the two major parties to proceed from the beginning to the end of a specific adventure, so that all are consulted in respect to all phases of the undertaking, I think it is a tremendously useful thing." But, he added, "to think that can be done as an everyday practice in regard to all of the multiple problems of international import which now descend upon the State Department every day, in my opinion is totally out of the question."

The Senator knew that he *had* to cooperate on the central, European issues of the day: "The Republican Party has this dilemma: if it does not cooperate in the world, it will be blamed for destroying the peace, as in 1920. If it cooperates too much with the Democratic administration, it will be charged with having no policy of its own." His answer was to back Mr. Truman's European policy where "we could lose everything," and attack on Asian policy where "there is no solution I can think of anyway."

There were enough Republicans like Vandenberg and enough Democratic conservatives to ensure Presidents Truman, Eisenhower, Kennedy, and, for a while, Lyndon B. Johnson of a workable and steady majority to back most of their foreign ventures. From 1945 to 1965, Presidents had what might better be labeled a solid majorityship than a free bipartisan ride.

As long as Presidents stayed in the political center with a moderate kind of anti-Communism, they could navigate between the ideological extremists. The left was singularly unpowerful. Truman could get elected in 1948 even after the defection of the left led by former Vice-President Henry Wallace. The right was larger, vocal, far more powerful than the left. But when Senator Joe McCarthy fell, moderates could see that the right was far from invincible.

Power was in the political center, and the foreign-policy center was owned by the Establishment, a relatively homogeneous group of bankers, lawyers, and Foreign Service officers, largely from the northeastern part of the United States, largely pragmatic and centrist in beliefs.

The anti-Communist-policy consensus was at the heart of centrism and majorityship, and gave it steadiness and direction. But it led to rigidity as well, and in this rigidity lay the seeds of the center's destruction. The doctrines at the heart of the consensus, and their political force, called for American intervention in Vietnam. Yet these doctrines retained their appeal only so long as the United States did not have to endure a prolonged crisis, and as long as no extended sacrifice of blood or treasure was required. The iron triangle of consensus, centrism, and majorityship could survive brief failures and setbacks—the loss of China, ruptures in the Western alliance with Britain and France over their attack on the Suez Canal in 1956, the Bay of Pigs fiasco in 1961, and even the trauma of not going all out to win during the Korean War—but it did not survive Vietnam.

The endless and seemingly hopeless agony of the Vietnam War destroyed the consensus, sprayed power out from the center toward the political extremes, and made the forging of majorities a trying affair. Moderates and liberals joined with the inheritors of the Henry Wallace tradition in a coalition of the left that, for the first time, enjoyed real political power. This coalition began to question the basic principles of postwar American foreign policy as rigidly ill-suited to the new and far more pluralistic world and ill-equipped to understand the limits of American power in such a world. Those liberals, conservatives and rightists who remained supporters of the war regarded the liberal-moderate defection as nothing short of betrayal. Their sentiments did not go unrequited, as the new left coalition roundly pilloried them as Cold Warriors and warmongers.

By 1965, the systemic breakdown in the American foreign-policy system had begun, and five years later it was well advanced. The center, the ballast for majorityship and consensus, was shattered. The extremes now had the preponderance of power. For being doctrinaire, the center was torn apart by the left in the 1960s over Vietnam. Then, because of the center's advocacy of détente and arms control with Moscow, the right rapped it for weakness. In time, the center came to stand for nothing. Centrists seemed to represent a geography, not a philosophy. Their position was defined solely by placement precisely between the extremes, wherever they might be. What they failed and refused to recognize was that the extremes were not simply engaged in a typical joust for power; by the late

1970s they were aiming at the defeat of the centrists as well as each other.

The making of American foreign policy had entered a new and far more ideological and political phase. The effects could be seen throughout our system of foreign-policy making: Public opinion was split, and with it our political parties. Ideological struggles within parties became as intense as those between them. Presidents became increasingly vulnerable and made themselves more so as they promised new foreign ideological triumphs that failed to materialize. The Establishment, which once helped keep things together, was now replaced by foreign-policy activists who ferociously tore the fabric apart. Battles for power among Presidential courtiers and departmental barons became a national spectacle. Congress and the news media tugged at the seams of what remained. Each of these changes reinforced the others, and all became rooted in new patterns of public opinion.

Ten years ago, political scientist John E. Mueller developed an influential model of public opinion. It held that up until the late 1960s public opinion on foreign policy fell into three categories: a leadership stratum of small numbers with shared views on ends and means; an attentive and educated group who "followed" Presidential and elite leadership in their internationalism and Cold War interventionist policies; and a noninternationalist mass public that knew and cared little for foreign affairs and generally backed a two-track policy of peace and strength.

By William Schneider's recent perceptive analysis, this pattern began to come apart in the late 1960s, because of ideological polarization within the leadership stratum. "Counter-elites emerged on both the right and the left to challenge the supremacy of the old foreign-policy establishment," writes Schneider. This, in turn, split the attentive followers and destroyed the consensus. The mass public, in its turn, became more activist and difficult to lead, in part due to the intrusion of television news on foreign affairs into their living rooms. More than before, the public wanted it both ways: no American military involvement and no Communist gains.

To make political calculations trickier still, in recent years the swings in public opinion on key issues have become wider and more frequent. In the space of a decade, the polls have shown the public calling for big defense cuts, then major increases, and then—once again—cutbacks in planned military spending. Clearly, the public had become less patient and less predictable.

Reflecting and reinforcing public opinion, party politics and beliefs have also fractured. Just as Barry Goldwater in 1964 took the Republican nomination away from Nelson Rockefeller and wrested control of the party from its liberal Eastern Establishment, Eugene McCarthy's followers in 1968 initiated a fundamental challenge to the Democratic party's powers that were. In the 1970s, Presidential primaries became ever more important, and ideological activists in both parties extended their sway. There is no doubt that today liberal Republicans and conservative Democrats play a sharply limited role in their Presidential conventions, compared to the pre-1965 years. In 1960, both parties in their platforms praised bipartisanship, called for more military strength and more aid, and approved the search for arms control with the Soviet Union—all in strikingly similar language. By 1980, the two parties took sharply divergent stands on dealing with Moscow, human rights, and most Third World questions.

Presidents themselves bore heavy responsibility for the fissures. If Presidential conduct of foreign policy up to 1964 can be described as "imperial," it is not stretching reality too far to see it thereafter as irresponsible. Before the breakdown, Presidents derived much of their power and authority over national-security matters from the belief that they stood above politics, that they would sacrifice short-term political gains for long-term goals, and that they somehow embodied the enduring national interest. Too many times since 1964 they have used foreign policy to enhance their personal positions, thus personalizing, politicizing and sometimes even trivializing the content and conduct of foreign affairs.

In so doing, they become almost like any other politician, and their words, facts, motives and actions became ever more subject to scrutiny and doubt. They thus squandered their own authority to construct steady majorities. By coming down into the political pits, they legitimized opposition on political grounds.

Presidents, especially from John F. Kennedy on, trapped themselves. By promising everything in their campaigns—to stay out of war and to stop Communist expansion—they set expectations that could not be met and that could lead only to public disillusionment.

It is inevitable that politics and policy come together. Democratic debate is more likely than doctrine to produce sensible foreign-policy decisions. There neither can nor should be a return to the days of doctrinaire consensus. The question, rather, is how responsibly we use the foreign-policy institutions that have become more open, more democratic. Will they be used to fashion mature policies of consistency and coherence, or will they be exploited for short-term political advantage? Too often the motivating force for our Presidents in making key decisions during the past two decades has been either gaining short-term political advantage—keeping political adversaries at bay, diverting attention from domestic problems, and scoring political points—or satisfying some set of values that bore little relation to reality but pleased political ideologues. (An ideologue can be defined as one who knows the answers before he knows the facts.)

What were some of the most egregious examples?

John F. Kennedy went ahead with the Bay of Pigs invasion in 1961 (even though it would have been clear, if properly examined, that it would fail) in part because of his campaign rhetoric and fear of being accused of being too soft. He told people privately that the war in Vietnam was hopeless, but did nothing to disengage or reduce American stakes—in fact, he heightened them with his own rhetoric and stepped up American military involvement.

Lyndon B. Johnson allowed the Vietnam problem to fester during the campaign of 1964, while he misled the public about where the logic of his rhetorical commitments and beliefs was taking the nation. Thereafter, he failed to make hard choices about the war. He refused to call up the reserves, which limited the military manpower available but kept some critics quiet: and he put off proposals to raise taxes to pay for the war, producing virulent inflation in subsequent years but postponing the painful immediate costs.

Richard M. Nixon oversold, along with Henry Kissinger, the idea that détente with the Soviet Union meant "a stable structure of peace" and "an era of negotiation not confrontation," when they both fully realized that serious problems were inherent in relations with Moscow. This helped to repel the challenge from his left and win the 1972 election, but standards were set for Soviet behavior that they knew Moscow would never meet.

Nixon and Kissinger also left a number of serious ambiguities in the text of the SALT I offensive-arms agreement of 1972, so as not to leave the Moscow summit empty-handed. Later, when Moscow exploited these ambiguities, they were almost forced to accuse the Soviets of cheating. Again, they ended up casting doubt on their own creation.

Gerald Ford decided against consummating the SALT II negotiations—although Kissinger and others felt that that was possible—for fear of giving political ammunition to his challenger for the Republican party nomination, Ronald Reagan. Later, Ford and others reckoned that this hesitancy may have cost him the Presidency in his race against Jimmy Carter. Not only arms control but his own political fortunes suffered.

Jimmy Carter carried his human-rights rhetoric and efforts to prevent the spread of nuclear-weapons capabilities to points where he succeeded in gratuitously alienating our allies. He exploited Iran's holding dozens of Americans hostage by playing on the crisis as a way of neutralizing Senator Edward M. Kennedy's challenge to him in the Democratic primaries. The same issue then helped to destroy him, as did his unsuccessful effort to pose as a latter-day Cold Warrior against Reagan's charges of softness.

Ronald Reagan, for clearly political reasons, lifted the grain embargo that Carter had placed on the Soviets in the wake of their invasion of Afghanistan, even as he pressed our allies not to sell industrial products to Moscow. That pleased the American farmer, but made no sense to our allies. Nor did it make much sense later when he invoked trade penalties against any ally selling certain oil and gas equipment to Moscow, when virtually all his advisers told him there was no chance the allies would refrain from selling.

In Lebanon, home of religious and factional rivalries dating from Biblical days, Reagan also shifted back and forth between ideology and political expediency. Singling out the East-West dimension of the conflict, he insisted that any retreat from support of the crumbling government of President Amin Gemayel would destroy American credibility worldwide. But then, with the Presidential election fast approaching at home, he reversed course and ordered the withdrawal of United States marines, a course he had previously dismissed as an unthinkable "surrender."

Reagan also became the first post-World War II President, as opposed to Presidential candidate, to maintain that the United States was militarily inferior to the Soviet Union. It is one thing to make the case that military trends are adverse and that defense spending needs to be increased. But it is quite another for a President to proclaim a presumed inferiority to the world, which can only discourage friends and embolden adversaries. Yet Reagan continued to so characterize the American military position, even after his successful 1984 re-election campaign.

To these words and deeds subsequent chapters will add many others. They made no sense on foreign-policy grounds. Nor were they the acts of stupid people, acting carelessly and without information or without the benefit of other points of view. From all evidence, they were calculated, driven by politics and ideology.

This is not to say that Presidents for the last twenty years did not make defensible and sensible decisions. But such decisions were in shorter supply than those made by their predecessors. Of equal importance, the good that they did was often colored, even overwhelmed, by the irresponsible. Lyndon Johnson's creditable efforts in Europe and the Third World were ignored because of Vietnam. Richard Nixon's policy of détente with Moscow and the opening to China were weighed down by his divisive rhetoric, by prolonging the war in Vietnam, by invading Cambodia, and by helping to "destabilize" a democratically elected government in Chile. Gerald Ford's steadiness in his first year paled beside his later walking away from his own policies under pressure from Mr. Reagan. Jimmy Carter's fine performances in achieving the Camp David accords, and gaining Senate approval of the Panama Canal Treaties—contributing to a greater sense of identity between the United States and developing nations—lost their luster in the political maneuvers of 1980. Ronald Reagan's success in establishing greater respect for American power was undermined by early anti-arms-control statements and his failure to deal sensibly with the Soviets.

But the breakdown is not just in the Presidency and Presidents. It is in our political system as a whole. It is, as Thomas L. Hughes has written, a case of collective irresponsibility "when repeated failures produce no discernible correction in basic behavior patterns or institutions." Presidential irresponsibility has been accompanied by the growing irresponsibility of our elites, Congress, and the news media. They have fed on each other and spread the disorders.

We have irresponsible elites, who often seem more dedicated to demolishing one another's world visions and careers than to undertaking the hard, slogging work of putting together a sustainable line of policy action. The old Establishment of relatively homogeneous, part-time, pragmatic and mostly bipartisan Northeasterners has been subsumed by a much larger, more diverse elite of full-time foreign-policy professionals. Their diversity and expertise are valuable. But they also are far more political and ideological than their predecessors.

The Establishment, for all its shortcomings and tendency toward being doctrinaire, served as a brake on politics. It stood for common sense, a willingness to hear out and accommodate other views within a certain range, and a sense of responsibility and proportion about policies and institutions. Today's foreign-policy elites help to drive policy into domestic politics and push debates toward the extremes. They are no longer a steady source of broad support for national policies; they support only those Presidents they actually serve—and not always then.

We have an irresponsible Congress, which often in the last two decades has posed obstacles to coherent Presidential policies without offering real alternatives. Members of Congress have grabbed headlines and sometimes power. But while making it harder for Presidents to exercise their responsibilities, Congress has not accepted its own attendant responsibility to share in tough decisions or propose serious alternatives.

To be sure, Presidents Johnson and Nixon did a lot to provoke Senators and Representatives of all political persuasions. Secret wars, double bookkeeping and duplicity are bound to generate Congressional reaction. So, in the 1970s legislators put more and more laws on the books to make themselves a part of the policy process. Yet, views in Congress itself were so diverse and power so dispersed that Congress was forever pulling in several directions at the same time.

As with Presidents, Congress did some commendable things. At its best, Congress probed and questioned administrations, and forced them to justify important and dubious acts. Congress properly would not take at face value the various schemes offered by the Carter and Reagan administrations for basing the new MX missile. Congress properly has a role to play in determining whether or not American forces should go to war. But for the most part, Congress has failed either to implement its laws or, preferably, to work with the Executive to make them succeed.

Just as Congress was emboldened by the Vietnam and Watergate experiences to assert itself, so were the national news media. Investigative journalism, necessary for ferreting out the abuses of those years, became the model. The news media generally, and television in particular, do not do well in dealing with ideas and institutions. They are more at home portraying personalities and headlining extreme statements. So, in an era of more politics and more ideology, the media have consistently amplified the worst features of the system and thus quickened the breakdown.

The price we are paying for the breakdown is very large indeed. At precisely the moment when we need to husband our strength and use it more efficiently; at a time when there is no choice but involvement in world affairs; in an era when others look to us for maturity and sophistication in dealing with international problems of growing complexity—at that moment we are taken less seriously than at any time since World War II.

In December 1981, in the Israeli Knesset (or Parliament), it was the night when Prime Minister Menachem Begin's government announced the annexation of the Golan Heights, Syrian territory. Ever since the 1967 Arab-Israeli war, when Israel captured that stretch of high ground from Syria, it had been a major element of American policy to prevent the Golan issue from permanently blocking Syrian-Israeli talks. An American correspondent asked a member of the Knesset if there would not be trouble with Washington over the annexation. "For two days, maybe," came the reply. "But we have seen that you can get over your problems with us very quickly."

In Saudi Arabia in 1982, during a trip to that country by Defense Secretary Caspar Weinberger (who was a well-known friend of the Saudis), a Saudi general was asked by an American reporter what his government had promised the Americans in return for the advanced arms just offered. It was clear to all that the Administration was facing mountainous opposition in obtaining Congressional approval of such sales. But the contempt in the answer from the Saudi was as plain as the disdain in Jerusalem—"You are just arms merchants and we pay cash."

For years, Western European diplomats have regularly clutched at the lapels of their American colleagues to plead, "Where is your government going in its defense planning? On arms control? Toward China? On the neutron bomb, human rights, nuclear non-proliferation? What are your priorities? What will they be a year from now?"

African diplomats too are left to wonder about American directions. Do we believe that closer ties to the South African government can actually help encourage an end to apartheid, as suggested by the Nixon, Ford and Reagan administrations? Or does the United States propose to distance itself from South Africa's whites so long as the blacks there are denied their rights, as was the trend under Johnson and Carter?

Nations cannot afford to disregard us, and they do not. American power remains enormous, and Washington is a factor in almost every world issue. But what can the United States accomplish in the Middle East, for example, when Israeli leaders know that because of American politics they have little to fear from flouting American interests and when Saudi leaders think we care more for cash than for policy? And why should Europeans follow us when they cannot predict where we shall lead tomorrow? That is what it means to be taken increasingly less seriously, or at the very least, less seriously than we should be.

The cost is substantial. For it is only when a great power such as ours can bring its weight to bear steadily over time that we have a chance of breaking some international deadlocks. The persistence and the weight are the greatest weapons in diplomacy. But such consistency and patience comes only with a widely accepted popular view of our national interests.

When a nation's conduct abroad is governed so much by the whims of politics and the dictates of ideology, by who the leadership happens to be every four years, it has no such definitions. To be sure, other countries alter and shade their policies. But, by contrast to the United States, they are almost all models of stability.

For them (as for us in the years after World War II), policy has been guided in the main by an enduring and consistent set of values, by geography, by certain economic needs, and by purposes shared among elites. These have carried over from government to government in almost all countries, whether the leaders were Conservatives or Socialists. The foreign policies of West Germany changed in no essential when Mr. Schmidt's Social Democratic party was replaced by the Christian Democrats under Helmut Kohl; nor France's by virtue of Socialist François Mitterand's succeeding the more conservative Valéry Giscard d'Estaing; nor the Soviet Union's when Leonid I. Brezhnev died and Yuri V. Andropov succeeded him.

For most nations, only war and revolution have overturned centuries of national interest. That happened in the Russian revolution of 1917; in Mao Tse-tung's revolution in China after World War II; in Fidel Castro's takeover of Cuba in 1959; when the Ayatollah Khomeini overthrew the Shah of Iran in 1979; and when the nations of Africa gained their independence. For others, it took fundamental changes; for us, merely an election or a change in political imperatives, bringing a call for sweeping new designs.

The United States was always different, as the French observer Alexis de Tocqueville noticed more than a century ago. So pragmatic and stable in our internal politics we were, yet so ideological and quixotic in foreign affairs. Other nations were deemed to be so decadent that we would not go near them, or so sinful that we had to redeem them.

For more than a century, we could afford this. We could live in isolation from the political wars of Europe, then go forth to impose our ideals, and then retreat again behind the ocean and our wealth. After World War II, we could not afford the isolationist illusion. And it seemed to others that our country understood this, understood that its well-being was now inextricably bound with the outside world, understood that international life was complicated and ambiguous. We had learned the lesson that we had to cooperate as well as compete with our adversaries and that in the nuclear age we could not safely keep the peace by strength alone. Participation in the United Nations, the Marshall Plan, foreign aid, international banking institutions, NATO—all were demonstrations of a new maturity.

For at the heart of the creative burst after World War II was a mature internationalism, which recognized that America's interests were served, in the long run, by seeking common purpose and mutual advantage with other nations. Hence the importance of helping Europe and Japan recover their strength, not only in opposition to the Soviet Union but also for the sake of a strengthened world economy.

The post-World War II leaders took the world for what it was, a place filled with enduring conflicts. They sought not to remake it in our image, but to act within the realm of the possible, to dampen those forces that threatened world conflagration, to nurture those that built cooperation through enlightened self-interest.

Then something happened. Perhaps in part from the shock and humiliation of Vietnam, America began to turn from this internationalist view of its interests to new forms of nationalism. This turn was later reinforced by the frustration of the Iran hostage crisis. It was not a return to the nationalistic isolationism of the 1920s and 1930s. The isolationist impulse had been beaten back. It was a new, more complex form of nationalism.

For many conservatives, it was and is a rejection of accommodation with allies or adversaries for the sake of mutual gain—the belief that with a new assertion of national will and military strength, the United States could somehow impose its way on the world. For the first time in decades, it was on the right in America that one found the most important assaults on our European alliance.

On the left, the new nationalism took the form of a doctrinaire insistence on the universal applicability of our ideals, whatever the cultural and political realities of other societies. While Cyrus Vance, an internationalist of the old school, spoke of promoting human rights with pragmatism and flexibility, his President was portraying the same policy in terms of a moral crusade. In this, Carter was repeating the mistake of Woodrow Wilson, who had failed to sell his vision of a postwar world because he put it in terms of an almost personal morality. Both seemed more concerned with the purity of their vision than with gaining the cooperation necessary—at home and abroad—for its fulfillment.

And for many liberal politicians who had an eye on the labor vote, there was an emerging economic nationalism in their support for protection against foreign competition.

The new nationalisms of both right and left recalled some earlier American attitudes. They played on a lack of knowledge about the world. Americans speak few foreign languages, and language is the only way into the bloodstream of another culture. And the new nationalisms reflected a traditional American impatience with the intractability of international problems.

Ideologues on the left and the right of our political system exploited these attitudes, promised solutions where there were only enduring problems, and withheld their support from any effort to manage those problems if it did not conform entirely to their own philosophies. Our system went into shock, into a systemic breakdown.

It is our aim to substantiate this harsh indictment before we turn to considering answers to our distress. There is no corrective until there is clear diagnosis, until we understand that we really are worse off than we were two decades ago. In the following chapters, we examine how the domestic politics behind our foreign policies have become increasingly ideological and partisan; how this trend has created, and been reinforced by, changes within the foreign-policy establishment; how new forms of irresponsibility have come with the enhanced importance of Congress and the press; how all these developments have been reflected in the bureaucratic wars within the executive branch; and how Presidents have succumbed to the temptation to manage the details as well as the direction of our diplomacy. The starting point is an examination of American politics and how our Presidents have fed upon the breakdown only to be themselves devoured.

I Presidents: The Triumph of Politics

NEAR the end of the first meeting with his advisers after the North Korean attack in June 1950, President Truman reprimanded Under Secretary of State James Webb for suggesting they "talk about the political aspects of the situation." "We're not going to talk about politics," Truman snapped. "I'll handle the political affairs." President Nixon is reported to have told Vice-President Agnew at a National Security Council meeting not to pursue a point about the Jewish vote—"I'll worry about that," Nixon said.

Like sex in Victorian times, the political dimension of foreign-policy decisions was, until recently, a subject rarely mentioned in polite company within the government. The political angle in major foreign-policy decisions appeared only rarely in the archives or in the memoirs of statesmen and their court historians. Indeed, according to some of his subordinates, Secretary of State Henry Kissinger ordered them never to include references to the dread subject in their written work. And Ronald Reagan is said to have laid down a similar injunction for Cabinet meetings. But in one way or another, for decades, politics has been on the minds of most when decisions have been made.

Especially in the years of "bipartisanship" just after World War II, foreign policy ostensibly has been above politics. Even intensely political leaders like Harry S. Truman took the high road, or tried to appear to be doing so. Today, when polite company is less polite than it used to be, the explicit discussion of politics in foreign-policy-decision making is still guarded—expressed mainly in terms of the effects of special-interest groups on specific issues: Israel, Greece, South Africa, textiles. Within the government, "Congressional reaction" is often used as a code word for broader political considerations when discussing a foreign-policy decision.

Yet despite such pretense, the reality is that foreign-policy making since World War II has become increasingly partisan in its aims and origins. Before the Roosevelt-Willkie campaign of 1940, foreign policy played only a minor role in our Presidential elections, with the partial exceptions of the 1790s, 1840, 1900, and perhaps 1916 and 1920. Except for Theodore Roosevelt and Woodrow Wilson, who created more ambitious standards for themselves, our Presidents were expected only to keep America out of trouble abroad.

World War II and the triumph of internationalism in this country did more than inject America into the world; foreign policy also was injected into American politics as a constant issue. Foreign policy and domestic politics have become inseparable, especially during election "years," which now stretch into eighteen months or more.

In a democracy, this is inevitable. In an era in which international events have such real meaning for the lives of Americans, every President must be held accountable for his decisions about how to try to shape those events. Nor can a President disregard the importance of building political support for his policies if they are to endure or even be implemented.

The importance of the military as well as economic strands in our foreign policies has also naturally propelled foreign-policy issues into our politics.

Since World War II, America has in one way or another been on a psychological-war footing, either cold or hot. Korea and the draft, and then especially Vietnam, brought foreign policy into every town in America. Foreign-policy decisions on such matters thus increasingly became *political* decisions. And now, when the Soviet military buildup receives such publicity in the national press, and the costs of our own buildup loom larger in a time of economic uncertainty, the military content of our foreign policies still brings foreign issues home to most Americans.

The growing importance of economic issues in our international relations has had a still greater impact on the politicization of foreign policy. Before World War II, international economic policy had been at the heart of American foreign policy almost continuously since the earliest days of the Republic. In recent years, its domestic importance has again been on the rise. When United States exports were some 6 percent of our Gross National Product, as they were in 1965, and when Japanese trade still meant toys more than Toyotas, international economic policy did not mean that much in political terms. Now, with exports at over 12 percent of GNP, with one out of every eight American manufacturing jobs and some 40 percent of our farmland dependent on exports, international economic policy is crucial. And global "stagflation" makes the people and politicians of the United States, like those everywhere, look to the machinations of foreigners for explanations of their domestic woes. Thus protectionism becomes good politics, if terrible policy.

Whether it is trade policy and protecting our auto workers; or a grain embargo over Afghanistan and the welfare of American farmers; or American interest rates and relations with our Allies; economic factors inevitably erase the line between foreign- and domestic-policy decisions. This means that a President must take the reins on such issues; no foreign-policy agency can impose its will on the domestic departments and constituencies involved. More important still, the White House will always want to control the political dimension of these issues.

So, foreign policy and domestic politics inevitably come together. The question is how much and how the two are related. When Presidents began more blatantly to use foreign-policy issues for narrow partisan advantage, this marriage of politics and foreign policy came to be managed in ways that are increasingly destructive for all concerned—for our foreign policy, for the public whose interests are at stake and, ironically, for the Presidents and politicians who have tied the marriage knot.

At the most obvious level, the story of politics and foreign policy can be told through the tales of wretched excess in our ever longer Presidential campaigns.

The pressures of a Presidential campaign create both the excesses and the self-serving justifications for them. Few candidates seem able to resist the view that the importance of giving the nation the benefit of their services, and saving it from the clutches of their opponents, justify behavior that in more normal times would make all but the most shameless blush.

Issues are raised in ways that make little or no sense. Eisenhower let his aides promote the illusory "liberation" of Eastern Europe in 1952, when he clearly knew better. Adlai Stevenson, in 1956, called for a nuclear-test ban in careless terms that led George Ball, his close adviser, later to write in his memoirs that Stevenson "violated the rules of prudence; he failed to articulate his nuclear proposal in a clear and definitive way. . . . Any new idea in a political campaign . . . should, first of all, be vetted by experts familiar with its pitfalls, political as well as technical. . . ." The Quemoy–Matsu debate between Kennedy and Nixon first magnified and then blurred the differences between them in ways that left the issue totally confused. In the same campaign, Vice-President Nixon attacked Kennedy for advocating support of anti-Castro exiles, even though within the councils of government Nixon was one of the strongest proponents of such support.

In 1968, Hubert Humphrey adopted an extremely vague formula that would govern an end to the bombing of North Vietnam, one that would *sound* different from Johnson's but would not necessarily *be* different in substance. In this case, George Ball was more forgiving. Explaining why he and others had urged this "fuzzy shibboleth" on Humphrey, he wrote that "No one expects the rational or relevant at the end of a Presidential race."

In 1972, an announcement by the normally thoughtful Edmund Muskie that he would cut $18 billion from the defense budget sent his advisers scurrying to figure out where the cuts might come. Four years later, Gerald Ford let the pressures of debate lead him to portray the state of freedom in Poland in a way that left all observers dumbfounded. Jimmy Carter took positions on Korea and Yugoslavia that he probably would not have taken as President. All these men were normally far more sophisticated in their thinking about foreign policy.

And every four years, challengers begin to portray the United States in ways that can only encourage our adversaries and dismay our friends: America has grown weak; our enemies are flourishing. Neither party has held a monopoly on the refrain. The memory of the Republican assault on Truman in 1952 is still in the collective memory of the Democratic party. Few probably remember, however, Adlai Stevenson's charge in 1956 that we were losing the Cold War through policies of drift. Republicans well recall Kennedy's "missile gap" charges and the USIA poll he used to show America's declining prestige. Few probably remember Richard Nixon's failed effort to create a "security gap" issue in 1968. Henry Kissinger, in

1976, was outraged by Ronald Reagan's charge that under President Ford the United States had become "Number Two." He advised Ford to take Reagan on, for his charge was endangering our position in the world by making us look weak. Four years later, addressing the Republican National Convention, Kissinger was charging that the Carter Administration had let the "political balance of power" tip in the direction of the Soviets, endangering the survival of the free world.

The legacy of campaigns in which such charges are bandied about is ideological, doctrinaire behavior by new Presidents in their first year in office. The new leader is all the more convinced that a "new" approach is needed to rectify the terrible errors of his predecessor. His subordinates, the most ambitious and committed of his political followers who were awarded key positions in the new administration, follow suit. In the first two years of the Reagan administration, for example, intractable national problems, both foreign and domestic, were regularly explained in terms of previous Democratic error rather than in terms of the problems themselves.

All of this, and the increasing length of the campaign season, offers foreign governments and groups further opportunity to exploit the vulnerabilities of a President running for reelection, as was seen in the efforts of the Saigon government in 1968 to outwait the Democrats in the hope of a better deal with the Republicans, in Hanoi's hopes of getting the best possible deal before Richard Nixon was reelected in 1972, or the way in which the Iranians exploited the American electoral season of 1980. And the temptation of foreign leaders to seek to influence the outcome of an American election can prove seriously damaging—as became apparent in the harm to German-American relations resulting from the mutual personal dislike of Chancellor Schmidt and President Carter. This may have had its roots in Schmidt's public preference for Gerald Ford in 1976. Thus our campaign carnivals can confuse the issues, our allies, our adversaries and ourselves.

But these problems are neither the worst nor the most profound part of the story of how our foreign policies have combined with our partisan struggles. For that we must look at a pattern of behavior that is both more subtle and more damaging, as our politicians ensnare themselves in the trap of promises unkept.

The conventional wisdom among academic analysts has been that foreign-policy issues are not voting issues, that public opinion does not constrain or impel Presidents in their decisions on such issues. Yet, since World War II most Presidential politicians and Presidents have acted otherwise. They have believed that voters tend to judge the personal qualities of a candidate for the Presidency, at least in part, by how well he will manage our international affairs. Will he be able to stand up to the Russians? Will he keep us at peace? And the politicians have found it expedient, even necessary, to promise that they can and will do both, at a cost acceptable to all. The promise has helped them to gain election, and then damaged them politically when they did not deliver.

This had seldom been the case before World War II. Americans generally had seen the world as a wicked place, torn by wars fought for ignoble purposes. Except for a period of illusion at the time of the First World War, the notion of a permanent peace was seen to be a chimera. For the first century of our national existence, the cardinal principle of American foreign policy was to avoid the wars fought by corrupt European princes for their own aggrandizement. The Spanish-American War was a reminder, for many Americans, of the wisdom of that view. Then for a time Woodrow Wilson was able to convince Americans that involvement in a European war could even end all war. But disillusionment with Wilson and his vision helped to restore the traditional view. Until 1940 most American Presidents thus had faced one political imperative when it came to foreign policy: that of keeping us out of war.

After 1945, the formula became more complex. The predominance of American power, the growing hostility of an ideological enemy in the Soviet Union, and the lessons of the 1930s combined to make isolation from the world impossible in conceptual or practical terms. Now there were two central foreign-policy goals: keep peace—and also stop Communism.

The problem has not been with the goals of preserving peace and constraining the Soviets. What has gone wrong is that these goals have been transformed, through excesses of political rhetoric, into unshaded political absolutes. American political leaders, in this relatively brief period of American global engagement, have fed the American public a simple-minded, cost-free view of the world.

Nations with a long history of engagement in international affairs know that with successes also must come failures. Most Europeans also know that there are costs, that a policy of opposition to an expansionist power will probably involve the loss of treasure and life.

Such resignation to realities, such patience, is somehow alien to the American spirit. It implies a moral laxity. For many Americans, the unstated assumption has been this: If Communism is evil, and we are just, how can we settle for less than total victory? And do not the virtuous deserve victory without suffering?

Candidates and Presidents have been only too willing to play on such expectations. America could defeat the Communists, not only most of the time, but all of the time. We could build a permanent peace if we defeated aggression everywhere. And often it was promised that this could be done with less military spending, less sacrifice, less danger than before.

Through the rhetoric of such promises, politicians and Presidents helped to create the myth of American omnipotence. And from that came a sense of American omniresponsibility. If America was able to remake the world, could find only victories and no defeats, then surely any failure to do so was a failure of will, a failure to meet the responsibilities that came with such great power.

The agony and humiliation of Vietnam created a reaction to this view. With disillusionment came an impulse toward retrenchment. But the popular responses to the Iran hostage affair, to the Reagan rhetoric of 1980 and 1984, to the invasion of Grenada—all showed that, despite a new cynicism and caution, a majority of Americans still rebelled against a recognition of limits to our power.

Having repeatedly encouraged the view that anything is possible for a determined America, Presidents then became trapped by it. Time after time, they were caught between the rock of their promises and far-flung commitments and the hard place of the world, in which American power has been immense but increasingly limited by the growing power of others, allies as well as adversaries. Their promises could not be kept.

Our first postwar Presidents, Harry S. Truman and Dwight D. Eisenhower, set the trap. Truman made the containment of Communism not only a basic goal but a global doctrine. Eisenhower, and especially his lieutenants, suggested that Communism not only could be contained but could be rolled back—and that we could prevail with reduced military expenditures.

Both these Presidents, however, were usually able to resist taking America on foreign adventures beyond her capabilities, whatever the political pressures to live up to the responsibilities of omnipotence. For Truman, the tragic exception was his doomed effort to liberate North Korea as well as help protect the South, a goal he quickly abandoned after the disastrous retreat from the Yalu in the winter of 1950–51.

Their successors were neither so fortunate nor so wise. They not only suffered politically when they were unable to deliver on their promises, but they also were driven into policy failures, especially in Indochina, by the conflicting imperatives of acting wherever the Communist challenge was raised, but adhering to the constraints of peace and keeping the costs of war at the lowest possible level. The result was policies of bold commitment but compromised means. In this sense, the Bay of Pigs and the Vietnam War were cut from the same cloth.

The pattern was set most clearly on March 12, 1947, as Harry S. Truman faced a joint session of Congress and made his historic plea for aid to Greece and Turkey. According to Truman, the speech initially had been drafted in the State Department, with a focus on the situation in Greece itself. Partly in order to garner conservative Republican votes for his aid program, Truman insisted that there be a more general thrust to his declaration; the State draft, he later wrote, sounded "like an investment prospectus" with its background data and statistical figures about Greece. The conservatives needed rhetorical red meat if they were to be convinced that Truman meant business. The result was the "Truman Doctrine." "I believe," he grandly proclaimed, "that it must be the policy of the United States to support free peoples who are resisting attempted subjugation by armed minorities or by outside pressures. . . . The free peoples of the world look to us for support in maintaining their freedoms."

On April 5, Truman drove the point home in a Jefferson-Jackson Day speech: "We must take a positive stand. It is no longer enough merely to say, 'We don't want war.' We must act in time—ahead of time—to stamp out the smoldering beginnings of any conflict that may threaten to spread over the world. . . ."

Thus the worldwide sweep of the policy of containment was proclaimed, with its corollary of preventive intervention. And, at least in retrospect, Truman meant exactly what he said. The issue was not only Greece or Europe. It was global. "After I delivered the speech," he later wrote of his address to the Congress,

> the world reaction to it proved that this approach had been the right one. All over the world, voices of approval made themselves heard, while Communists and their fellow travelers struck out at me savagely. The line had been drawn sharply. In my address I had said that every nation was now faced with a choice between alternative ways of life.

The global terms of his pronouncement were not welcome to some leading foreign-policy officials, and they were questioned publicly by such analysts as Walter Lippmann. Two days after the Truman Doctrine was proclaimed, George F. Kennan, a major author of the containment policy in Europe, was meeting with a class at the National War College. While he supported the President's decision to come to the aid of Greece and Turkey, Kennan raised questions about the sweeping language of Truman's declaration. The most important of these had to do with American capacities. Would the United States be able to effectively help *all* nations facing an internal threat? Specifically, would it be possible in China, where the performance and predicament of Chiang Kai-shek was increasingly perilous? Kennan was skeptical. Writing later in his *Memoirs,* he noted his objection to "the congenital aversion of Americans to taking specific decisions on specific problems, and by their persistent urge to seek universal formulae or doctrines in which to clothe and justify particular actions."

Dean Acheson, then the Under Secretary of State, was similarly cautious. In testimony before the Senate Foreign Relations Committee on March 24, 1947, Acheson stated that

> requests of foreign countries for aid will have to be considered according to the circumstances in each individual case.... It cannot be assumed ... that this government would necessarily undertake measures in any other country identical or even closely similar to those proposed for Greece and Turkey.

But Truman's own global predisposition was reinforced by calculations of political advantage. In action, containment might remain Eurocentric. In rhetoric, it would be global.

On November 19, 1947, Presidential aide Clark Clifford sent Truman a campaign-strategy memorandum which, while concentrating on domestic issues, recommended a tough approach on foreign policy. The "battle with the Kremlin," he argued, could be turned to the administration's advantage. Henry Wallace, who threatened to drain votes from Truman on the left, could be blunted if liberal Democrats loyal to Truman were to "identify him and isolate him in the public mind with the Communists." At first hesitant about this tactic, Truman then allowed the Democratic National Committee to state that "a vote for Wallace . . . is a vote for things for which Stalin, Molotov and Vishinsky stand." On March 17, 1948, Truman took up this cudgel himself. "I do not want and will not accept the political support of Henry Wallace and his Communists," he told a St. Patrick's Day dinner audience. Peace and containment, everywhere, were the goals of America: "Free men in every land are asking: where is this leading? When will it end? I can bring you tonight no simple or easy answer. But I can express my firm conviction that, at this moment in history, the faith and strength of the United States are mighty forces for the prevention of war and the establishment of peace."

There can be little doubt that Truman was sincere in his views and was responding to real Soviet actions in Eastern Europe and elsewhere. But the rhetoric was political as well, and the President was playing the right tunes for public opinion. At the beginning of 1948, polls indicated that despite the Truman Doctrine, 73 percent of those questioned felt that the United States was being "too soft" on the Soviets. At the same time, in the wake of events in Czechoslovakia, fears of war were beginning to grow. The twin demands were in place: stop the Soviets, but get along with them and maintain the peace. And Truman promised both during the course of the 1948 campaign.

Thus, by the November election, Truman, through his rhetoric of the prior two years, had helped his conservative opponents establish three notions: that containment was an American responsibility wherever "free nations" were threatened; that there were dupes of the Soviets in the United States like Henry Wallace and his followers (a view encouraged also by Truman's 1947 "loyalty program" designed to manage security risks in the State Department); and that peace could be maintained by "faith and strength" but at little real cost. Military spending was being held at very low levels, although aid levels were on the rise.

After 1948, despite his tremendous achievements in helping to shape the creation of a new international system, Truman and his party came under assault on all three of the central notions he helped to establish. For, as the events of 1949 showed, there was a gap between the global rhetoric and what was achievable—indeed, between the rhetoric and Truman's actual policy. The gap offered Truman's enemies on the right enormous political advantage.

The trap he had helped set in 1947 and 1948 was triggered by China in 1949. That autumn, after Mao Tse-tung controlled the Chinese mainland and proclaimed the People's Republic of China, the United States refused to invervene militarily. More than that, the Administration had lost all faith in Chiang Kai-shek and his followers, and the State Department announced that American forces would not be used to defend Formosa—"The United States government will not pursue a course which will lead to involvement in the civil conflict in China." The path was open to the Communists to take Formosa, and it was expected that they would do so.

The more conservative Republicans were not about to let Truman get by with it. Frustrated by the defeat of Dewey in 1948 and ascribing it at least in part to his "me-tooism" on foreign-policy issues, they attacked. On European issues the Republican leaders in the Congress had been consulted, and they had lent crucial support on the Marshall Plan, the Truman Doctrine and the creation of NATO. Not so regarding Asia. Here they were free of responsibility, and thus free to find fault with Truman's management of containment as a whole—in the terms of his own previous rhetoric. Senator William Knowland of California put the case succinctly when he said that Communism in Asia had made gains which many times offset the losses of Communism in Europe. Moreover, Alger Hiss's conviction for perjury in January 1950 seemed to confirm the view that American losses in Asia could be attributed to Communist sympathies in the State Department, a charge that Senator Joseph

McCarthy played up in the dark weeks thereafter. Other, mainstream politicians played on the same themes. Senator Robert A. Taft of Ohio denounced the "pro-Communist group in the State Department who . . . promoted at every opportunity the Communist cause in China." Truman's popularity was in severe decline. War fears were again on the increase, and a narrow majority of Americans thought that we were losing the Cold War to the Russians.

That was the political context at the time of the North Korean attack on South Korea in June 1950. There is little doubt that Truman's firm response, with the dispatch of American troops, was made in the belief that to fail to oppose this act of aggression would be to encourage such acts elsewhere. There also can be little doubt that if he had failed to act, there would have been a massive popular and political explosion. As it was, after an initial burst of enthusiasm and support for American military intervention, the Republicans returned to their attack on Democratic weakness; McCarthy was in the forefront of the charge, calling in speeches around the country for the removal of the "Commicrats." In the fall Congressional elections, the Democrats' majorities were heavily cut both in the Senate and the House. The Democrats' administration of the nation in general was unpopular, but the losses were especially heavy for defenders of Truman's foreign policies.

In response to the attack in South Korea, Truman had made a series of decisions that brought his policy of containment to Asia; they included a reversal of policy toward Formosa—which would henceforth be protected—and the provision of great quantities of aid to the French in their fight for Vietnam and the rest of Indochina. But these actions cut no ice with his conservative enemies, who had tasted political blood after the fall of China and would not be satisfied with a limited "police action" in Korea. Truman was ensnared. China and Korea showed that he could not deliver on the rhetoric of 1947 and 1948, the promise to stop Communism everywhere while maintaining the peace; yet, after the reaction to the "loss" of China, he could not back away from his global goal, even if he had wanted to do so—as evidenced by his fateful blunder in letting General Douglas MacArthur cross the 38th parallel in Korea in October 1950. Louis Halle, a distinguished historian and member of the State Department's Policy Planning Staff in 1950, has written:

> This was . . . a time when the American people were becoming convinced that the foreign policy of the United States had fallen into the hands of Communist conspirators. . . . For the Government now to have ordered MacArthur to desist from giving the beaten Communists the *coup de grâce* would have appeared to confirm this view. Without the actual test, the people, having MacArthur's word for it, would never have believed that Korea could not have been quickly unified under a friendly democratic regime. . . . Truman's action would have gone down in history as the great betrayal.

The war dragged on for the remaining two years of Truman's Presidency, and its growing unpopularity paralleled Truman's own. Walter Lippmann caught perfectly the nature of his quandary. Truman, he wrote,

> was not able to make war (against China) because the risks were too great. This dilemma of Truman's was resolved by the election of Eisenhower. . . . President Eisenhower signed an armistice which accepted the partition of Korea and a peace without victory because, being himself the victorious commander in World War II and a Republican, he could not be attacked as an appeaser. President Truman and Secretary Acheson, on the other hand, never seemed able to make peace on the only terms that the Chinese would agree to. The Democrats were too vulnerable to attack from the political followers of General MacArthur and of . . . Senator McCarthy, and indeed to attack from the whole right wing of the Republican party.

The irony was that this was happening to a President who not only has been justly acclaimed for his foreign-policy accomplishments, but also was responsible for the policy of containment. It is impossible to measure how much his own rhetoric had helped to create the global criteria for foreign-policy success by which he was now found wanting. But wanting he was found. The rhetoric portrayed a global challenge in which Truman genuinely believed. But it implied an American ability to order events—an ability that was beyond Truman or any other President, as he found in Korea and others were to find in Vietnam.

What can be said is that Truman had helped string the rope with which he was hanged by the Republicans. In 1947–48, he might have seized the middle ground, where the votes usually are, by attacking both the right and the left and talking sense about the limits to both Soviet and American power. But instead of rejecting rhetorical extremes in order to position himself in the middle, Truman chose to adopt them—in part to sell his international programs, in part out of belief, and in part because it protected his right flank, where he must have felt most vulnerable. It worked toward the defeat of Dewey, but it helped make his second term hostage to the anti-Communist fears of the right, the illusions of an easy peace, and the myth of omnipotence.

If Truman helped to create the trap of unkeepable promises, Dwight Eisenhower strengthened it in 1952 through the Cold War rhetoric he allowed first his party and then himself to use. Unlike Truman, however, he had the political and personal standing to escape its teeth.

Eisenhower began the 1952 campaign with an instinctive caution that was to serve him well throughout his Presidency. But as the campaign progressed, Republican rhetorical excesses flourished. In effect, the promise of this rhetoric was that the United States, while reducing the defense spending that had tripled in Truman's last years as a result of Korea, could actually go beyond containment to rolling back the Iron Curtain. We could defeat and humiliate the Soviet bully with one hand tied behind our back. The basis for this extraordinary act of American power would be our nuclear arsenal.

The 1952 Republican party platform, picking up themes that had been advanced by Senator Taft, John Foster Dulles and others, attacked "the negative, futile and immoral policy of 'containment' which abandoned countless human beings to a despotism and godless terrorism." It would be replaced by a policy that would somehow "revive the contagious, liberating influences which are inherent in freedom."

By August 25, Eisenhower picked up the theme himself. In a speech before an American Legion convention, he called for a great moral crusade—"We must tell the Kremlin that never shall we desist in our aid to every man and woman of those shackled lands who seeks refuge with us, any man who keeps burning among his own people the flame of freedom or who is dedicated to the liberation of his fellows."

A few days later, Dulles, one of Eisenhower's senior campaign foreign-policy advisers, elaborated: Having stirred up resistance through Voice of America broadcasts, we would air-drop supplies to the freedom fighters in the captive nations and then, after their liberation, welcome them into the free world.

After a Democratic counterattack charging that the Republicans were promising a third world war, Eisenhower backed away. We would promote liberation, he said, only by peaceful means. In the last days of the campaign, he stayed away from the subject. But Republican campaign materials continued to call for lifting the Iron Curtain, even promising to free the people of Poland without going to war. Polish-American voters defected heavily from Democratic party ranks.

After becoming President, Eisenhower dropped "liberation" completely. But the commitment to undifferentiated containment in Asia, undertaken by Truman in 1950, was enthusiastically embraced in the Eisenhower Administration's rhetoric. If the Communists were allowed to make gains anywhere in Indochina, the result would be the loss of freedom everywhere in Southeast Asia. Eisenhower put it more graphically than Truman had done. During their first year in office and into 1954, as the situation in Indochina collapsed around the French, the new American President and his officials constantly raised the stakes: Indochina was a "cork in the bottle"; its loss could provide the beginning of a negative "chain reaction" in the area. On April 7, 1954, as the French faced defeat at Dien Bien Phu, Eisenhower explained the stakes in terms of "falling dominoes."

Despite having thus dramatized the issue, Eisenhower went grudgingly along with the French surrender, and shrewdly citing Congressional and Allied views, he refused to approve the proposal of some of his military leaders that we commit American air power in the French behalf.

Eisenhower, a military hero, was not so easily driven into military action as Truman had been and Kennedy would be. But once again, the gap between rhetoric and reality, between promise and performance, had grown. And at the same time as he was raising the rhetorical stakes in Asia, Eisenhower was working to reduce the military budget. This fit nicely with the emphasis of Secretary of State Dulles on using the threat of nuclear weapons to deter Soviet adventures.

Eisenhower himself seems to have been skeptical of "massive retaliation" as an easy and cheap answer to military challenge, and toned down such language in the Republican party platform in 1952. But a year after his inauguration, in the first major description of his defense policies, Eisenhower emphasized in his State of the Union address the role both strategic and tactical nuclear weapons would play. The military budget he then presented to the Congress included a cut of $3.5 billion from the previous year.

Five days after Eisenhower's address, Dulles went further in a January 12 speech at the Council on Foreign Relations. The United States would not seek to match "the mighty land power of the Communist world." Instead, we would "depend primarily upon a great capacity to retaliate, instantly, by means and at places of our choosing."

As Samuel F. Wells argues, this speech was more than a statement of military policy. Since "liberation" had been abandoned in favor of the more limited dominoes of containment, there was a need to show that the Eisenhower Administration, as it promised in 1952, had a new approach to the world. The speech "was Dulles' attempt to discharge the responsibility that the Republicans had assumed during the campaign of 1952 to develop a foreign policy fundamentally different from that of the Democrats."

Thus, in the public mind, the promise was clear. There would be containment of the Soviets and Chinese and—to those who still remembered the words of 1952—even liberation of captive peoples. And it would be done with declining military budgets. Through the *threat* of using nuclear weapons, there could be victory, lean budgets and peace.

It could not work. The disproportion between the threat of nuclear attack and the limited significance of local events around the world meant that the United States was muscle-bound. Nor could the threat of nuclear blackmail remain credible as the Soviets developed their own nuclear forces.

Moreover, where "liberation" had once been promised, there was the impotence of the United States in the face of bloody Soviet repression in Hungary in 1956. Where containment had been promised, there was actual, if not formal, American acceptance of the French defeat in Indochina—and, toward the end of the decade, the "loss" of Cuba. Lower defense spending was used by the Democrats, at the end of Eisenhower's second term, to suggest that the Soviets had gained a military advantage even in strategic weaponry. And while there was no war, by 1960 there was no peace—as evidenced by new tensions over Berlin, the U-2 incident and the collapse of the Paris summit meeting.

Again, more had been promised than had been achieved. And under Eisenhower, we first saw a refinement to the promise-performance trap that has persisted to this day: while all Presidents are required both to stop the Soviets and to maintain peace, the imperatives are given different weights for Presidents of different parties. As Truman discovered over Korea and as his Democratic successors found over Vietnam and arms control, the Democrats would not be able to make peace, for with them it would appear weakness. The Republicans, on the other hand, could not make war, for with them it would appear more reckless. Barry Goldwater would find this to be true when running for President in 1964; Richard Nixon would too, when, as President, he sought to buy time for the Vietnam War; and so would Ronald Reagan, when he was forced in 1981 to cool the El Salvador issue publicly and move to more oblique tactics. And even that strategy ran into trouble, as the Congress placed obstacles in the way of his efforts to give covert aid to the guerrillas fighting the Sandinista regime in Nicaragua. Up through 1984, the limit for the Republicans has been quick military operations: a Mayaguez rescue operation or an overwhelming action in Grenada.

In every case, where choices had to be made, Eisenhower chose the peace rather than the containment side of his dilemma: in letting the first Indochinese domino—North Vietnam—fall; in sliding by the anguish of Hungary in 1956; and in accepting the triumph of Fidel Castro in Cuba. Yet his political standing, while scathed at the end, remained strong. He accomplished this through his personal appeal; by maintaining an image of being somehow above the fray; through taking advantage, in the early years, of the fresh memories of Korea; and, most of all, by being a military hero. No other President has been able, or thought he was able, to consistently choose peace over containment and accept the foreign setbacks that come with such a policy. As John Mueller puts it, "If a President wants to leave office a popular man, he should either (1) be Dwight David Eisenhower, or (2) resign the day after inauguration."

Eisenhower might escape the trap, but his Vice-President, running to replace him, could not. John F. Kennedy was able to do to Nixon in 1960 what the Republicans had done to Truman in 1952—portray a foreign policy that had failed on its own terms. The Democrats, Kennedy promised, would do better, both in containing Communism and in building peace. Foreign-policy issues did not elect Kennedy. But his attacks helped, to a large extent, to keep Nixon from exploiting international issues to *his* advantage.

When Adlai Stevenson and Chester Bowles were named Kennedy's principal foreign-policy advisers in July 1960, the two caught the twin imperatives perfectly: they stated their belief in the importance of rallying the free world against the Soviets "without war or surrender." But it was the struggle against Communism that received the emphasis.

> Astonishingly [Robert Divine writes] Kennedy . . . planned to attack the Republicans on their strongest point. For eight years, the Eisenhower administration had kept the nation at peace, ending the war in Korea and preventing the outbreak of any new conflicts . . . yet the Democratic candidate boldly asserted that . . . the nation had passed from a position of strength and respect to one of weakness and shame. Gambling that the nation's sense of confidence had been undermined by the U-2 affair and the rise of Castro, Kennedy sought to burden Nixon with Eisenhower's mistakes and thus neutralize the peace issue. . . .

More astonishing still, Kennedy actually compared Eisenhower's performance to that of British governments in the 1930s—the years in which "England slept," as Kennedy's book had put it in 1940.

> Twenty-three years ago [Kennedy said in 1959] in a bitter debate in the House of Commons, Winston Churchill charged the British Government with acute blindness to the menace of Nazi Germany, with gross negligence in the maintenance of the island's defenses, and with indifferent, indecisive leadership of British foreign policy and British public opinion. The preceding years of drift and impotency were "the years the locusts have eaten." Since January 1953, this nation has passed through a similar period. . . .

As Samuel Lubell wrote in 1962, the public was not prepared to repudiate Eisenhower's foreign policies.

> But the voters weren't willing to give the Eisenhower policies a ringing endorsement either. On one hand, voters would say, "We're not at war," and this was a considerable Nixon asset. But deep concern was also voiced over the course of events since the U-2 incident, particularly over Castro in Cuba. Nixon's contention that the prestige of the United States was higher than ever collided with the oft-repeated feeling that "the Russians are kicking us around. We need a tougher foreign policy."

Playing on these post-Sputnik fears and new trends in academic thinking about nuclear weapons, Kennedy hammered at the existence of a "missile gap," and he promised to close it. A resurgent America would recover lost respect and offer people around the world a clear answer to Communism. No more would we rely on discredited massive retaliation; we would get actively involved in the struggle for the hearts and minds of the peoples of the southern hemisphere. The rhetoric was designed to appeal to an American public that, according to polling data, was once again becoming increasingly worried about both Communist successes and the prospect of war.

The promise of a new, strong, more militant approach to the world was laid out in exalted terms. "I believe," he proclaimed at the end of the campaign, "that we can check the Communist advance, that we can turn it back, and that we can, in this century, provide for the ultimate victory of freedom over slavery."

Such rhetoric may or may not have done more, politically, than work against Nixon's use of the "peace" issue. But when mixed with the attraction of Kennedy's personality and the sense of power that he exuded, it was exciting stuff for a new, young President on the eve of a new administration. Who could question such grand goals? Who would not want to see the United States accomplish all that? Few questioned, at the time, whether it all could be accomplished. And there is no evidence that Kennedy or his advisers asked whether they were creating public expectations that might push in the direction of overreaching foreign-policy errors. Yet that is just what happened in the first months of the new administration. Where Truman and Eisenhower had remained cautious in approach despite their rhetoric, Kennedy was driven by the importance of imagery. He certainly could not do all that he had promised. But his expansive claims helped push him to expensive action.

The new President came to power committed to doing something about Castro. He had demonstrated his anti-Communist credentials in the campaign by hammering at Eisenhower's failure to keep Castro from coming to power "eight jet minutes from the coast of Florida." On the evening of October 19, 1960, building on Kennedy's own general statements on the subject and having observed that attacks on Castro brought an even bigger popular response than those on Khrushchev, campaign aides had released a specific statement in Kennedy's name: "We must attempt to strengthen the . . . democratic anti-Castro forces, in exile and in Cuba itself, who offer eventual hope of overthrowing Castro. Thus far, these fighters for freedom have had virtually no support from our government." *The New York Times* gave the story its lead headline: "Kennedy Asks Aid for Cuban Rebels to Defeat Castro."

We cannot know how strong a role this pledge played in Kennedy's mind as he gave his approval to the plan for an attack on the Bay of Pigs by Cuban exiles. It *is* clear, however, from Peter Wyden's fascinating account of the affair, that one of Kennedy's chief concerns was the public reaction if he canceled the CIA's plan. What would be done with the Brigade, the exiles who were already being trained for the invasion? What would be the reaction if they were returned from their training camp in Guatemala, without a chance to take on Castro? Wyden summarizes Kennedy's concern on this point as expressed at a key meeting with his advisers on March 11, 1961: It was not only that the exiles would spread the word around Latin America that the United States had turned tail, thus encouraging new revolutions. "The Republicans would call him chicken. The political repercussions would be nasty." Kennedy was in a stronger position than Truman had been to manage such assaults. But an impression of weakness would nonetheless be very damaging. It would be a denial of Kennedy's whole approach to foreign policy, of his toughness, his courage, his capacity for cool decision making in a crisis—even if the crisis were of his own making. When one of Kennedy's closest advisers, Theodore Sorensen, tried to question Kennedy about the operation, the President cut him short: "I know everybody is grabbing their nuts on this," he said.

Kennedy hoped that the operation could be limited, both by disguising the American role and by letting the anti-Castro exiles fade into the countryside if the invasion ran into trouble. But the operation had to go forward. And the consequence was humiliation.

Similarly, Kennedy imposed limits as he made the decisions that deepened American involvement in the growing conflict in Vietnam. He rejected, for example, the introduction of a contingent of American combat troops when it was proposed by General Maxwell D. Taylor and Walt W. Rostow in October 1961. But, as on Cuba, the central impulse was for involvement, without sufficient questions about the capacity for success. Much of the compulsion was undoubtedly produced by genuine anti-Communist sentiment. As with Truman's Korea decisions, however, the impulse also seems to have been rooted in a concern with the political implications of failing to act. And as with Truman, those political pressures were, to some degree, the product of the President's own rhetoric. For how could a President who had promised in his extraordinary Inaugural Address that America would "bear any burden, pay any price," fail to prevent a Communist victory in Vietnam? In Laos, where military intervention appeared technically impossible, a search for a coalition government could be attempted. Not in Vietnam. American military advisers were not only sent in large numbers; they were sent out into the field with South Vietnamese combat units. The American press followed. The war began to come home to Americans; defeat became unthinkable. As Truman could not afford politically to make peace in Korea on terms the Chinese could accept, so Kennedy, remembering Truman's fate over China, Eisenhower's dominoes, and his own campaign rhetoric, could not allow a show of weakness in Vietnam.

Walt W. Rostow recalls the ultimate reasoning behind Kennedy's decisions on Vietnam: "He began with domestic political life. He said if we walked away from Southeast Asia, the Communist takeover would produce a debate in the United States more acute than that over the loss of China. . . . The upshot would be a rise and convergence of left- and right-wing isolationism that would affect commitments in Europe as well as in Asia."

Arthur Schlesinger recalls the same line of Kennedy reasoning, but in terms less elevated: "Kennedy told Rostow that Eisenhower could stand the political consequences of Dien Bien Phu and the expulsion of the West from Vietnam in 1954 because the blame fell on the French; 'I can't take a 1954 defeat today.' "

Kennedy's White House Chief of Staff, Kenneth O'Donnell, has written that Kennedy later concluded, partly on the advice of General Douglas MacArthur (what an irony Harry Truman might have found in that), that further involvement in Vietnam would be a mistake. In response to criticism of his war policy by Senator Mike Mansfield, Kennedy is reported to have told the Senator in late 1962 that he accepted the need for a complete military withdrawal from Vietnam. "But I can't do it until 1965." "President Kennedy felt, and Mansfield agreed with him," O'Donnell writes, "that if he announced a total withdrawal of American military personnel from Vietnam before the 1964 election, there would be a wild conservative outcry against returning him to the Presidency for a second term."

By mid-1962, Kennedy was the prisoner of the promise of his new approach. His performance in Laos, in Berlin (where, while denouncing the Wall, he accepted it), and in Cuba (where Castro remained, cockier than ever) could not match the rhetoric of 1960. And as the November Congressional elections loomed near, the Republicans began to strike at Kennedy where he had hit Nixon—from the right. In late summer as rumors of Soviet missiles in Cuba began to emerge, the Republicans made Cuba their issue. The Chairman of the Republican National Committee put it succinctly: Cuba was the "symbol of the tragic irresolution of the Administration." Kennedy was hoist with his Cuban petard.

Kennedy's response was twofold. On the one hand, he played down publicly the possibility that the missiles, in fact, were there. On the other, he took a tough line with the Soviets on what he thought was a hypothetical case. At a press conference on September 13, he warned: "If at any time the Communist buildup in Cuba were to endanger or interfere with our security in any way . . . or if Cuba should . . . become an offensive military base for the Soviet Union, then this country will do whatever must be done to protect its own security and that of its allies."

The case was not hypothetical, as Kennedy was to discover a month later. And while his press-conference statement, even in retrospect, seems wise policy, its public expression helped to create a political climate in which the President's freedom of maneuver could be limited by political pressures. He escaped this danger by maintaining a high degree of secrecy until he announced the "quarantine" that ultimately proved successful. But the political pressures for reckless action were clear when Kennedy finally did brief Congressional leaders on his decision. Senator Richard Russell of Georgia dismissed the blockade as a halfway measure that would do the Communists no real harm. Even Senator Fulbright, who had opposed the Bay of Pigs, supported Russell in calling for an invasion of Cuba.

The quarantine succeeded, and Kennedy emerged a hero. The crisis earned him a respite on his right flank, and he could move on, in 1963, to efforts at détente with the Soviet Union and negotiation of a limited ban on the testing of nuclear weapons. Yet his popularity declined during the last year of his Presidency and his life.

For Kennedy, as for Truman before him, taking a rigid view of the policy of containment and promising its fulfillment had proved damaging to both President and nation. At the Bay of Pigs and in Vietnam, it led to ill-considered adventures in which goals were beyond means. Where moderation had prevailed—on Berlin, on Laos—the President was found weak in his own terms.

Nineteen sixty-four marked a new stage in the politicization of our foreign policies. Before the electoral campaign of that year, the problem lay primarily in Presidents' trapping themselves through their promises. From 1964 on, they compounded the problem by using foreign policy also for immediate political advantage, sometimes acting more like candidates than like Presidents.

Running against Barry Goldwater in 1964, Johnson promised everything but Arpège. True, he won by a landslide as he turned both anti-Communist and peace themes to his advantage. But he also bought trouble for himself and the nation. Acting dramatically as commander in chief in response to the Tonkin Gulf attacks (real and imagined), he ordered retaliatory strikes against North Vietnam and gained, in the Tonkin Gulf Resolution, a Congressional blank check for future escalation. At the same time, he promised that the costs of taking "all necessary measures . . . to repeal aggression in Southeast Asia," as the Resolution had it, would not be high. "We don't want our boys to do the fighting for Asian boys," he said.

Johnson was doing more here than reasserting the old promise of low-cost containment. He was also letting the election-year politics intrude in Presidential decision making in new and more damaging ways. As the situation in Vietnam deteriorated during the course of the election year, Johnson refused to face the fact that preventing defeat in Vietnam would necessitate American military intervention. This was all too evident during the course of the following year, as the bombing campaign against North Vietnam was followed by the introduction of American Marine units into combat. It may be, as *The New York Times* version of the Pentagon Papers suggested, that Johnson knew he would intervene and was simply getting the election out of the way before moving. More likely, Johnson found it politically advantageous simply not to address the logic of events, even in his own mind. Whichever was the case, political calculation led to bad policy as the situation in Vietnam was allowed to slide for a year. And it was undemocratic policy making; the American people never were allowed to hear debated, as they should have, the fateful decision to send combat troops to Vietnam.

This is not to say that Presidents had never previously taken politics into account in making foreign-policy decisions. But Johnson was the first postwar President to let major foreign-policy decisions be twisted by election-year politics. As Presidents, Truman, Eisenhower and Kennedy may have used their rhetoric for political purposes; Johnson, in 1964, allowed electoral purposes to shape actual policy.

The record shows that Harry Truman was indeed a very political man. But while he found the rhetoric of global containment irresistible in 1948, his actual decisions do not, to any significant degree, seem to have been politically driven. It is true that his idea in 1948 of sending Chief Justice Vinson to Moscow to negotiate for peace does seem to have been stimulated by two speech writers worried about the peace vote. But he backed away from the notion when it was opposed by his Secretary of State. It is also true that Truman's motives for ordering American recognition of the state of Israel in 1948 are commonly found in domestic politics. His political advisers did press Truman on the issue, to the dismay of his Secretary of State. But the fact is that Truman dragged his heels on the issue for as long as he could before deciding; he was clearly impressed by the last-minute foreign-policy argument that the Soviets were about to recognize the new state; and, when at last he moved, he refused to grant *de jure* as well as *de facto* recognition until after elections had been held not only in Israel but in the United States.

In the 1952 campaign, there is little evidence that Truman tried to shape foreign-policy issues to the advantage of his party, perhaps in part because Adlai Stevenson was doing all he could to distance himself from his unpopular President.

In 1956, Eisenhower, even more clearly than Truman, did not let electoral considerations move his policies: he opposed our allies and Israel in the Suez crisis and avoided belligerent posturing over the Soviet rape of Hungary. Eisenhower most certainly benefited from the two crises. He reported to the nation as "your President" and by looking especially Presidential was able to reinforce the natural tendency of the voters to stick with their leader at a time of international danger. But, in each case, the substance of his decisions was not calculated to gain the greatest number of votes.

In 1960, Richard Nixon tried, as Stevenson had done eight years before, to put daylight between himself and the incumbent—in this case, not because of a President's unpopularity, but to insulate himself from charges of America's "decline" and perhaps to demonstrate his own political and psychological independence from the man who had occasionally treated him with such exquisite condescension. As in 1952, the incumbent did little to help his party's candidate when it came to the substance of foreign-policy decisions. Eisenhower refused to increase defense spending in response to Kennedy's charges of a "missile gap," for example, although he did reveal certain defense measures under way that would tend to refute Kennedy's alarmism.

Lyndon Johnson, however, leaped over the line in 1964—from political-foreign-policy rhetoric to political foreign policy. It was not only a question of Johnson's ambition and insecurity; the conditions of American politics were changing as well. Issues and personalities rather than parties and organization were starting to dominate voting behavior, as television brought campaigns into living rooms across the country. Presidents were thus tempted to pay more attention to how the issues were shaped during an election year.

In 1948, voters had not divided along party lines when it came to issues of foreign policy, but that was because there was little difference between the parties as Dewey ran the "me-too" campaign that so infuriated the isolationists. By 1951, however, polls showed that the voters had followed party leaders into sharp foreign-policy splits along party lines. The result, of course, was that foreign-policy differences were prominent in the 1952 campaign. But Eisenhower, through his person and popularity, tended to swamp these differences thereafter.

By 1964, voters were moving away from party identification in forming their views on both domestic and foreign party issues. Ideology, once so powerful in American politics at the turn of the century, in the early 1920s and again in the late 1930s was again dominant. In the Republican party, the grip of anti-Communist doctrine was strengthening, as reflected by the Goldwater nomination. And as Republicans moved right, Democrats would move left in 1968 and 1972 in reaction to Vietnam. Ironically, the decline of party identification produced still more politics when it came to making foreign policy. For it meant that candidates and Presidents would now find it attractive to take politically motivated positions on foreign-policy issues that would appeal to the ideologically committed. And the ability of the parties to provide even a modicum of coherence to foreign-policy debates was eroded. Party platforms would no longer be a source of consensus building; now they would become the occasion of blood-letting within parties, leading not to agreement but to further splits. Loyalty to party became subordinate to strongly held views on policy substance; ideological differences became more pronounced. The "realignment" of voters that so preoccupies political scientists has not, as some point out, been between parties, but from party identification to political "de-alignment." There is now the self-definition of great numbers of voters by issues and ideology.

In addition to the decline of parties, changes in the geography of power within parties, and in party rules, began to produce still greater ideological conflict.

From 1940 to 1960, the Republican party had been strongest in the Northeast. As Robert A. Taft discovered in 1952, the northeastern Establishment generally won the Presidential nominations. Political power and the postwar internationalist consensus were in harness.

The nomination of Barry Goldwater and humiliation of Nelson Rockefeller at the Republican convention of 1964 showed that the center of power had shifted dramatically to the West and South, and to a new generation of party activists who were ideologically more conservative and nationalistic, as well as resentful of vestiges of Eastern influence. The old internationalist primacy within the GOP was gone.

While the West and South rolled over the North and East in the Republican party, the Southern barons were losing power among the Democrats, as the voters of their region turned increasingly to the party with the more conservative outlook. More than the Republicans, the Democrats were rocked by the tidal waves of Vietnam and by the domestic unrest of the late 1960s. The divisions within the party crystallized at the bloody convention in Chicago in 1968. The 1972 nomination of George McGovern and his campaign slogan of "Come home America" signaled the shift of many (but by no means all) Democrats to both domestic preoccupation and opposition to weaponry and foreign interventions of almost any kind. Internationalist consensus on the shape of American foreign policy had disappeared for the Democrats as well.

And within both parties, changes in party rules meant that the road to nomination, if not then to election, led through a series of primaries in which fervency on the issues was the key to the votes of those most likely to turn out at the polls. Thus, in seeking primary votes, candidates were led away from the middle; they moved toward the left in the Democratic party and the right among the Republicans. Foreign-policy differences between the candidates in the general election were therefore more sharply drawn than the actual views of either probably justified. As each then has sought the middle, where the votes are to be found in the November election, he has tended to caricature the views of the other as extremist, drawing on the ideological statements made by his opponent in the primary races. The result has not been an elevated discussion of issues. Caricature and calumny produce a mutual bitterness that greatly reduces the possibility of civility and even consensus on important foreign-policy issues, once the election is over and a new or reelected President must try to govern.

In addition, as new nominating rules took the power to anoint candidates away from the professional politicians and placed it in the hands of party activists and media advisers, the prize of nomination became far more subject to capture by appealing personalities and promisers who had limited governmental experience and, sometimes, low ratings with the peers who knew them best.

It is not coincidental that both the decline of the parties and the increased attraction of foreign-policy issues for ambitious politicians came at the same time as the completed development, in the early 1960s, of national media. *The New York Times, Time* and *Newsweek* had become more important than local newspapers in shaping opinion. More significant still was the rise of television. In 1963, for the first time, more Americans said they learned about the news of the day from television than from newspapers. By 1981, the margin between television and newspapers as a prime source of information about the world had widened to 64 percent to 44 percent. The result has been that Presidential and even many state elections have become *national* in their focus. It is no longer a question of stitching together regional coalitions. If you want to get elected, you must get time on television and be quoted in the national press. And how do you do it? It is foreign policy that usually opens the show for the network news; world events often shape the images on the covers of *Time* and *Newsweek.* To get national attention, you take a position on a hot issue—and foreign policy provides the most glamorous subjects. It is on international issues that you get to look "Presidential."

Thus, around 1964 trends in the nature of our politics began to make our foreign policy ever more political in its character. And the result was that foreign policy was becoming less and less manageable. For the preceding twenty years, the unifying experience of World War II had provided a legacy of internationalism on which Presidents could try to build. Congress-based isolationists who had fought against Roosevelt's cautious internationalism were gone or discredited by the early 1950s. The Democratic party had emerged from the war overwhelmingly internationalist. Republicans were more divided, but the famous Vandenberg transformation had established a basis for cooperation at least on Europe when, as Senate Foreign Relations Committee Chairman, Vandenberg brought critically needed support to the Truman Doctrine, the Marshall Plan and NATO. There was public support for the United Nations, for defense readiness, for the saving of war-torn Europe, and for political-military vigilance in general.

Politicians would squabble on the second-order issues but rally round the President's flag in East-West confrontations. There were Congressional leaders with whom Presidents and Secretaries of State could deal. And the belief that there *ought* to be bipartisanship helped to curb or isolate extreme critics.

Now, in the middle 1960s, Vietnam changed all this.

After the easy promises of 1964, the decisions to escalate in 1965 and the two following years had a profound effect. With each new increment of American forces and each new move in the air war against North Vietnam, Johnson was forced to wrestle with a knottier political problem at home than had faced any of his predecessors.

They too had needed to play on peace as well as containment to sell their foreign policies and themselves. But for them, peace had been a generalized public desire.

Now, as the costs of Vietnam grew, as draft calls increased, as the savagery of the war came home on television screens, peace developed an active constituency. Before, peace could be promised *through* containment. If we could avoid the mistakes of Munich, where British Prime Minister Neville Chamberlain had tried to assuage Hitler's territorial appetites and merely whetted them, then aggression could be deterred and peace maintained. Now, for more and more Americans, Vietnam seemed to show that global containment meant war, not peace. The conceptual basis of American foreign policy was now shaken, and the politics of foreign policy became far more complicated.

Public and Congressional disillusionment after the escalation of 1965 required Johnson to look to both left and right flanks, to prevent either one from so eroding that it began to cut the diminishing middle ground from under him. He had three concerns here. First, he was fighting to maintain popular support for his war policies, in which he believed. Second, he was seeking to preserve the political base of his party and his own future. And third, he was trying to keep the war from destroying his dream of a Great Society. Its government programs required money and energies that were increasingly drained by the struggle in Vietnam. Yet, paradoxically, the dream of a Great Society also pulled him in the direction of deeper involvement in Indochina, for he feared a loss of effectiveness with Congress if he appeared weak. "If I don't go in now," he once said, "and they show later I should have gone, then they'll be all over me in Congress. They won't be talking about my civil-rights bill or education or beautification. No sir, they'll push Vietnam up my ass every time. Vietnam. Vietnam. Vietnam. Right up my ass."

The threat on the left flank was the most obvious problem in 1965–67, the one that seized the headlines and most of his attention—demonstrations and chants of "Hey, Hey, LBJ, How Many Kids Did You Kill Today"; hearings in the Senate Foreign Relations Committee, where Senator Fulbright challenged the premises and conduct of the war; and Senator Robert F. Kennedy, ready in the wings to step in and claim the peace vote. To shore up that flank, or to keep its appeal from infecting middle-of-the-road opinion, Johnson refused, despite the entreaties of the military, to call up the reserves or to put the economy on a war footing. He offered negotiation, wrapping a nonnegotiable position in the language of peace. He put limits on the bombing. He labeled his opponents "Nervous Nellies," stopping short of using names that could raise accusations of McCarthyism. And always a man of Washington, he sought to cajole and bully wavering members of Congress and the press. (When Senator Frank Church cited Walter Lippmann in arguing for a negotiated settlement, Johnson glowered and said, "Frank, the next time you want a dam in Idaho, you just go to Walter Lippmann for it.")

While the threat from the left was the more obvious, Johnson at least claimed to be more concerned, in the long run, with the threat from the right. In later explaining to Doris Kearns his decisions to send combat units in 1965, Johnson put it this way:

> "I knew that if we let Communist aggression succeed in taking over South Vietnam, there would follow in this country an endless national debate—that would shatter my Presidency, kill my administration, and damage our democracy. I knew that Harry Truman and Dean Acheson had lost their effectiveness from the day that the Communists took over in China. I believed that the loss of China had played a large role in the rise of Joe McCarthy. And I knew that all these problems, taken together, were chickenshit compared with what might happen if we lost Vietnam."

To try to keep the right on board, Johnson always gave the American military enough soldiers for Vietnam to prevent their splitting with him (as MacArthur had turned on Truman), even while he trimmed the soldiers' requests. He escalated the war whenever necessary to prevent defeat. And he played to the right when he called the left names.

Most important, Johnson tried to manage his problems on both right and left through his rhetoric—with disastrous consequences. The rhetoric contained two strands: constant, grandiose, albeit shifting, statements of American purposes and stakes in Vietnam, and optimism about the progress of the war designed to buy more public patience and, thus, more time.

Not content with portraying the American objective in Vietnam to be the denial of a Communist victory there, as the objective was defined in internal policy papers, Johnson wrapped it in more positive and popular language: it was "self-determination," "free elections," and "permitting the South Vietnamese freely to determine their own future." The dominoes of Southeast Asia described by President Eisenhower now became global, psychological dominoes. In 1965, Johnson argued that "We are there to strengthen world order. Around the globe, from Berlin to Thailand, are people whose well-being rests, in part, in the belief that they can count on us if attacked . . . To leave Vietnam to its fate would shake the confidence of all these people. . . . The result would be . . . even wider war." And always, there was unrelenting optimism, the corner turned, the light at the end of the tunnel.

The doses of rhetoric and optimism may have done some good, for Johnson's purposes, in the short run. In the long run, they did him, his policies and the nation great harm. With each grand statement of stakes and goals, there was a deepened commitment and a widening gap between expectation and performance should Johnson ever have wished to settle for less than victory. For each paean to democracy, there was a growth in public cynicism as reports about the abuse of their people by our Vietnamese allies appeared in our newspapers. After each statement of optimism, there were new reports of stalemate or worse, new requests for more troops. The optimism was midwife to the birth of the credibility gap. We had seen bomber gaps and missile gaps that never existed and could be closed by new rhetoric. The credibility gap, once opened, could not be closed.

Pushed on by the right, constrained by the left, unable to win and unable to lose, Johnson pursued a compromise course that denied the uncompromising character of his rhetoric. It could not last. The enemy offensive of early 1968 provided some military successes for American forces in Vietnam; but, in refuting the Administration's claims of previous progress, it led to the political defeat of Johnson's policies, and Johnson himself, at home.

A majority of Americans still supported the goal of containment in Indochina. But the left and the right were coming together in their disillusionment with the war and its conduct, the former disillusioned about its purposes and costs, the latter by its limits. In the New Hampshire primary on March 11, Senator Eugene McCarthy stunned Johnson and the nation by coming within 230 votes of defeating the President's stand-in. And Johnson, it turned out, was right about the threat from the right as well as the left. Later analysis revealed that for every two dovish, prowithdrawal votes for McCarthy in New Hampshire, there were three who opposed the Administration from the right.

On March 31, 1968, Johnson, as Truman before him, announced that he would not seek reelection. The irony is deep; driven by the memory of reaction to Truman's loss of China, Johnson chose instead the Korea model, a limited war in Asia. And then, like Truman, he was destroyed by the contrast between rhetorical goal and actual events. Unlike Truman, however, he attempted to use a key foreign-policy decision to help his party's candidate in the election to choose his successor. Despite the successful efforts of the Saigon government to block the initiation of peace talks, and lacking firm guarantees from Hanoi about its future behavior, Johnson nonetheless announced on October 31, 1968, that the United States would halt its bombing of North Vietnam. It is hard to believe that this effort to create the impression of progress toward peace, coming on the eve of the election, was anything but politically inspired.

Richard Nixon, who during the 1966 Congressional campaigning season had called for prosecuting the Vietnam War as "a war that has to be fought to prevent World War III," ran in 1968 on a pledge to "end the war." He implied that he had a plan to do so, and he did not deny it when others concluded that the plan existed. According to columnists Rowland Evans and Robert Novak, Nixon's campaign theme on Vietnam "was not dovish and not hawkish but very Delphic, susceptible to favorable interpretation by dove and hawk alike." But the effect was clear: Nixon, with his impeccable hawk credentials, was promising his way to power by playing on the growing desire for peace. His containment flank was secure, like Eisenhower's, and he could concentrate on the peace imperative.

As President, Nixon then faced a complex problem in dealing with his promises of peace. He could not lose in Vietnam; it was unthinkable in his own terms and would hurt him with his conservative constituency. While a majority of the American people had concluded by now that Vietnam was a mistake, it was not clear that they would accept a defeat, even one that Nixon could blame on his predecessors. Yet there was little more patience for a continuation of the bloodshed with no end in sight.

A complex problem brought a complex strategy. Nixon would buy time by gradually reducing the American presence in Vietnam through the "Vietnamization" program. He would proclaim as his goal, "peace with honor." He would seek that peace through secret negotiations. He would strengthen his hand in negotiation by threatening the North Vietnamese with massive bombings if they did not make fundamental concessions. And he would enlist the help of the Soviets through threats and promises about the future of the United States–Soviet relationship.

At home, there was something for everyone. For the left, there was Vietnamization and the goal of "peace." For the right, there was a lot more: peace—"but only with honor"—more bombing, the invasions in 1970 and 1971 of Cambodia and Laos, and more rhetoric about the importance of Vietnam. As American troops crossed the border of Cambodia on April 30, 1970, Nixon stated that "If when the chips are down, the world's most powerful nation—the United States of America—acts like a pitiful, helpless giant, the forces of totalitarianism and anarchy will threaten free nations and free institutions throughout the world."

With such complexity came, inevitably, contradictions. As National Security Assistant Henry Kissinger pointed out at the time, Vietnamization brought with it its own political imperative. Once Nixon started withdrawing United States troops, the American public became fixed on regular dosages. And the requirement to continue the withdrawals constantly undercut the American position at the negotiations. How could the United States insist on the withdrawal of North Vietnamese troops from South Vietnam in exchange for our own withdrawal, when the latter was taking place unilaterally? The central American demand for North Vietnamese withdrawal was ultimately dropped in 1971–72. In addition, as with his predecessors, Nixon's rhetoric about the American stakes in Vietnam put *more* American chips on the table. But now it was a time when American negotiators had progressively fewer high cards to play.

With regard to foreign policy as a whole, the Nixon Administration, to its credit, had a coherent central concept that reflected a more realistic view of the world and American power than had the grandiose pictures painted by Lyndon Johnson. In early 1970, the President's first "State of the World" report to the Congress, shaped almost completely by Henry Kissinger, emphasized that the world had changed: the United States no longer had the power to make the efforts of our allies unimportant. Referring to the President's Guam press-conference remarks that became labeled as the "Nixon Doctrine," the report stated that "America cannot—and will not—conceive *all* the plans, design *all* the programs, execute *all* the decisions and undertake *all* the defense of the free nations of the world. We will help where it makes a real difference and is considered in our interest."

It was a welcome recognition of reality. But it did not reduce expectations, for it was overshadowed by the rhetoric of Vietnam, and by the fact that, in its global activism, the Administration was in fact pursuing maximum feasible United States involvement from Chile to Bangladesh. The Nixon Doctrine represented a realistic change in tactics, but not in unrealistic goals. It was a new form of promising global success at reduced costs. Now Communism would still be contained everywhere, but others would pay more of the price and bear more of the burden.

Despite the tumult following the invasion of Cambodia in 1970 and the growth in public opposition to his conduct of the war in the following two years, Nixon was able to make foreign policy work for him in the election campaign of 1972. He did it through a combination of important achievements, shrewd political timing and, once again, rhetorical promises that sowed the seeds of future disillusionment.

On February 9, 1972, Nixon issued the third of his foreign-policy reports to the Congress. The report contrasted the successes of the past three years with earlier failings in the record of the Democrats. The report, which Max Frankel in *The New York Times* called a "campaign document," outlined what would become Nixon's major campaign issues: progress in Vietnam and the Vietnamization program; summit meetings in Moscow and Peking; and agreement on limiting strategic arms.

On Vietnam, he used public revelations of peace proposals, indications of progress in the negotiations, and Kissinger's famous "peace is at hand" statement just before the election to keep his opponents off balance and the public on board. Kissinger's statement was aimed, in part, at a Vietnamese audience; but its political effect in the United States can hardly have been unintentional, especially in view of Kissinger's skillful and lengthy background meetings with reporters through the day or two after his statement. Through such techniques, Nixon was not able to persuade the left; but he could and did split it from middle-of-the-road opinion. And he rallied the right by bombing Hanoi and mining Haiphong harbor in response to the North Vietnamese spring offensive.

Nixon also used his 1972 foreign spectaculars for maximum political effect. It is true that the actual importance of his summitry was profound, both in achieving the SALT I agreements of May 26 and in the opening to China, which his successors were able to expand. It may be that only "Nixons" can make such moves; certainly more liberal politicians would be much more vulnerable politically. But not all Nixons *do* "go to China," and Nixon's achievements must be recognized.

Yet their timing and handling smacked heavily of political calculation. Was it necessary, in 1971, to "tilt" toward Pakistan during its savage repression of the people of Bangladesh, at least partly so that the Pakistanis could help to arrange the most expeditious channel to Peking by 1972? The extraordinary secrecy surrounding Nixon's surprise announcement of this China breakthrough did help to neutralize the old China lobby, and win overwhelming public support for a step that Kennedy had considered politically unthinkable less than ten years before. But is it possible that Nixon was oblivious to the electoral benefits that the secrecy also provided? The shock to Taiwan and Japan diminished the foreign-policy advantages of Nixon's historic move.

All this helped Nixon take the peace issue away from George McGovern, the "peace candidate." And, as on Vietnam, Nixon sought additional political mileage through heavy promises. A combination of threats, détente and negotiation would provide a new world, "a structure of peace." In Moscow, in May 1972, Nixon told his Soviet hosts that "we meet to begin a new age in the relationships between our two great and powerful nations." On his return to Washington, the President made a dramatic helicopter trip directly from Andrews Air Force base to the Congress, where he reported on his summit meeting. A constructive but modest SALT I was described in terms that made our negotiators "squirm," according to one of them. Nixon told the Congress that the accords marked "the beginning of the end" of United States–Soviet tensions.

The long record of their writings and statements shows that both Nixon and Kissinger knew and believed otherwise about the Soviets. The only reason for their overblown rhetoric about détente can have been politics—to seduce the left and neutralize the right.

Such hyperbolic hopes for a new world of peace worked politically in 1972. But just as the Watergate escapades, at a more dramatic level, were designed to widen Nixon's electoral margin but later destroyed him, so his hyperbole in 1972 led to postelection reaction. If peace in Vietnam was "at hand," why the savage bombing of Hanoi in December 1972? Why the continuation of the fighting in Vietnam, even after the withdrawal of American troops, until the collapse of the Saigon forces in 1975? If détente was to bring peace, why were the Soviets still competing so persistently with us in the Third World? If SALT I would mean an end to tensions, why the massive military spending?

These contradictions, and the political, cynical motives ascribed to Nixon and Kissinger, strengthened by Nixon's pathetic effort to divert attention from his Watergate woes by a trip to Egypt in 1974, further widened the credibility gap. "Truth" on foreign-policy matters seemed to exist only on the extremes. The center, already diminished by Vietnam, was eroded further. The cynicism about Nixon's motives clouded the sound policies that he had pursued, as in the Middle East.

It is true that, to the end, Nixon's handling of foreign policy retained higher approval ratings than anything else he did as President. But by the time he was compelled to resign, in August 1974, his foreign policies were under increasing attack within elite opinion and among political activists in both parties. From the left came cries that we had more *realpolitik* and threat than peace and accommodation. From the right came charges of having gone soft on the Soviets. Nixon had done better at making foreign policy work for him politically than any other President save Eisenhower—and under circumstances more difficult than those of the 1950s. His foreign-policy actions still made headlines in 1974. But on Vietnam, on détente, on the "structure of peace," he, like his predecessors, had promised more than he delivered. And the reaction to his claims for "détente" had started to set in. The reaction would bedevil his successors.

Gerald Ford promised to continue "a foreign policy . . . that has been most successful in the achievement of peace," by retaining Henry Kissinger to maintain it. Beyond this pledge of continuity, Ford had had little time to promise very much. Nor, as President, did he create the opportunity to accomplish much more. Although in 1974 the new President was able to negotiate an agreement with the Soviets on the outlines of a new measure to limit nuclear arms, building on Nixon's SALT I achievement, it was all downhill after that. Conservative reaction to Nixon's promise of peace through détente solidified as the Soviets and Cubans pressed their intervention in the civil war in Angola. As Ford's memoirs show, the greatest part of his administration became devoted to heading off a challenge to his policies and—most importantly—reelection prospects by the right.

As the primary campaigns of 1976 gathered steam, Ronald Reagan discovered that foreign policy was his best issue against the President. The more Reagan talked about the weakness of Ford and Kissinger in pursuing both détente and negotiation over the Panama Canal, the better Reagan did among GOP primary electorates. Ford's reaction was to try to meet Reagan on his own ground. "Détente" had been oversold and was unpopular with conservative Republicans; Ford banished the word from the lexicon of his Administration. On March 1, Ford told an interviewer that "I don't use the word 'détente' any more." Negotiations on SALT were put on ice, canceling Ford's earlier accomplishment. The signing of a treaty on underground nuclear explosions was suddenly postponed until after the Michigan primary, prompting a Soviet official to tell a *New York Times* reporter, "Every four years, the United States becomes unpredictable and it is very difficult for us." The *Times* itself issued an editorial tut tut: "The Presidency and this country's status as a world power are not enhanced by the injection of election politics into international diplomacy."

To his credit, Ford did side with Kissinger and against his political advisers on two issues: proceeding with the Helsinki agreements that traded border recognition in Eastern Europe for Soviet human-rights pledges, and letting Kissinger take on the white Rhodesians in seeking a peaceful settlement of the conflict there. But Kissinger was kept from playing the role he might have played at the 1976 nominating convention and—to appease the right—Ford accepted a "morality in foreign policy" plank that he later called "nothing less than a slick denunciation of Administration foreign policy."

Squeaking past Reagan, Ford then faced attack by Jimmy Carter from both right and left. Playing to the right, Carter attacked Ford for giving away too much in his negotiations with the Soviets; for being prepared to give up "practical" control of the Panama Canal; and for Ford's refusal to meet with Alexander Solzhenitsyn, the dissident Soviet novelist, at the White House. While appearing on these issues to be Ronald Reagan redux, Carter also played on Ford's weaknesses on liberal issues—which, again, were a legacy of Richard Nixon. There would be no more immoral *realpolitik*, no more Watergate-type secrecy, no more destabilizing CIA interventions, as there had been in Chile. There would be human rights and respect again for American virtue, destroyed by the Nixon-Kissinger-Ford policies in Indochina and by their support for corrupt dictatorships around the world.

Ford's political advisers recall all too well the impossible position in which Ford found himself. For defending himself against these attacks from right and left, Ford had also to prove his personal competence. He had to show that Lyndon Johnson had been wrong in saying (in the cleaned-up version) that Ford couldn't chew gum and walk at the same time. He had to show that he, and not Henry Kissinger, made American foreign policy—both Reagan and Carter made an issue of Kissinger and Kissinger's influence. Yet, having cooled the negotiations on arms control and hunkered down on foreign-policy issues for defensive purposes against Reagan, he had given up the chance to show what he could accomplish. By forgoing foreign-policy accomplishments for political reasons, he lost an opportunity to prove himself a capable President.

Ford was thus doubly trapped. First, by acting in the doubtful tradition of his immediate predecessors and shaping his foreign policies for electoral advantage, Ford missed an opportunity to gain an important arms-control agreement and damaged himself politically in the process. Writing later in his appealingly honest memoirs, Ford recognized that this might have been the case, as he reviewed the reasons for his loss to Carter. "What if," he asked, "we had been able to achieve a SALT II accord with the Soviets? Brezhnev would have come to the United States in 1976. Would our joint commitment to a lasting peace have tipped the scales in November?" And second, Ford was caught by the trap of promises unkept. He had allowed his approach to foreign policy to be shaped by the crosscurrents of reaction, on right and left, to Nixon's policies and promises.

Jimmy Carter used these crosscurrents in his drive for the Presidency. His would be a new approach to the world, and it would restore Americans' good feelings about themselves. Our foreign policy, like our government, would be as "open and honest and decent and compassionate" as the American people themselves.

As Stanley Hoffmann put it, Carter in his first year in office "did much to help Americans overcome the bitter divisions, and the sense of shame and guilt, engendered by the war in Vietnam and by the Watergate scandal." But as candidate and as President, Carter talked his way into his own, novel version of the trap of promises unkept.

In the campaign and during his first year in office, Carter promised peace and security through "world-order politics." Containment of the Soviet Union was played down, even dismissed. During the following three years containment gradually returned as the central purpose of American policy. During both phases, Carter and his staff found ways to frame the issues in such enhanced terms that his actual policies and accomplishments seemed weak in comparison. For previous Presidents, promise and disillusionment followed sequentially. For Carter, they became almost concurrent.

As candidate, Carter held out the hope of a better world through his approach. Summing up in his debate with President Ford on October 6, 1976, he put the point in sweeping terms—"This election will . . . determine what kind of world we leave our children. Will we have a nightmare world threatened with the proliferation of nuclear weapons . . . of hunger and hatred . . . a government of secrecy? Or will we have a world of peace with the threat of atomic weapons eliminated. . . ." Such a world could be created through "world-order politics," never clearly defined—"What we need is to . . . establish world-order politics, which means that we want to preserve peace through strength. We also want to revert back to the stature . . . that our country had in previous administrations. Now I can't say when this can come. But . . . it will come if I'm elected."

Unlike his predecessors, Carter said he accepted the idea that the United States had become overextended in Indochina, that the war had been wrong. Building on the cautionary experience of Vietnam, he might have tried to invoke greater public realism about American power. Instead, he concentrated on trying to change American foreign-policy goals. The United States would concentrate less on containment and more on peace, human rights and preventing nuclear proliferation. "There can be no nobler nor more ambitious task for America," he said in his Inaugural Address, "than to help shape a just and peaceful world that is truly humane."

The problem was that the lofty rhetoric about eliminating nuclear weapons and creating a humane world made pragmatic steps in pursuit of Carter's goals seem to the public to be like moral compromise. When Secretary of State Vance gave a speech on the practical problems involved in pursuing human-rights concerns, and the ways in which the Carter Administration would seek to surmount them, it was erroneously seen by reporters covering the State Department not as a sign of a serious approach but as a backing away from the President's absolute commitment on the issue. And while there was public backing for a human-rights campaign, there was often public opposition and confusion when practical compromises did not meet absolutist rhetoric. The same pattern held true as the Administration wrestled with the practical application of the President's pledge to limit American arms sales abroad.

By the end of his first eighteen months in office, the crusade for a better world was in trouble with the public. It was inherently difficult to demonstrate any successes when it came to nuclear nonproliferation. And the human-rights policy had been blurred by the inevitable need to take different approaches to different cases abroad. Conservatives objected to the cutting of aid to friendly dictatorships as punishment for their transgressions; liberals wondered why Carter let rhetorical assaults on Soviet repression endanger arms-control negotiation.

In addition, Carter now faced a growing suspicion that he was not tough enough on the Soviets—a view fueled by his dismissal, in a speech at Notre Dame, of "inordinate" fears of Communism. Polls in mid-1978 showed that most Americans wanted to see better relations with the Soviets. But a majority also believed that Carter should take a harder line.

In response not only to Soviet actions in Africa and the Persian Gulf area but also to such polls, Carter began by 1978 to place greater emphasis on the Soviet threat and less on creating a "humane world." There would be less concern about acting as "arms merchant" to the world and more concern about supporting friendly nations. Carter was shifting, fitfully, from the peace theme to containment.

Having previously promised too much on peace, now Carter promised too much on containment. As conservative assaults on his policies began to score more heavily, Carter sought to beat them back by adopting more of their tone, if not their program. This meant that the new promises took an especially damaging form—rather than concentrate on what it was accomplishing, the White House (and especially National Security Assistant Zbigniew Brzezinski) went beyond describing the Soviet threat to looking for ways to dramatize it. The result was that the accomplishments, the measures to deal with the threat, constantly paled in comparison, and Carter looked weaker rather than stronger.

The irony was a bitter one. It was clear that the shift in tone was being produced at least in large part by political calculations. It was no secret that Carter's White House political advisers wanted him to appear "tough" on East-West issues. How else can one reasonably explain the fact that after the political wars of 1978–80, after Reagan had been elected and Carter was giving his last speech on foreign policy before returning home to Plains, he returned to the themes of the first months of his Administration—to peace, and human rights, and halting the arms race? The irony was that neither the President nor his White House ever understood that he was being damaged by hyping the threat instead of concentrating on his positive accomplishments. Certainly, the threat was real enough. But over and over again, its dimensions were portrayed in ways that made it impossible for any reasonable action taken by the Administration to seem sufficient.

The pattern had been formed in the Ogaden crisis of 1977–78. In the early spring of 1978, as the invading forces of Somalia were driven back by Cuban and Ethiopian military units from Ethiopian territory, the United States warned the Soviets not to let their clients cross the Somali border. As the Somalis fled into their own territory, the Cubans and Ethiopians did, indeed, pull up at the boundary of the two nations. It was a success for American diplomacy. But instead of seeking credit for what had been accomplished, White House officials used the occasion to emphasize the threat posed by the presence of the Cubans in Ethiopia. Certainly their presence was a real and serious issue. But there was no point setting as a public goal their expulsion, since this was beyond the capacities of the American government to achieve for any foreseeable future. By transforming the issue into one on which the United States had little influence, the Administration lost an opportunity to demonstrate its strength.

The pattern was repeated in May 1978, when the Carter Administration gave the French and Belgians essential assistance as they intervened, for the second time in two years, in the Shaba region of Zaïre. An attack by dissidents who had been in exile in Angola was defeated, and the hostages they had taken were freed. Coordination with our allies was excellent. Carter acted with firmness and skill in a delicate situation. But he received little credit; soon after the event, White House aides, acting on a body of highly suggestive but not conclusive evidence assembled by the CIA, ordered Administration spokesmen to play up Cuban involvement in the affair.

On May 29, Brzezinski, in the course of what *The New York Times* called "one of the sharpest denunciations of the Soviet Union by a high Administration official in years," claimed that the Cubans and, in some measure, the Soviets bore responsibility for the dissidents' invasion. The President himself added his accusation of Cuban responsibility for the attack. The evidence could not, however, be released, and anonymous officials were quoted by reporters as disagreeing over its meaning. Instead of gaining credit for effective crisis management, Carter was mired in a crisis of credibility. Instead of applause, there were questions. An analysis in *The New York Times* put it bluntly: "Were Mr. Carter's advisers, intent on drawing the line against Soviet and Cuban advances in the region, too eager to make political capital out of the Central Intelligence Agency's findings?" The intention had presumably been to impress both the Soviets and American conservatives with the Administration's toughness. Judging by subsequent events, the tactic worked in neither policy nor political terms.

As the Soviets increased their presence in South Yemen and the Horn of Africa, the Administration developed its planning for such American countermeasures in the region as seemed possible, including the formation of a Rapid Deployment Force. But rather than wait to be able to emphasize the response, the White House once again gave priority to the threat. The region had become an "arc of crisis." Picking up the phrase, *Time* magazine ran a cover portraying a Russian bear about to savage the Middle East. There was little indication of how the United States would make it turn tail. Once again, the domestic political effect was to portray weakness rather than strength, more threat and promised reaction than actual performance.

In August 1979, intelligence analysts pieced together evidence that certain Soviet military personnel in Cuba were operating together in brigade-size patterns. This appeared to be a step beyond the advisory role in which they had previously been engaged, perhaps a violation of the agreements ending the Cuban missile crisis in 1962. When informed of this finding, Senator Frank Church of Idaho, up for reelection and himself the object of attack for softness on the Soviet Union, linked the removal of the brigade to ratification of the SALT II agreement. Partly in an effort to convince other Senators that they need not join Church in pushing for firm action, the normally careful Secretary of State, Cyrus Vance, stated that the United States would not accept the *status quo.* But after lengthy negotiation it became apparent that the Soviets would not accept anything else. (The Soviet position was strengthened when the CIA belatedly discovered records of the presence of the Soviet force in Cuba many years earlier, although not performing in the same way.) Carter backed away, under cover of semantic niceties.

Meanwhile, Carter's national-security adviser had publicly warned the Soviets of possible retaliation if they did not cooperate in finding a solution. Again, the Soviet threat and, in this case, threatened American action had been portrayed as larger than the actual United States response. The combination of tough talk and moderate action again had produced international and political embarrassment. A crisis had been created, and nothing effective had been done about it.

Late December and early January 1980: the same pattern but with new events, this time far more serious—Soviet forces were invading Afghanistan. Moscow was lying about its purposes and the events leading up to the invasion. Showing political courage, President Carter went beyond symbolic sanctions against the Soviets and ordered a grain embargo that would require sacrifices both by American farmers and by the taxpayers who would be asked to cushion the costs to the farmers. All in all, it was a perfect opportunity for a President accused of weakness not only to act with strength, as he was doing, but to be perceived as strong.

It did not happen. The pattern was repeated. The strength of the response was diminished by the portrayal of the threat. The invasion of Afghanistan, said Carter, was "the most serious threat to world peace since the Second World War." Of course, the President could not gain public support for sacrifices without demonstrating the seriousness of this Soviet action. But such hyperbole put his own judgment in question. He added to the damage by stating that the invasion had changed his view of the Soviets.

By now, editorialists and cartoonists were portraying the President in cruel, diminutive terms. In his State of the Union address at the end of January, the President made another effort to strengthen his position and image, as he pledged that any attempt by an outside power to gain control of the Persian Gulf area would be "repelled by use of any means necessary including military force." Whether this was good policy—whether its deterrent effect outweighed the danger of making a commitment beyond the capacity of our conventional military forces; whether a public declaration made more sense than private warnings to the Soviets—it seemed to be good politics. But in the long run it was not. After the initial applause for the stand he was taking, the situation in the region remained as threatening as ever. Soviet repression in Afghanistan increased. And the hostage crisis in Iran became a crushing symbol of the President's perceived international impotence.

Iran was a symbol that Carter himself had helped to create, almost a perfect case of a President trapping himself both by promising more than he could deliver and by appearing to use a foreign-policy issue for political advantage, thus demeaning both his office and himself. There is no doubt that the issue itself caused the President, like so many other Americans, real anguish. But there can also be little doubt that his tactics conveyed an impression of political as well as international concerns at work. The initial publicity about the unlit Christmas tree; the successful "Rose Garden" strategy of refusing to go out to joust with Senator Kennedy in the primaries because of the pressures of dealing with the Iran crisis; the inaccurate claim, on the morning of the Wisconsin primary, that a breakthrough on Iran was imminent; even the abortive rescue effort—all contributed to this impression. By the end of April 1980, the Rose Garden had lost its appeal. Carter was again sinking in the polls. Iran was hurting him badly—as it was to do through the remainder of the campaign.

Announcing that the hostage crisis had been "alleviated to some degree," the President took up active campaigning on May 1. No one can know the degrees to which Carter had been motivated by his genuine concerns on the issue and by the race against Kennedy. It is clear, however, that in political terms the Iran issue, which had first picked up the President on its wave, later dashed him on the beach. In retrospect, it would have been far wiser to try to diminish rather than increase the public furor about the issue. The greater the furor, the more the issue appealed to the Iranian terrorists and then worked to the advantage of Carter's political opponents.

The growing impression of a President twisting foreign policy for political purposes was fueled also by a fiasco at the United Nations in March, when the United States reversed its vote on a Middle East

Resolution critical of Israel. The initial vote, which was arguable on its merits, offended supporters of that nation, of whom there were more than a few in the upcoming New York primary. The political damage in New York may have been slightly reduced by the reversal. But the impression of fumbling and political calculation was far more damaging in the long run.

During his race against Ronald Reagan, the President sought to use the peace theme, portraying his opponent as dangerous and reckless—1964 redux. It had worked for Lyndon Johnson, but it did not work for Jimmy Carter. Despite the leak of PD-59, a nuclear-strategy document that put a tougher face on the Administration's military stance, and the clumsy revelation of plans to build the Stealth (a new strategic bomber), Carter's containment credentials remained suspect, and his political emphasis now on peace added to the perception of irresolution in the face of extraordinary threats. And Ronald Reagan, muting his hawkishness, refused to play the peace-threatening role called for in Carter's campaign strategy.

Despite his real successes in both policy and personal terms—the Camp David accords, negotiation of a SALT II agreement, normalization of relations with the People's Republic of China, the Panama Canal treaties, peace in Zimbabwe, the reversal of the decline in defense spending—by 1980 Carter had few public defenders of his foreign-policy record. His early achievements had come through political courage, as over Panama. His later years had seemed to show more political ambition. Liberal supporters were disillusioned by his turn to global containment. Conservative opponents found him to be wanting in terms of his own latter-day containment rhetoric. Truman, Kennedy and Johnson had failed to meet their promise of an America that could preserve freedom everywhere. With Carter, it was a failure to deal with the threats and challenges he and his aides had portrayed. The gap between words and deeds was the same. And after the promises of a new approach in 1976 and 1977, the sounds of Carter as Cold Warrior rang false. In the end, no one knew who he was; and, rightly or wrongly, many suspected that the President did not, either.

Ronald Reagan came to office promising the simplicity of confrontation with the Soviets as a substitute for the complexities of Carter's efforts to create a new world. Reagan would play Henry V to Carter's Hamlet. Essentially, the Reagan promise was this: by recapturing American military strength, America would be "number one" again. And simply by being in first place militarily, we could preserve the peace. As he put it in the October 29, 1980, debate with Carter, "America has never gotten in a war because we were too strong. We can get into a war by letting events get out of hand.... Good management in preserving the peace requires that we control the events and try to intercept them before they become a crisis."

This sounded like a recipe for interventionism, much like the Truman and Kennedy rhetoric of earlier years. So, Reagan qualified his rhetoric with a cautious note, which itself contained a promise that was actually more difficult to achieve than theirs had been. For, he went on, we need not actually become involved militarily while "controlling events." "I have seen four wars in my lifetime. I'm a father of sons. I have a grandson. I don't ever want to see another generation of young Americans bleed their lives into sandy beachheads in the Pacific and jungles in Asia or the muddy, bloody battlefields of Europe." In short, we could dominate events in the world by *having* military strength: we could not have to *use* it.

This was simply another cost-free version of omnipotence. The Republican party warned of the greatest peril since 1776 and also called for cutting taxes and abolishing registration for the draft. For purposes of gaining election, it all fit well with the American mood. As John Rielly wrote in the spring of 1979, the polls showed that Americans wanted a "foreign policy of self-interest." The public wanted to see increased defense spending and a more vigorous assertion of American economic and political positions abroad. But a majority of Americans also were "wary of the kind of direct involvement in the affairs of other countries that characterized U.S. foreign policy" in the 1960s. We should defeat our enemies and impose our will; we should not pay any substantial price for it.

The world turned out to be far more unruly than Reagan had imagined—or at least had portrayed. Simply asserting that the United States would again be the Number One, with greatly enhanced military spending, did not make our adversaries quail. And indeed, within a year, our allies sounded almost as fearful of the United States as of the Soviet Union. Nor did the new rhetoric of strength make the kinds of choice that had bedeviled Carter go away. As Reagan wrestled with the limits to American influence in the face of repression in Poland, of continuing Soviet aggression in Afghanistan, or of our relations with Beijing, Jerusalem and even San Salvador, he had to make compromises with reality. Despite pledges of linkage between arms-control negotiations and Soviet behavior elsewhere, such negotiations were undertaken even while Soviet troops continued to sweep the countryside of Afghanistan, even after martial law was declared in Poland, and even after the Soviets shot down a Korean civilian airliner. While he had promised full support for Taiwan, Reagan was forced by the Communist leaders of China to agree to new limits to (and even the eventual elimination of) American arms sales to the non-Communist Chinese.

When he sought to persuade our allies not to help the Soviets build a natural-gas pipeline between Siberia and Western Europe, he failed. When he then imposed economic sanctions against the Europeans after their refusal to heed him on the issue, he was forced first to weaken his punitive measures, and later to abandon the whole effort behind a thin smoke screen of diplomatic word play. When a Korean airliner was shot down in cold blood, the rhetoric from Washington was tough as nails; the action was so restrained it went almost unnoticed. In Lebanon, humiliating withdrawal of the Marines contradicted the rhetoric surrounding their deployment.

This was a reassertion of America? This was being Number One again?

As the President developed a record noted more for words than for acts, the right became uneasy about the leader who had promised it so much. At first the attacks came against Reagan's Secretary of State, Alexander Haig. As Haig was jettisoned, for reasons of personal behavior more than for policy difference, conservative unease remained as "neoconservative" ideologues such as Norman Podhoretz constantly attacked Reagan for apostasy.

His constituency on the right had believed him; now its faith seemed shaken. And after a year of near silence (save on El Salvador), in 1982 critics on the left began to pick up the cudgels, charging Reagan both with bellicosity in his rhetoric and failure in his policies, especially with regard to the state of our alliances.

On arms control, Reagan met a surprisingly strong public reaction. In 1981, the European peace movement—its demonstrating crowds swollen by loose Presidential (and Secretarial) rhetoric in Washington—drove the Administration to the negotiating table on limiting theater nuclear forces. In 1982, the burgeoning nuclear "freeze" movement at home joined with European concerns to produce the START proposal for strategic weapons reduction. But if Reagan's proposals bought him political time, their asymmetric focus on Soviet force cuts blocked practical progress, assuring renewed domestic pressure on Reagan. This pressure was eased, in 1984, by the clumsiness and intransigence of Soviet policies, and in early 1985 by the return of the two nations to the bargaining table.

Central America exemplified Reagan's problem. To "lose" El Salvador or Guatemala would be a denial of his rhetoric of global containment. If we could not "defend ourselves there," he said in April 1983, ". . . our credibility would collapse, our alliances would crumble, and the safety of our homeland would be put at jeopardy." But to try to defeat the guerrillas there through increasing military intervention would mobilize the left and probably the political center against him. Despite Haig's early rhetoric of American strength and the portrayal of El Salvador as a test case of an American foreign policy now free, at long last, from the "Vietnam syndrome," Reagan was forced, for at least his first term in office, to rely on small numbers of advisers and more aid to the government of El Salvador; military exercises in the region; and highly visible "covert" aid to rebels against the leftist Nicaraguan regime to which the Congress put at least a temporary halt. Rather than a policy that would "control events," Reagan had to hope that events in Central America would break his way.

In short, Reagan faced the same old dilemma. The domestic politics of the issue required both containment of leftists in Central America and no military intervention or loss of American life. The push of the Munich analogy was joined by the restraint of an equally simplistic Vietnam analogy, which seemed to argue that American intervention in the Third World led not to peace through deterrence but simply more war. The conceptual basis of American foreign policy was still fractured. The politics of foreign policy remained far more complicated than in the pre-Vietnam era. Polls in 1982 showed undiminished demand for American strength and success in the competition with the Soviets. But an NBC poll in March 1982 also showed that 65 percent of Americans "with some knowledge about U.S. policy in El Salvador" opposed United States involvement there. It was true that there had been some increase in public willingness to help defend alliance areas and the Persian Gulf region, after support for any form of intervention had reached a post-World War II low in the middle 1970s. The successful invasion of Grenada in the fall of 1983 was popular. But the taste for paying a real price for containment remained low. By the second year of Reagan's Presidency, polls showed that defense spending was now near the bottom of the voters' priorities. And by February 1983 a *New York Times*–CBS poll showed that almost twice as many Americans thought too much money was going to new weapons as thought that spending levels were about right. Only 11 percent favored new increases.

Reagan was expected to stop the Communist and even, perhaps, defeat them, for he had implied that this too might be possible. Yet he would have to do so without becoming embroiled in lengthy or costly foreign adventures. A quick Grenada boosted his popularity; a drawn-out affair in Lebanon posed political dangers, and the President quickly cut his losses. Like his predecessors, by using illusion for his brush as he painted his picture of the world and American power, Ronald Reagan set the political trap for himself.

The trap did not close on him in his 1984 campaign, for events in Central America and elsewhere had not forced him to choose between containment and concession. The public responded well to his rhetoric of national supremacy, just as it thrilled to the American performance at the summer Olympics. But this was no mandate for assertive policies abroad, no relief from the popular injunction against costs. On the issues, polls showed public support for the more cautious approach of Walter Mondale. And in early 1985, increasing numbers of taxpayers were calling for cuts in defense spending. In his second term, if the President were to move toward military intervention or fail to find more of a handle on the arms race, there seemed little doubt that opposition to his policies would grow again. The cross-currents of public opinion and the politics of foreign policy remained as treacherous and contradictory as ever.

How had we come to this?

Certainly the contradictory demands of the public, the rapid shifts in opinion, have made it terribly difficult for any President to manage our foreign policies. But the harsh fact is that our Presidents and politicians have helped to make it so.

As many analysts have argued, public opinion and political pressures are not autonomous creatures. The public, to be sure, reacts spontaneously to events and shapes its views in consonance with prevailing values. And our elites, the so-called "attentive public," play a central role in the formation of public opinion and in putting pressure on politicians through editorials and letters. But while the press and elites pose issues and points of view, the politicians sometimes perceive public demands and reactions, and political impulses and constraints, where in fact there would be a possibility for public education. Sometimes the public is more sophisticated than the politicians believe, and politicians react to the fears they have generated for themselves. As Kenneth Waltz has pointed out, for all the furor over who lost China a few years before, a Gallup poll in 1954 showed that 73 percent of those polled blamed the ignorance of the Chinese people, the skill of the Communists, and the corruption of the Nationalists: only 10 percent blamed the American government for the "loss."

In short, it is a symbiotic process, with politicians, elites and public reinforcing prevailing ideologies and political imperatives. Time after time, politicians running for President have encouraged the voters to believe that there can be peace *and* containment without losses, and all at a relatively minor cost. Whether it is the contrast of a global Truman Doctrine with Korea; or "liberation" with Hungary and Cuba; or the rhetoric of 1960 with the events of the Bay of Pigs and the Berlin Wall; or the promises of 1964 with the escalation and frustrations of 1965–68; or the peace plan of 1968 with the war of 1969–75; or the broad promise and the narrow reality of détente and human rights with the containment of late Carter and early Reagan—in every case, Presidents have promised more than they could do; felt compelled and constrained by the public attitudes they had a major share in creating; and then suffered at the polls as disillusionment set in. Indeed, for recent Presidents, the problem has not so much been disillusionment as the reinforcement of post-Vietnam cynicism. While in Truman, Kennedy and Johnson the constraints and penalties of the trap were specific to their own Presidencies, since Vietnam the credibility gap has become institutionalized. Now there is cynicism about most Presidents and just about all politicians.

This has hurt our foreign policies. And it has hurt our Presidents. But our concern here should not merely be for them personally. After all, by promising their way to power, they achieved their immediate personal ambitions. Rather, our concern should be for the Presidency and for America's credibility as a steady force in world affairs. We all have a stake in a central institution that can bring coherence to our foreign policies and rally popular support behind them.

The decline in public confidence in our government as a whole, over the past two decades, has been striking. Between 1964 and 1976, the number of Americans expressing a feeling of alienation from their government doubled, from 31 percent to 61 percent, according to the Center for Political Studies at the University of Michigan. Harris polls show a decrease, from 41 percent to 17 percent, in confidence in the Executive Branch, from 1966 to 1979. While polls show continued support for our institutions of government as institutions, public trust in the people who fulfill the duties of those institutions is low.

The Presidency is thus in trouble. The political survival rate of our leaders bears witness—between 1933 and 1961 three Presidents held office over a span of seven four-year terms. Between 1961 and 1980, five Presidents served for exactly five such terms. It is no accident that our last two Presidents, Jimmy Carter and Ronald Reagan, gained office through campaigns that emphasized their opposition to the ways of the federal government. In effect, we now are nominating and electing anti-Presidents.

The issue goes far deeper than the traditional one of the powers of the presidency versus those of the Congress. It concerns the relationship between the people and their government. And that relationship, the key to the health of a democracy, is not well.

A number of sensible explanations for this loss of confidence have been offered. Clearly, events—Watergate, the Vietnam War, instances of corruption—have played a part. So has frustration born of the decline in America's relative economic position. Anthony Downs has argued that each President creates, over a four-year period, a powerful opposition coalition of minorities who had lost out on his specific decisions. But the events, the economy and a President's decisions do not go far enough in explaining the problem. To understand our disillusionment, we must examine the nature of our illusions.

What makes America, American social progress and American foreign policy distinctive is the hold of our ideals on our imagination. This produces impulses toward greatness. It also creates extraordinary tensions in our political life. "The more intensely Americans commit themselves to their national political beliefs," Samuel Huntington has written, "the more hostile or cynical they become about their political institutions. . . . The legitimacy of American government varies inversely with belief in American political ideals." For our institutions—or any form of government, for that matter—cannot make real the dream of a perfect society that has always animated American politics.

If this clash between belief and possibility is true about our own society, is it not also true for our approach to the world? Both liberal and conservative Americans, in different ways but for the same reasons, tend to promote an absolutist morality in the world—an "Americanism" that, as Louis Hartz argues, "is inspired either to withdraw from alien things or to transform them: it cannot live in comfort constantly by their side." Some might argue that this "Americanism" was tempered by the Vietnam experience. The popular response to human-rights crusades and distaste for pragmatism in their pursuit, to the Reagan rhetoric of 1980, and to the Grenada invasion—all these suggest otherwise.

This belief in a special American mandate and the temptation to believe in American omnipotence collide not only with the stubborn realities of a world in which the United States is powerful but not dominant; they also collide with our democratic process. First, democratic institutions and the inherent American mistrust of strong central institutions make it hard for any President to carry out the strong foreign policies called for by the American vision of our role in the world. In addition, democratic pluralism tends to produce policies of compromise, of limited means dwarfed by our grand goals. And compromise, in a moral struggle, is easily seen as sin. Thus, the way in which we make foreign policy is inherently in tension with the absolute morality that we continue to impose on our view of the world.

Logically, these dilemmas of democratic foreign-policy making could be resolved by putting tighter boundaries on democracy itself when national security is at stake. And this, indeed, has been the tendency of most Presidents, whatever their previous rhetoric about civil liberties and openness in government. Clearly, some such bounds are necessary. Successful diplomacy requires a large measure of secrecy. But it is much too easy to go too far with this prescription. The history of Watergate shows how much can be lost when we begin to destroy our democracy in order to protect it.

The question should not be how to *reduce* our democracy, but how best to *use* it. It is whether our politicians, elites and public will act in responsible ways and refuse to abuse our institutions by asking too much of them and of ourselves. The answer in these times has been a sad one; by constantly playing on and raising public expectations about what can be done to bring America's peace and America's ideals to the world, a generation of Presidents and candidates too often have capitulated to irresponsibility.

Just as the New Deal, in its rhetoric as well as in undoubted successes, encouraged Americans to hold the government accountable for the quality of their personal lives, so the politicians' expressions of belief in the myth of American omnipotence have encouraged us to expect somehow that our government can transform the world. Our political leaders have acted—or, rather, spoken—as if the world is a simple place and the public simple-minded.

Our argument is not with the basic goals of American foreign policy, with the containment of the Soviet Union or the promotion of human rights or efforts at peace. It is with pretending that there can be an easy way or easy choices. It is with our tendency to overestimate the power of our nation—and our Presidents—in the world. It is with our ability to forget traditional American pragmatism when embarking on global crusades. It is with promoting the illusion that there can be all victories and no defeats, and holding our politicians hostage to the illusion, as they continue to hold one another.

The government of our nation becomes nearly impossible when the public—disillusioned by the gap between political promises and the ability of Presidents to deliver in a world of new limits to American power—instinctively starts to turn on its leaders within a year or so of their inauguration.

When a new President takes office, his policies fairly quickly take hold within the foreign-policy bureaucracy. Contrary to the impression of most analysts and Presidents themselves, the wheels of government do start to turn in the direction set by the new leader. There may be a loose pulley here in the machinery of government or a grinding of gears there, but the wheels do turn—if the new leader's directions are reasonably clear.

Outside the government, however, a balance wheel starts to move in the opposite direction. Led by the President's political and ideological opponents, public opinion starts to build against what the President wants to do. As President Carter pursued arms control, sentiment for a "margin of safety" or United States military superiority began to grow. As Reagan pursued a massive military buildup, sentiment for a nuclear freeze welled up while support for military spending declined.

This is healthy to the degree that it imposes moderation on new administrations anxious to demonstrate that their ideology can change the world overnight. And in the past decade, as each administration has committed itself to even more significant changes in the foreign policies of its predecessor, the need for this moderating reaction has become more important. But over and over again, the contrary balance wheel turns too far, preventing Presidents from managing effectively and providing the political momentum for the new Presidential challenger to ride his own promises into office. And so the public helps the politicians swing the pendulum back and forth between right and left, confounding our Presidents, their policies and, ultimately, our hopes for both.

This cycle of promise and reaction could be ameliorated by our elites, by those in our society who should understand the complexities of the world, the limits to our power and the importance of consistency in our policies. But, far from providing moderating advice to Presidents they support, or responsible opposition to Presidents of another party, our elites have become still more ideological, more partisan than the public. Instead of a steadying force in public opinion, and in the government, they have become a major cause of confusion and domestic conflict. It is to their role in the foreign-policy breakdown that we now turn.

II From "Establishment" to "Professional Elite"

DURING the 1960s, a revolution was taking place in the structure of America's foreign-policy leadership. Power was passing almost imperceptibly from the old Eastern Establishment to a new Professional Elite, from bankers and lawyers who would take time off to help manage the affairs of government to full-time foreign-policy experts, from an essentially homogeneous group of centrists and pragmatists to those with views that tended toward (and sometimes were at) the ideological extremes of American political thought, and from an essentially bipartisan or nonpartisan approach to a highly political one.

The men (and, rarely, women) who run American foreign policy have always operated in a small world, so the transformation was something of a revolution in a teapot. But from this teapot came the ideas and actions that shaped the great issues of war and peace. This transformation in the 1960s and 1970s thus helped to unhook the United States from the moorings of more than two decades of policy. From about 1970 on, our foreign policy tumbled first in one direction and then in another as views polarized within the country and as groups within the new Professional Elite contended for power. The anchor provided by the old Establishment was gone, for good and for ill.

The anchor had been personified by men like Robert A. Lovett. When he was named Deputy Defense Secretary on September 28, 1950, *The New York Times* applauded his "impressive" record as Assistant Secretary of War for Air during World War II and as Under Secretary of State from 1947 to 1949. "He has worked quietly and efficiently, he has avoided rash statements, he has kept out of needless controversies and he has made himself felt as a man of character, industry and intelligence," the editorial stated. A year later, the *Times* was no less kind when it bannered the retirement of George C. Marshall as Secretary of Defense and his replacement by Mr. Lovett.

A decade later, when President-elect John F. Kennedy was searching for ballast for his young Administration, he invited Lovett down from his Wall Street office for a chat in Georgetown. He offered the older man his choice of portfolios—Secretary of State, Defense or Treasury. It is said that the old man, whose soft eyes belied his strength of character, gently told the President that he had voted for his opponent, Richard Nixon. Kennedy said this did not matter. Then, pleading poor health, Lovett declined all the positions. He recommended instead Dean Rusk, President of the Rockefeller Foundation, Robert S. McNamara, President of the Ford Motor Company, and C. Douglas Dillon, a partner in the Wall Street firm of Dillon and Read, the very men Mr. Kennedy was to select for these posts.

Lovett was to serve in various capacities on prestigious Presidential commissions on arms control and intelligence during the 1960s. But mostly he stayed put in his Wall Street firm of Brown Brothers, Harriman and Company. Years before, he had married the daughter of one of the Brown brothers. Like so many of the old policy establishment, he had all the right tickets for any marriage and any position. At twenty-three, fresh from Yale, he had joined the Great War as a pilot and won the Navy Cross. After the war, he had gone on to Harvard Law School.

Lovett was a man who could look a fact in the face. Like his partners in the Truman Administration, he continued to urge support for Chiang Kai-shek and the Chinese nationalists until it was clear that money would not help, that Chiang's regime was hopelessly corrupt, and that the wave of the future was with Mao Tse-tung and his Communists. As hard as it was, the bond of support for Chiang had to be cut, and Lovett was prepared to do it. He showed the same kind of flexibility when it came to recognition of the new state of Israel.

"Few men in the State Department were more coldly pragmatic than Robert Lovett," wrote Dan Kurzman in *Genesis 1948.* Drawing on accounts of Mr. Lovett by his contemporaries, Kurzman judged that Lovett had neither sympathy for Zionism nor the Lawrence-like attachment for Arabs so prevalent in the State Department. He had been persuaded that America had far more to gain from backing forty million Arabs than from backing a few hundred thousand Jews in Palestine. Despite all the arguments he had been making against the recognition of the state of Israel, he finally concluded that the establishment of a Jewish state was inevitable. He and the State Department had fought against it and lost. Now, as a practical matter, the United States had to adjust, and Lovett played an important role in the ultimate conversion of the State Department to that view.

If Robert Lovett was the prototypical man of the Establishment, Zbigniew Brzezinski seemed to embody the new Professional Elite. Like so many key members of this new elite (Harvard professors like Henry A. Kissinger and Stanley H. Hoffmann and Georgetown Center for Strategic and International Studies pundits like Edward Luttwak and Walter Lacquer), he was foreign born. Son of a Polish diplomat, a Harvard Ph.D., Brzezinski first made his mark as a scholar. His career pattern was the reverse of the Establishmentarian's; he was to write first and serve in government later.

Power came to Lovett; Brzezinski had to claw for it. Lovett, like most of his contemporaries, went far out of his way to avoid making news or saying anything catchy; Brzezinski, like his contemporaries, wrote for effect and raced after headlines. Lovett was a man of little or no theory and a lot of action. For Brzezinski and the Elite, words, articles and theories were the route of elevation. Lovett's power base was Wall Street; Brzezinski's were his ideas and his ties to politicians.

In 1959, Harvard had one tenured opening for a young professor of international politics. As was to happen often in Brzezinski's career, the mantle was placed on Kissinger. Brzezinski retreated to Columbia University and began to climb a ladder parallel to, but always one rung behind, Kissinger's. They both built reputations as scholars, though Kissinger's was more luminous. They both wrote articles in magazines like *Foreign Affairs*, the organ of the Council on Foreign Relations, but Kissinger's always seemed to get more attention. They both derived their views from the school of power realists, from the writings of Hans Morgenthau, a Chicago University professor who spoke the language of power politics with a German accent. Both Kissinger and Brzezinski believed in balance-of-power diplomacy, in containment of Soviet power, and in the Vietnam War. Yet, they were always competitive and quarreling. Members of the new Professional Elite always seemed to be quarreling with one another.

Henry Kissinger was the first from the new elite to make it to the top, now defined not just by power but by publicity as well. To be sure, Walt W. Rostow, an MIT professor, was the national-security assistant to President Lyndon Johnson, but his work was still behind the scenes. Kissinger, under President Nixon, was to transform that position into *de facto* cabinet rank, virtually the protocol equal of the Secretaries of State and Defense, and soon more than the policy equal. Kissinger, protégé of the old Establishment, was to become the first powerhouse of the new elite, the model.

Kissinger made Nelson Rockefeller his base. He advised Rockefeller in his perpetual quest for the Republican Presidential nomination. He ran a variety of foreign-policy projects for the Council on Foreign Relations and the Rockefeller Brothers Fund, one of which led in 1957 to his path-breaking book, *Nuclear Weapons and Foreign Policy.* Brzezinski fastened onto David Rockefeller, head of the Chase Manhattan Bank. Together, in 1973 they fashioned the Trilateral Commission, a kind of international Council on Foreign Relations dedicated to fostering better relations among North America, Western Europe and Japan. It was Nelson Rockefeller, Nixon's perennial rival, who opened the doors for Kissinger into Nixon's world. It was David Rockefeller, whose contacts were everywhere, who provided the opportunity for Brzezinski to meet Jimmy Carter.

The Trilateral Commission was a club, and Brzezinski and David Rockefeller got to choose its members. They chose the then virtually unknown Georgia governor. At a time when few members of the Elite had ever even heard of Jimmy Carter, let alone dreamed of his going anywhere on the national stage, Brzezinski befriended him and began advising him. Few were surprised when President-elect Carter named Brzezinski to be his Assistant for National Security Affairs.

Nor would it have been surprising if Brzezinski had gotten this post under almost any Democratic President. By the time Carter's long-shot campaign was under way in 1976, almost every Democratic hopeful had been the beneficiary of private conversations with the Columbia professor. He had positioned himself substantively. His articles and advice carried the perfect blend of anti-Communism and liberal humanism, of checking Soviet power and of advancing human rights. He would have the Democrats contain Moscow better than Kissinger and be more humane than Kissinger at the same time. Under Kissinger, he told the Democratic hopefuls, America had lost its sense of values; it had stopped caring and standing for anything. He was selling himself as a kind of "Good Henry Kissinger."

It was not as if Brzezinski had to break down the doors to meet the Democratic candidates. By the time he went to them, they all wanted him. He gave them a kind of legitimacy, the most important kind for the 1970s: expertise. Like his contemporaries who were working in the same vineyard, he had met the politicians at conferences, dined with them, sent them copies of his articles, and took their telephone calls to provide quick advice for a comment to the news media.

Like Kissinger, Brzezinski knew how to talk to men of power, to appreciate politics, to combine the language of scholarship and expertise with the world of power. He could explain problems and ideas simply, put them in words that politicians could use in speeches and television appearances, give them a clever phrase to catch a headline. He understood their dilemmas, the need to combine high moral purpose with new-sounding approaches and phrases that could win elections. It was not a waste of time for politicians to talk with this professor.

Before Carter named Brzezinski to be his White House national-security aide, he chose Cyrus R. Vance as Secretary of State and Harold Brown as Defense Secretary. No surprises here either. Vance, a Wall Street lawyer, was a man who had held high office previously in the Pentagon. He was every inch the safe and sound Establishmentarian, or so it seemed, despite the fact that he had become a critic of the Vietnam War. Harold Brown, the former President of the California Institute of Technology, former head of Pentagon research, and Secretary of the Air Force during the Johnson administration, also was a natural choice. But together, Brzezinski the professor, Vance the Establishment lawyer with liberal views, and Brown the technocrat were to mark the crossover point. With them, and the people they brought with them, the revolution was complete. The new Professional Elite had come of age.

It was an irony that Vance was to help usher in the new era. He was, by birth, style, temperament, character and career, an exemplar of the old Establishment. To many, it seemed that Vance would be the natural successor to John J. McCloy, the Wall Street banker and confidant of Presidents, as the unofficial head of the Establishment. But from the time when Vance left his post as Deputy to Defense Secretary Robert McNamara in 1966 and returned to Simpson, Thacher and Bartlett, his law firm, something happened to him. His thinking about foreign policy changed. He moved from safe centrist positions to a more liberal line, from being a man whose career had defined the center to someone who would take the point position on controversial issues he cared about. As Secretary of State, he was to surprise almost everyone. Instead of using his well-honed skills to shape centrist consensus as he had done in the past, he became the point man in the Carter Administration in arguing for arms-control agreements with the Soviet Union and tolerance in accepting change in the Third World.

But while his views had moved leftward, his style and sense of values and fair play remained very much of the Old World. He saw very early in 1977 that Brzezinski was not playing by the same rules. From reporters, legislators and friends at the White House, it was clear that Brzezinski had already begun to position himself as the practitioner of *Realpolitik* in the administration, painting Vance and his subordinates as left-wingers. But Vance would not respond in kind. He would not try to make alliances with Harold Brown or with key White House aides against Brzezinski. He would not call in newsmen to correct stories about him planted by Brzezinski and his aides, nor would he countenance his own aides doing that work for him.

Early on, a story appeared in *Time* magazine attacking Brzezinski, with the calumny ascribed to a State Department official. Vance called in the assistant secretary suspected of the leak and said, "Did you do it?" The response was yes. "Don't do it again," said the Secretary. "That's the wrong way. It will only spread the poison and make it worse. I'll take the issues up with the President. But I'm not going to talk to him about Zbig or any bureaucratic nonsense. I'll talk to him about the issues. That's the way to do it."

His strategy worked for a time. He did have the President's ear, and most decisions went his way in the first year. But the country was moving to the conservative side of the foreign-policy debate, the White House wanted to bend in that direction, and Brzezinski was caricaturing his position. But by temperament and conviction, Vance would live by the gentlemen's rules from the old era—and eventually be hit by the new rules. He knew that their policy differences were substantial. He did not want to recognize the lengths to which Brzezinski and his allies would go in trying to win.

But Brzezinski, Brown, their staffs, and Vance's aides were products of the new game and the new rules. The people they brought in with them were at the very heart of the new Professional Elite. By the dozens, they came in, to take over almost every top position in the State Department, Defense Department and National Security Council staff. There were scores more who were placed in lower-level positions and in the critical special-assistant slots. To be sure, the Nixon administration brought a number of Republican foreign-policy specialists into government in 1969 and removed a good many professionals with Democratic connections. At the same time, however, many professionals—civil servants and Foreign Service officers—were kept on. Henry Kissinger's National Security Council staff was a blend of outside experts and career professionals, Democrats and Republicans, liberals and conservatives alike, pro- and anti-Vietnam. Foreign Service officers also held their own in many key State Department positions. The biggest turnover under Nixon occurred in the Pentagon, where many civilian experts had constituted the hotbed of opposition to the Vietnam War, and where McNamara's "whiz kids" had done much over the years to alienate the professional military.

The takeover by the new types in 1977 was not partial as it had been in 1969; it was virtually total. More than one hundred critical foreign-affairs positions were filled by people coming from outside government. A sizable percentage were serving in the Executive Branch for the first time.

Perhaps more important than numbers was the fact that almost all the new policy makers were from the center, center-left and left on the ideological spectrum. It was not just a physical turnover, but an intellectual one. There was as much continuity as change in policy in the transfer of power from the Johnson administration to the Nixon and Ford administrations. From Ford to Carter, there was far more change than continuity. It represented a takeover of the Vietnam War critics, advocates of arms-control agreements with the Soviets, and those who felt strongly that the power of the United States should be used to affect human-rights issues in other countries. Conservative Democratic foreign-policy experts were excluded, sometimes by calculation, sometimes by their own choice, and most often simply by the force of the old-boy network on the center and left.

Those who could choose their own staffs selected people who had fought by their sides in past battles and those who would serve with them in future battles.

They came in especially at the Assistant Secretary rank. In the State Department could be found Richard Moose as Deputy Under Secretary of State for Management and later Assistant Secretary for Africa; Richard C. Holbrooke as head of Asian and Pacific Affairs; Douglas Bennet to manage Congressional Relations; Anthony Lake to run the policy-planning staff; Leslie H. Gelb to manage political-military matters; Marshall Shulman to serve as Vance's special adviser for Soviet affairs; Matthew Nimitz as Counselor; and Daniel Spiegel as Vance's special assistant.

Harold Brown took as his key people: David McGiffert, a Washington attorney and former Under Secretary of the Army in the Johnson administration, to be Assistant Secretary for International Security Affairs, the Pentagon's little State Department; Walter Slocombe, a Washington tax lawyer and arms-control specialist who had worked on the Presidential campaign of George S. McGovern in 1972, to oversee work on strategic-arms-limitation talks with Moscow; Russell Murray, one of McNamara's "whiz kids," to be Assistant Secretary for Systems Analysis; and Lynn Davis, a Columbia specialist in defense policy, to run the policy-planning staff. Later, Robert Komer, an NSC aide under Kennedy and Johnson, moved in as Under Secretary for Policy.

Brzezinski filled his critical White House billets with similar types: David Aaron, a former Foreign Service officer and then aide to Senator (later Vice-President) Walter F. Mondale, as Deputy Assistant to the President for National Security; Robert Hunter, a former aide to Senators Hubert Humphrey and Edward M. Kennedy, for Western European Affairs, Michel Oksenberg, a professor from the University of Michigan, to be his China expert; William Quandt, another professor from the University of Pennsylvania, as the main man on Middle East negotiations; and as Special Assistant Rick Inderfurth, a former member of the Church Committee staff that investigated wrongdoing in the Central Intelligence Agency.

Paul C. Warnke was named by President Carter as Director of the Arms Control and Disarmament Agency. Warnke, as Assistant Secretary of Defense in the Johnson Administration, had come to symbolize opposition to the Vietnam War from within the government and advocacy of arms control. At the beginning of the administration, Warnke was in many respects the darling of the Carter foreign-policy team for his outspokenness and courage. Later, when the public mood shifted rightward and Brzezinski went on the attack against what he called left-wing policies, Warnke became the main target of the NSC staff. As his deputy, Warnke chose Spurgeon Keeny, an arms-control specialist from the agency in the 1960s. John Newhouse, a foreign-policy writer with previous government experience in the agency and the Senate, was selected as an Assistant Director. Another was Barry Blechman, who had headed the defense-studies staff at the Brookings Institution.

Along with these established experts on traditional foreign- and defense-policy matters came a number of people who were to be the experts in the new areas of diplomacy, people with essentially political backgrounds. Vance chose Patt Derian, a former Mississippi civil-rights activist, to be the Assistant Secretary for the new bureau of human-rights affairs. Brzezinski picked Jessica Tuchman Mathews, an aide to Representative Morris Udall, to run his global-issues "cluster" dealing with nuclear nonproliferation, human rights and arms sales. President Carter made the most daring move himself in naming Andrew Young, a protégé of Martin Luther King and a man with highly unorthodox notions about foreign policy, as United States Ambassador to the United Nations. These people were a new breed within the new Professional Elite. They operated on the frontiers of late-twentieth-century diplomacy in ways that were to symbolize the Carter Administration to its conservative detractors. Promoting human rights in countries friendly to the United States and preventing the proliferation and export of nuclear capabilities from allies to Third World countries were delicate matters and bound to cause great controversy. And they did.

None of these Carter administration appointees stayed on in the Reagan administration. Nor, with very few exceptions, did career officers with any policy identification with the Carter foreign-policy line. Instead, the right side of the new Professional Elite came to power. Secretary of State Alexander M. Haig, Jr., Defense Secretary Caspar Weinberger, and Richard Allen, as head of the National Security Council staff, made a sweep that was broader than the 1977 one, extending to Foreign Service officers and civil servants. And just as the Carter Administration had excluded conservatives, the Reagan team eliminated not only those who might conceivably have any liberal and left leanings, but also those with moderate Republican tendencies. Foreign Service officers who were being considered for lower-middle-level positions in the State Department were summoned for interviews by the political staff of the White House. This was unprecedented. But so was the commitment to conservative ideology that characterized the new administration.

These feelings were so strong that even experts with ties to former Secretary of State Kissinger, hardly a liberal, were either prevented from getting jobs or were made to pronounce their political and ideological allegiance to the new wave. Haig was permitted to make Lawrence S. Eagleburger, a former Kissinger aide, his Assistant Secretary for European Affairs. But the price was accepting William P. Clark as Deputy Secretary. Clark was a political aide to President Reagan when he was Governor Reagan of California, and a man who admittedly knew nothing about foreign affairs. White House officials did not hesitate to acknowledge that "the Judge," as he was called, was being sent to Foggy Bottom as the watchdog. Not least, he was dispatched to keep an eye on Haig himself, who had once been Kissinger's deputy at the National Security Council staff.

Haig's other appointments were very much the mirror image of the Vance appointments. Paul Wolfowitz, a Democrat with ties to conservative Senator Henry M. Jackson of Washington, became Director of the Policy Planning staff. Richard S. Burt, a reporter for *The New York Times*, assumed the management of the Bureau of Politico-Military Affairs. Elliot Abrams, another conservative Democrat, replaced Patt Derian in the Human Rights Bureau after Congressional resistance forced Ernest Lefever, who showed little sympathy for the purposes of the Bureau, to withdraw his name. Chester Crocker from the conservative Georgetown Center for Strategic and International Studies in Washington was named to head the African Affairs Bureau.

Weinberger's appointments went much further to the right, a fact that was to lead to constant friction between the Defense Department and the State Department, much as Carter's State Department and National Security Council staff warred with each other.

Fred C. Ikle, the head of the Arms Control and Disarmament Agency under Nixon and President Ford, became Under Secretary for Policy. Richard Perle, *eminence grise* to Senator Jackson, and one of the most formidable opponents of past arms-control treaties with the Soviet Union, became Assistant Secretary for International Security Policy.

Richard Allen won for his NSC staff the award for the greatest ideological purity. He wanted all "Reaganauts," as those who had supported Mr. Reagan all along were known. His staff, even within the Administration itself, gained low marks for competence but high grades for ideological devotion. Harvard Professor Richard Pipes was put in charge of Soviet Affairs; he was regarded as far to the right by even the most conservative members of the Administration. Among the more moderate members of the staff was Geoffrey Kemp, a Middle East specialist. Kemp was a professor at the Fletcher School of Law and Diplomacy and Tufts University and a strong conservative himself.

Two key symbolic figures were Eugene V. Rostow and Jeane Kirkpatrick. Rostow was named as Director of the Arms Control and Disarmament Agency. He had been the chairman of The Committee on the Present Danger, a powerful conservative lobby that pressed for increased military spending and opposed the SALT II Treaty with the Soviet Union. He was widely regarded as an opponent of arms control. But in two years, he was to surprise some of his closest friends, perhaps himself, and certainly the White House, when he started to advocate compromises with Moscow to reach arms-reduction accords.

Kirkpatrick was the anti-Derian, a professor at Georgetown University who had spent much of the previous four years attacking the human-rights policies of the Carter Administration. She was the author of a famous article in *Commentary* magazine proclaiming the distinction between totalitarian and authoritarian governments. Totalitarian governments were of the left, anti-American, hopelessly dictatorial, and had to be opposed. Authoritarian governments, she argued in the article, tended to be friendly to the United States, were clearly preferable to the totalitarian ones, and could be made to be less dictatorial. But she insisted in the article that their viability should not be jeopardized by pressuring them to follow human-rights dictates from Washington. Just this kind of idealism, she claimed, had caused Washington to call on the Shah of Iran to liberalize his regime, leading to the Shah's political weakening and ultimate overthrow. The United States had done the same with Anastasio Somoza in Nicaragua, and gotten the Sandinistas as our reward. There were only two choices, and better *our* sons of bitches than theirs: this was the bottom line of her argument.

After the Carter and Reagan Administrations, the transformation was complete. The Establishment had been submerged by both wings of the new Professional Elite. For more than twenty years after World War II, the debate over American foreign policy covered no more than an octave, and now it ran over the whole keyboard. The narrow range that bounded the real choices for two decades first broke left under Carter and then right under Reagan.

For all practical purposes, the Establishment center was gone. The story of this transformation can be told in five parts: in the decline of the Establishment and then of its club, the Council on Foreign Relations; and in the ascent of new, more partisan "think tanks," of ideology, and of the Professional Elite itself.

The Decline of the Establishment

Typically for an informal institution, the Establishment came into prominence just as its days of glory were drawing to a close. Richard Rovere, with tongue firmly in cheek, revealed its existence in an Autumn 1961 article in *The American Scholar*, then expanded his diagnosis in the opening chapter of his 1962 book, *The American Establishment and Other Reports, Opinions, and Speculations* (New York: Harcourt, Brace and World, 1962). He found that "there is an Establishment in America—a more or less closed and self-sustaining institution that holds a preponderance of power in our more or less open society." Its "chairman" in 1958, he asserted, was John J. McCloy, Chairman of the Board of the Chase Manhattan Bank and Chairman of the Council on Foreign Relations. It "constitutes itself a ready pool of manpower" for leadership positions. "The perfect Establishment type," wrote Rovere quoting John Kenneth Galbraith, "would be the Republican called to service in a Democratic administration," or "vice versa." He added that Galbraith himself, just appointed Kennedy's ambassador to India, did not meet this criterion, "for he could not hope to be held over in a Republican administration."

British correspondent Godfrey Hodgson, writing in the Spring 1973 issue of *Foreign Policy,* reached a similar working definition: "a self-recruiting group of men (virtually no women) who have shared a bipartisan philosophy towards, and have exercised practical influence on, the course of American defense and foreign policy." Hodgson went on:

> I would add that to qualify for membership a man must have a reputation for ability in this field that is accepted by at least two of three worlds: the world of international business, banking and the law in New York; the world of government in Washington; and the academic world, especially in Cambridge, but also in a handful of the other great graduate schools and in the major foundations. And I would further suggest that this group of men was in fact characterized, from World War II until the late 1960s at least, by a history of common action, a shared policy of "liberal internationalism," an aspiration to world leadership, an instinct for the center, and the habit of working privately through the power of the newly bureaucratized Presidency.

Foreign affairs was the peculiar preserve of the Establishment. Almost anyone could become involved in domestic politics. Positions in local, state, and even federal government in the domestic area had been open to people of virtually all backgrounds since the beginning of the Republic. But to be a diplomat was something special. It required education, money, and time for travel.

Almost from the beginning of the Republic, foreign policy was the glamour field—and more so into the twentieth century, when issues of war and peace became paramount. For an ambitious young man playing for the highest career stakes and for service to his government, there was nothing to match it. The name of an Assistant Secretary of State might well be better known to the readers of *Time* magazine and on the Washington social circuit than that of the Secretaries of Commerce, Labor or the Interior.

Most prominent in the early twentieth century were Elihu Root,

Secretary of War under William McKinley and Secretary of State under Theodore Roosevelt, and Henry Stimson, Secretary of State under Herbert Hoover and Secretary of War under William Howard Taft and Franklin D. Roosevelt. Others who followed them were not so well known to the public, but were recognized by the powers that were in the United States and around the world. After World War II, they included W. Averell Harriman and John J. McCloy. These men were reliable. One could have confidence in them and they in each other. They had dealt with the Europeans in the war, so they knew the world. No one else in America at these times knew the world so well.

The Establishment was white, Anglo-Saxon, Protestant, Ivy League, and comfortably well-off. There was a relatively small number of men competing for a relatively small number of positions in the State Department or the civilian sector of the military establishment. There was a place for them in foreign policy; they were secure.

These men, when they were finished with their high government positions, went back to their banks and law firms. Back in private affairs, they rarely wrote or gave formal speeches about foreign policy. Mostly, they supported whatever the President was doing in foreign policy. If a President needed help in resisting some politically motivated effort in foreign affairs, he would call on them, regardless of party, to help. And they did. They were always ready to heed the President's calls to help preserve the pillars of postwar American foreign policy: to lobby Congress against a pullout of American troops in Europe, for example, or for foreign aid.

The Establishment, in many ways, gave the President what it felt was his due. He alone had access to all the facts, knew all the angles. The problem and the responsibility were both his. He generally wanted to go in the direction of containment and internationalism desired by the Establishment. Who knew better than the President? Give him the benefit of the doubt. And the Establishment did.

The Establishmentarians were ideological, but their dogma was that of the center. Its members were basically centrists and concerned primarily about methods and procedures. It was almost more important to them how things were done than what things were done. Thus, the way the Establishment framed its objective in the

Vietnam War showed a great deal about what really bothered them and why. The objective was not simply to prevent a Communist takeover of Vietnam—it was to prevent such a takeover *by force.* They remembered Neville Chamberlain's miscalculation with Hitler at Munich—military aggression had to be resisted and turned back or it would be encouraged. Presumably, if the Communists could win at the ballot box or the negotiating table, the accession to power would be acceptable. Maybe it would have been and maybe not. But this was how most of them thought about the problem and explained it to themselves and others.

The basic ideology of the Establishment was set by two of its most shining lights: Paul Nitze and George Kennan. The latter was considered not quite reliable, perhaps because of his tendency to challenge assumptions. But his intellectual strength and lucidity of expression still made him a leading Establishment figure. The former was later to play a leading role in the battles among the Professional Elite on arms control. Together with Dean Acheson, they were the principal framers of the doctrine of containment, of holding the spread of Russian influence to Eastern Europe. They saw Moscow as hostile and expansionist; the prime goal of American policy should be to stop the expansion of Russia and Communist power by a blend of force and diplomacy. These precepts had the weight of religion. They constituted the consensus on foreign policy within the United States, and the Establishment was mainly responsible for shaping that consensus.

Prior to the Vietnam War, the only time their comfortable world was disturbed was during the McCarthy period in the early 1950s. The anti-Establishment Irish-Catholic, Senator Joseph R. McCarthy from Wisconsin, terrorized them. He said that they were soft on Communism, said that many of them were indeed Communists. There was no harsher epithet. But it was one thing for an outsider like McCarthy to hurl stones and another for one of their own to attack them. John Foster Dulles was one of their own, and yet he too drew blood of Foreign Service Establishment types as he sought to shield himself from the right-wing attack. Together, but for very different reasons, they traumatized the Establishment and drove it to the right, making most of its members even more anti-Communist and anti-Soviet than they were before.

All this set the stage for the most conspicuous failure of the Establishment: the war in Vietnam. That was the ultimate test of the containment doctrine that they held so dearly, and with few exceptions, the Establishment rallied around Presidents Kennedy and Johnson in its pursuit. Only as the war wore on, as American and Vietnamese deaths piled up, as the Treasury was drained, as their children took to the street in protest, as America seemed to fall apart, without victory in sight—only then did many members of the Establishment see another light than the one "at the end of the tunnel." When they did, the Establishment split asunder, and a new American foreign-policy elite began to replace it—just as a plethora of new, competing foreign-policy "think tanks" emerged to diminish the importance of the Council on Foreign Relations.

The Decline of the Council

The Council on Foreign Relations was the embodiment of the Establishment. In 1961, Richard Rovere called its directors "a sort of Praesidium for that part of the Establishment that guides our destiny as a nation." Conceived at the Paris Peace Conference of 1919 to resist isolationism and promote American involvement in the world, the organization was nurtured by the internationally minded rich of New York, the high church of the elect. During the 1930s, with the growing threat from Nazi Germany, members of the Council were in the forefront of efforts to drop American neutrality and support France and Britain. After World War II, the Council led the fight once again against isolationism, for a bipartisan foreign policy, and for containment of the Soviet Union and Communism.

But it had been just before and during the war that the members of its house on Sixty-eighth Street and Park Avenue in New York City began to reach the apogee of their influence. In 1939, backed by Rockefeller money and encouraged by Secretary of State Cordell Hull, the Council established four planning groups to help shape the political, economic and strategic objectives of the United States for the war and its aftermath. In 1942 the studies, and many of the Council members involved in them, were transferred lock, stock and barrel to the State Department. There, their work took shape as idea papers for the United Nations, the World Bank, and the International Monetary Fund.

John J. McCloy, then Assistant Secretary of War for Air, is widely quoted as having once said that whenever the War Department needed someone, "we thumbed through the roll of Council members and put through a call to New York." From then until recent years, the Council became a recruiting ground for the plum jobs in the State Department, the Defense Department and the National Security Council staff. From President Truman through President Carter, more than 50 percent of each administration's senior foreign-policy appointees came from Council ranks, and many others became Council members upon acquiring high office in Washington.

It had all the earmarks of a conspiracy—a few hundred Wall Street bankers, lawyers, foundation executives and businessmen, meeting to arrange the deals far from the prying eye of the public and their elected officials. Even the home of the Council lent weight to such suspicions. It was named for its former owner, Harold Pratt, a man who described himself unashamedly as a "Capitalist." But despite the worst imaginings of the left and the right, what went on inside the Pratt House was all too often pretty tame. (John Kenneth Galbraith resigned his membership "out of boredom.") The anointed, with invited experts and guests, would meet in different study groups or listen to a distinguished speaker and ask questions, retire for a dinner and further discussion, and adjourn by nine-thirty. The Council, on occasion, would foster a book that had some wider impact. The most famous of these was Henry Kissinger's *Nuclear Weapons and Foreign Policy,* published under Council auspices as an outgrowth of a Council study group.

It was not as if Council members in these years had identical views. They had their differences, sometimes spirited, over the tactics of dealing with Moscow or the wisdom of a foreign intervention, and while they were mostly Republicans, there were a good number of Democrats as well. But they did share a centrist outlook and a disposition to back the President in foreign policy. Because of these attitudes, columnist Joseph Kraft wrote in a 1958 article for *Harper's* magazine, "The Council plays a special part in helping to bridge the gap between the two parties, affording unofficially a measure of continuity when the guard changes in Washington."

Whatever the internal differences, it was a cozy world—until the Vietnam War started to heat up. The Council leadership scrambled to accommodate the critics of the war, first by providing them an opportunity within the walls of the Pratt House to speak their piece as guests, then later as Council members. In the traditional manner of a sophisticated elite, their initial instinct was to co-opt new leaders, to make them part of the club. But the critics would not play by traditional rules; they would not confine their policy objections to the paneled rooms of the Pratt House. The Council could no longer play its traditional role, that of containing differences, or settling matters behind walls, or working toward a consensus and helping to recruit the officials who would govern by its precepts. The more so because many of the Council lions were being blamed by Vietnam critics for their role in getting the United States involved in Vietnam. Epitaphs like "war criminal" were being thrown around; the wounds were too deep.

Council troubles came uncharacteristically into public view in the matter of William P. Bundy's appointment as editor of *Foreign Affairs Quarterly,* which the Council had published for fifty years. As Assistant Secretary of State for the Far East, Bundy had been a key architect of Vietnam War policy, and when it became known in the summer of 1971 that the Council's board had offered him the editorship, critics struck with a letter calling for a referendum on Bundy. David Rockefeller, chairman of the board, responded with a public letter reaffirming the choice. Bundy's supporters grumbled about "McCarthyism of the left." Much to the unhappiness of the insurgents and after a good deal of name-calling, Bundy took the job.

Ten years later, insurgents won a different battle. As part of the opening-up process triggered by the Vietnam War, procedures for electing the Council Board of Directors had been democratized in 1972. Under a complicated formula, the Nominating Committee would propose more names than the eight slots required; usually nine to twelve. Others could be added to the list by petition. Valid ballots had to include votes for at least eight candidates, to avoid bullet voting for one or two candidates, and also to help insure the election of the best-recognized names. Under this procedure, former Secretary of State Henry Kissinger was renominated as a Council Director in 1981, one of nine names for eight slots. He had been the golden boy, the star of the Council for two decades. But in the eight years he had ruled over American foreign policy, he had also become the bête noire of many of those hundreds of new Council members. In particular, the insurgents held him personally responsible for the prolongation of the Vietnam War and its extension into Cambodia. With no suggestion of a conspiracy, many of these insurgents skipped over Kissinger's box and checked the eight others, and he lost.

The Council had other travails. During his campaign for the 1980 Presidential nomination, George Bush quietly resigned his membership. As a moderate Republican, he already had one strike against him in conservative circles. His association with the Council, long a symbol of appeasement and capitulationism for the right wing of the party, was deemed to be a dangerous second strike. In the judgment of some of Bush's political advisers, the resignation also made it easier for Ronald Reagan to choose Bush as his Vice-President. (A year later, when ultraconservative Senator Jesse Helms (Republican, North Carolina) was giving his ideological purity test to Reagan foreign-policy nominees, a standard question was "Are you a member of the Council on Foreign Relations?" The prize for the best answer went to conservative former Senator James Buckley, who replied, "No, but I have a well-known brother who is." William F. Buckley, Jr.'s, old right was comfortable with such establishment ties. The new right was not.)

Four years earlier, during the campaign of Jimmy Carter, his closest political advisers showed they had no love for the Council either. Hamilton Jordan, in an interview at the time, said that he would not serve in an administration that included a Cyrus Vance or a Zbigniew Brzezinski, two Council stalwarts. To populists such as Jordan, the Council was the symbol of political elitism, a symbol and source of power from which they wanted to wean the Democratic party. (Jordan was able to overcome his squeamishness when faced with the actual choice.)

Writing in *The New York Times Magazine* on November 21, 1971, J. Anthony Lucas concluded that "the public's tolerance for a self-elected and self-perpetuating foreign-policy elite is rapidly diminishing." He pointed out that this did not mean an end to the Council, but rather a clear decline in its influence as an institution on policy makers. Council President Bayless Manning, former Dean of

Stanford University Law School and just chosen by the Council Board as a "new face" for a new era, told Lucas: "We're moving into a period when we don't have any idea what we're doing in foreign relations. Vietnam was the last spasm of one way of looking at the world. The Council's role, as I envision it, will be to help the country evolve a new consensus." In 1977, Winston Lord, Manning's successor, was to make the quest for a new consensus his goal too.

But there was no consensus to be found or developed by the Council. The splits were too deep to be reconciled by gentlemanly discourse. And the New York bankers and Wall Street lawyers were being supplanted by the New Elite, whose base was not New York but Washington. The Council had lost its principal historical function, shaping the foreign-policy consensus and using this consensus as a kind of third force between the political extremes. It had also lost its power to co-opt new leaders, although most of the new professional elite came to join. Thus, after a decade of trying to recapture a major role for itself, the Council had to settle for something less. It is now an institution that reflects rather than shapes the policy debates, and one that now confirms status rather than confers legitimacy.

By the early 1970s, the Council was merely one of many foreign-policy organizations. It remained the most prestigious, but was no longer the most influential. The new model was the Brookings Institution.

The Ascent of New Centers

Founded in 1927 by Robert Somers Brookings, another businessman with a hunger to contribute to public policy, the institution on Massachusetts Avenue in Washington, D.C., quietly soaked up prestige for several decades as a producer of respectable academic books. But in 1969, the Establishment-like board and Brookings President Kermit Gordon decided to chart a new course. They would beef up the staff, mostly from the ranks of middle-level officials from the outgoing Johnson Administration, and they would offer balanced "alternatives" to the new policies of the Nixon Administration. Brookings rapidly acquired a reputation as a Democratic "government in exile."

The Brookings model was to be more emulated than that of the Council. The Washington location was critical. Political power in Washington was no longer seen to be subordinate to financial power in New York. Political factors as seen from the nation's capital would be overriding, not money concerns. The people did not have to go to New York, and usually did not have the time to make the airline shuttle trip. New York would have to travel to Washington now and not the reverse. The Council's being in New York was now a disadvantage, which the Council would seek to overcome by initiating a program of regular study groups and speakers in the nation's capital.

Brookings made a special effort to target Senators, Congressmen and their aides. The Vietnam War had caused Congress to assert itself passionately and institutionally in the foreign-policy-making process. With roll-call votes and committee meetings, there was not time for them to go to New York. Brookings was convenient. The legislators and their aides could stop by for drinks and dinner from six-thirty to nine-thirty, and still work a full day. And if they went to the Brookings meetings, it was in the interest of officials in the Executive Branch to go as well.

It was Kermit Gordon's idea that what the people from Congress wanted most was information and, above all, alternatives—new ideas for which they might themselves get some attention. That meant hiring a high-powered full-time staff of people who had the knowledge or knew where to get it, who had experience in government, who knew how things worked. So, Gordon went out and recruited Henry Owen, the former head of the State Department's Policy Planning Council, and made him director of Brookings' foreign-policy studies. Owen in turn hired people such as Edward Fried, an international economist from the National Security Council staff; Morton H. Halperin, former head of policy planning for international security in the Pentagon, and a former Kissinger aide at the White House; and A. Doak Barnett, a prominent Columbia University China scholar.

The boldest move made by Gordon and Owen was to establish a defense-policy staff, with financing from the Ford Foundation. For the first time in Washington, there was a respected alternative source of expertise on military matters outside the Pentagon. In a departure from the role traditionally played by the Council on Foreign Relations, Brookings began to turn out an annual set of alternatives to the Administration's budget, a book entitled *Setting National Priorities.* And this book included alternative defense budgets. Nor could this document be lightly dismissed; it was being produced by experts, including military officers, who had done just this kind of analysis for the Defense Department itself.

Another Brookings consumer in search of facts and alternatives was the national news media. While the headquarters of almost all major-media outlets remained in New York, their Washington bureaus were becoming increasingly important. That meant more and more reporters based in Washington, looking for stories. Like the Congress, the media had also been jolted by the Vietnam experience. For them as for the legislators, the word of the Executive Branch was no longer taken for granted. Brookings' books, pamphlets and meetings became an alternative "source."

The Brookings product was self-consciously "balanced" and centrist. But Brookings could not escape the fact that what it had to offer was being done mostly by Democrats, former officials and scholars not particularly sympathetic to President Nixon or conservative ideas. And no matter how "balanced" and "centrist," the product was also an alternative. Nor could conservatives escape the fact that Brookings, through its experts and their ideas, had found a new formula for power.

And Brookings was shortly joined on the activist, moderate-liberal side of the policy spectrum by the Carnegie Endowment for International Peace. For decades, Carnegie was based in New York, across the street from the United Nations, very much a centrist neighbor of the Council on Foreign Relations. Dwight Eisenhower and John Foster Dulles had been Carnegie trustees in 1952. But during the Nixon administration, the Board chose Thomas L. Hughes as Carnegie's new president. He swung the organization leftward in its policy orientation while shifting its primary focus from international organization to American foreign policy. In a new Washington office on Dupont Circle, he put together a stable of former Foreign Service officers, young and ambitious, to work on new international issues such as human rights and Africa. Among the Hughes stars were C. William Maynes and Donald McHenry, who were to gain high office in the Carter Administration.

Perhaps the most important step that Hughes took was to provide a home for a new quarterly called *Foreign Policy.* With managing editors John Franklin Campbell and then Richard C. Holbrooke, both former Foreign Service officers, the magazine became a focal point for shaping liberal alternatives to Kissinger foreign policy. *Foreign Policy* became "the place" to publish critiques of Kissinger and new ideas. Its principal themes became the guidelines for the Carter Administration—reaching back to traditional humanistic American values rather than Kissingerian balance-of-power diplomacy as the foundation of American foreign policy; emphasis on new issues such as human rights, law of the sea, nuclear nonproliferation, control of conventional arms; less emphasis on containing the Soviet Union directly and more on shoring up the American position in Western Europe, Japan and the developing world; and more attention to the economic and political instruments of diplomacy.

So as not to leave the field to Brookings and Carnegie, conservatives borrowed the model and joined the new scramble for influence with the Congress and press. The first conservative to see and act on the need to compete with liberals in the world of ideas and information in Washington was William Baroody, Sr. In the late sixties and early seventies, Baroody went to conservative leaders and businessmen seeking funds for the expansion of the American Enterprise Institute for Public Policy Research, of which he was president, into a conservative Brookings. With his drive and their money, he succeeded. Like Brookings, it would cover American politics and economics as well as foreign and defense policy. Here, on the top floors of an office building at Seventeenth and L Street, denizens of Capitol Hill and the press corps could go to hear the arguments in favor of Nixon and Ford policies, although Baroody was always careful to present a variety of viewpoints.

Baroody's enterprise was less book-oriented than Kermit Gordon's. He knew that Washingtonians were not great readers. What they really wanted were facts and arguments to buttress their political predilections. Conservatives also needed some bucking-up in a town dominated by liberal ideas. They needed to be able to argue back. And Baroody gathered some conservative thinkers who could help them out. Among the leading lights of AEI were Ben Wattenberg, a former aide to Lyndon Johnson and coauthor of polling expert Richard Scammon; Herbert Stein, former chief of Nixon's Council of Economic Advisers; and Irving Kristol, guru of the so-called neoconservatives and coeditor of *The Public Interest Quarterly*. These men were less concerned with the nitty-gritty details of the defense budget than were the Brookings experts; they were big-picture men.

The conservatives still needed a place that could compete on foreign-policy expertise. Into this breach stepped David Abshire, the shrewd Assistant Secretary of State for Congressional Relations in the early days of the Nixon administration, to energize the moribund Georgetown Center for Strategic and International Studies. The Georgetown Center had actually been formed in 1962, but its conservative founders such as Richard V. Allen, later to become for a short while President Reagan's national-security adviser, did not pay effective attention to institution-building until the Brookings experiment proved irresistible. Over the years, Abshire was able to round up luminaries on the order of Henry Kissinger, former Defense Secretary James R. Schlesinger, and Zbigniew Brzezinski. And Abshire, with his soft Southern twang and judicious manner, was highly successful in creating superboards, trustees, advisory groups, and the like, filled with conservatives who wanted some contact with the world of foreign affairs. For them and for an eager group of conservative legislators and their aides, he put together an almost continuous program of conferences. Again, the subjects were treated in a serious scholarly manner, as with Brookings and AEI, but the slant was moderately right of center.

Neither AEI nor the Georgetown Center was sufficiently conservative to please the right wing of the Republican party. They wanted organizations that would make an unadulterated hard-line pitch—the Russians are coming, they're already superior militarily to the United States, forget arms control and concentrate on building up American armaments. Right-wing money and plenty of it began pouring into places such as the Hoover War and Peace Institute at Stanford, California, and the Heritage Foundation in Washington. With funds principally from the Scaife-Mellon Foundation, a new right-wing think tank was created in Cambridge, Massachusetts, with Washington offices, called the Institute for Foreign Policy Analysis. All of them started producing reports and holding conferences.

And when it came to financing, the liberals were no match for the conservatives.

Even before a number of *Foreign Policy's* principal authors left to people the Carter Administration and try to put their new ideas into effect, another journal had jumped into the limelight to present the conservative alternative. *Commentary* magazine, under the editorship of Norman Podhoretz, former socialist and now a leader of the neoconservative movement, launched an all-out barrage against the Carter team. Some of its heavy hitters were Edmund Luttwak and Walter Lacquer of the Georgetown Center and Robert W. Tucker, a professor at John Hopkins University's School of Advanced International Studies in Washington. The main lines of their critique were: America was becoming overwhelmed by the "Vietnam syndrome"; there was a liberal unwillingness to see the world as it was (which, in power terms, required a relentless struggle against the Soviet Union) and a hesitancy to use American power; the United States had to rebuild its military strength and beware of letting arms control lead to unilateral American disarmament; there should be less concern about traditional American ties with a Western Europe falling inevitably into a position of moral and military neutrality between East and West, a Europe becoming "Finlandized."

If *Commentary* provided the ideas, the Committee on the Present Danger provided the action. Under the leadership of Eugene V. Rostow and Paul H. Nitze, both former high officials in the Johnson Administration, this group became the most potent political force against the Carter foreign policy. The Committee's special target was the strategic-arms-limitation talks between Moscow and Washington. If any one man can take credit for scuttling Senate ratification of the Treaty signed in June 1979 it was Paul Nitze. And there was no other group that contributed more high foreign-policy officials to the Reagan Administration.

On the left, meanwhile, the Institute for Policy Studies continued to provide support for activist scholars who challenged many of the basic assumptions of American foreign policy that mainstream liberals held dear.

By the middle 1970s the foreign-policy landscape was littered with think tanks, conferences, reports, quarterlies and chaos. Think tanks now provided homes and money for adversaries to wage perpetual war against one another. Experts wrote competing articles for the op-ed pages of *The Washington Post* and *The New York Times,* and otherwise extended traditional battles within the bureaucracy by other means.

The Ascent of Ideology

For a brief moment at the end of the Ford Administration and the beginning of the Carter term, it appeared as if the center-left and left were ascendant. The Nixon-Ford-Kissinger foreign policy was on the defensive, as much from attack by the right as by the left. Most of the top spots on the Carter team went to Vietnam war critics, liberals. Much to the later woe of the White House, conservative Democrats had been excluded by and large. Many of those excluded worked against the Carter foreign policy through the Committee for a Democratic Majority and the Committee on the Present Danger.

But the halcyon days of the liberal-left faded quickly under the pressure of events, and the power and money of the conservatives. By the end of 1979, the momentum had shifted dramatically. The Soviet Union had transported Cuban troops into the Horn of Africa. Vietnam, Moscow's key ally in Asia, was fighting a savage war of repression in Cambodia. It did not matter that Washington was now defending Somalia, the aggressor against Ethiopia in the Horn of Africa and Moscow's friend for more than a decade. Nor did it seem to make a difference that Washington now found itself supporting the likes of mass murderer Pol Pot in his battle against the Vietnamese puppet government for the Cambodian seat at the United Nations. The fact remained that the Soviet Union was gaining influence in new areas and exercising military power. It was easy to portray the United States as doing nothing about it. Above all, conservatives had succeeded in convincing much of Congress and the national news media that the Soviet Union had gained military superiority over the United States.

The last point was a classic example of how the extremes managed to manipulate public opinion through simple arguments and a one-sided statement of the facts. Some on the left did it in the wake of Vietnam with the pitch that economic and military aid to Third

World countries fighting insurgencies inevitably would lead to deepening American commitment, and eventually to American combat involvement. The argument was a *reductio ad absurdum.* It meant that doing anything would later drag the United States into everything, that no lines could be drawn, that there was no possibility of calibrating policy. It would have meant abandoning virtually every Third World country facing an insurgent challenge. It played to one of the deep-seated fears of the American people—fear of another Korean or Vietnam war. It was also quite effective politically.

The right was no newcomer to distortions of its own about Soviet military power, but in the 1970s it was to raise them to a new art form. There was no denying the fact that, over the course of the preceding fifteen years, Moscow had consolidated conventional or nonnuclear military advantages in Europe and that it had achieved effective parity with the United States in strategic nuclear power. The Soviet military budget had been increasing steadily since Moscow's humiliation at having to back down during the Cuban missile crisis of October 1962. During this same period, the United States was mired down in Vietnam and, in its aftermath, leveled off military spending in favor of domestic priorities. It was also true that Moscow had opened up about a three-to-one lead over Washington in tactical aircraft, tanks, artillery pieces and other conventional armaments; and it was true, too, that Moscow had developed land-based intercontinental missiles of far greater destructive power than their American counterparts.

But these simple and powerful facts told only part of the story. In the first place, they took no account of the overall geo-strategic situation, where the Soviet Union had to face the prospect of adversaries on two fronts, NATO in Western Europe and China to the east. Nor did the three-to-one bean counting include the forces of America's allies on the scales. Nor did it reflect the well-known intelligence judgment that Moscow knew that it could not count on most East European forces in any conflict with the West and, indeed, Soviet troops would be required to garrison these satellites during a war. Nor did it reflect continuing American superiority in quality of weaponry, albeit this gap had been closed in a number of areas. As for the fact of Soviet superiority in land-based intercontinental missiles, that was counterbalanced by the fact that Washington remained superior in the number of warheads, in less vulnerable strategic submarines and in their long-range missiles, and in bombers. True, American bombers were older than the latest Soviet models. But truer still, the U.S. Air Force continued to regard our old B-52s as far better in both range and payload than Soviet bombers.

But it was easy for the right to make the charges, to state the "facts" and let them speak for themselves. It was far harder for its targets to put the more complicated situation in reasonable perspective. Television and daily and weekly news publications gave more attention to the simple accusations than to the complicated responses. For the accusations played on deep-seated public fears after the humiliation of Vietnam.

The Carter Administration was on the defensive for its liberalism almost from the beginning, even though it contained several centrists in senior positions. Both Brzezinski and Defense Secretary Harold Brown were backers of the Vietnam War, and both had good standing with conservative Democrats. Brzezinski also made it a point to hire several experts for his NSC staff who also had good conservative credentials—such as Harvard professor Samuel Huntington, CIA strategic analyst Fritz Ermath, and Army Colonel William Odom. Brown, too, picked a number of subordinates with conservative ties—such as R. James Woolsey, a Washington attorney who was close to Democratic Senator Sam Nunn of Georgia, and William Perry, a businessman from the California military-industrial world. Woolsey was Under Secretary of the Navy and Perry filled the number-three job in the Pentagon, Director of Research and Engineering. These men were far from the kind of right-wingers who came to people the Reagan Administration. But they leaned to the conservative side of the ledger. Thus, even at the height of liberal-left power, Carter could not govern without some conservative ballast. Reagan, on the other hand, saw no need for cover to his left.

From World War I and the Russian Revolution in 1917, it was always harder politically for the left than for the right to hold sway in popular foreign-policy debates. The left undertook the burden of arguing that the United States should make an effort to get along with the new Communist giant, while the right was in the more comfortable position of being skeptical, suspicious and hostile. These were attitudes toward Communism more in keeping with American history and values. Communism represented a kind of triple threat to America from the beginning. Even before the Russian upheaval, the philosophical atheism in Communist doctrine rubbed a religious American the wrong way. Even before the revolution, but especially thereafter, the state control of the economy inherent in Communism ran directly counter to the free-enterprise ethic of America. And when Communism was harnessed to Russian nationhood and, after World War II, to growing Soviet military might, it became a direct security threat to the United States as well.

To make matters worse, Communism was seen also as a threat from within, from subversives controlled by Moscow and dedicated to the overthrow of the American government. Then anti-Communist fever subsided during the late 1930s and when the United States was allied to the Soviet Union in World War II. But it came back with a vengeance in the late 1940s and early 1950s during the heyday of McCarthyism.

The red scares and witch hunts came to be deeply ingrained in the American psyche. Even tough-minded conservative Democrats like Dean Acheson, Truman's Secretary of State, and Paul Nitze, Acheson's policy-planning chief, were vilified as being too conciliatory toward Moscow. And these were two men in the forefront of organizing the NATO alliance and arguing for an American military response to North Korea's attack on South Korea in 1950. The cruelest and most devastating epithet to hurl at someone's career was to say that he was "soft on Communism." By contrast, few if any were to lose political office or their position in the Executive Branch for favoring right-wing military dictatorships or American military buildup, or being anti-Communist.

While the liberal-left in the Carter Administration could not govern without conservatives, the conservative right in the Reagan Administration thus could and did get along without any liberals. There is no doubt that the spectrum under Carter that ran from Brzezinski to Patt Derian or UN Ambassador Andrew Young was far greater than the ideological distance under Reagan that ran from Defense Secretary Caspar Weinberger to Secretary of State Alexander M. Haig, Jr. The striking feature of the Reagan team was its ideological purity. White House political honchos who oversaw the appointments process in the various departments even reached down to ensure purity in positions normally free from politics. For example, anyone associated with the SALT II enterprise, whether at the Foreign Service or the civil-service-expert level, was removed from the strategic-arms negotiations under Reagan.

The policies of the Reagan Administration swung so far to the right that they soon became vulnerable to political attack as well. A conservative administration was one thing; but one that pursued a hard anti-Communist line, one with uncompromising rhetoric that did not admit to prospects of serious negotiations with Moscow, one that appeared hell-bent on an arms buildup with disdain for arms control, went too far. The news media and Congress have usually felt comfortable with a right-of-center foreign policy. Whatever their personal philosophical and political orientation, they have generally found a moderately conservative foreign policy to be politically unassailable.

The media and Congress also held their peace in the first year of the Reagan administration, waiting to see how far the new team would go. But by the second year Reagan too was paying a price for his foreign policy. Slightly more than midway through his first term, public-opinion polls began to show that while Reagan's overall popularity was once again on the rise, his conduct of foreign affairs was being greeted with wide disapproval. For example, a *New York Times*–CBS news poll conducted in March 1983 showed that by about two-to-one the respondents agreed with Reagan's description of the Soviet threat, but that by about three-to-one they disagreed with his strategy for dealing with it. Even in the wake of the popular Grenada invasion, there was broad concern about the state of United States-Soviet relations.

That said, there remained no doubt that Carter's perceived soft-line policies were much more injurious to him politically, in his first three years, than were Reagan's perceived hard-line policies. Even before the fiasco of Americans held hostage by Iran and the Soviet invasion of Afghanistan, foreign policy was already a political noose for Carter. This was so despite the fact that before the end of the third year of his administration he had put together the Panama Canal Treaty, the SALT II treaty, normal relations with China, and the Camp David accords between Israel and Egypt, and had helped to achieve a settlement in Rhodesia. At a comparable time in his administration, Reagan had failed to produce a single concrete accomplishment of comparable significance. The lesson not lost on political leaders or foreign-policy experts was that the American people and political system still preferred to err on the side of what they saw as toughness than on the side of weakness.

The Ascent of the Professional Elite

The swings of the foreign-policy pendulum, from Nixon to Carter to Reagan and then seemingly away from Reagan did not occur simply because the liberal left and the conservative right were having at each other. Nor did the rise of the New Elite occur only because of the fissures caused by the Vietnam War. The volatility in the small world of the foreign-policy maker and expert was a reflection of larger changes taking place in the country. The United States itself was undergoing a metamorphosis that was, in turn, transforming the political culture, including the foreign-policy subculture.

American society and politics were becoming democratized, leveled, fragmented and specialized. Establishments and entrenched power brokers of almost every kind were becoming less in tune with the times, less relevant and less effective.

The two world wars, the Depression, labor unions, and more nearly equal access to education had all contributed to making Americans more middle class and more equal than ever before. But economic sameness did not produce uniform political views. Despite the reassertion of ethnic loyalties, Americans looked more like one another in dress and lived more like one another in their homes, but they still did not think like one another. There was a spectacular rise in the number of special-interest groups and single-issue groups, and an increase in their power. In the process, the sense of the general or public interest was being submerged, and it was this larger sense that had given the old Establishment some of its leverage.

There were virtually no more captains of industry or Hollywood moguls or big-city bosses. Giant industries had become too complicated for one-man rule, and the giants who used to run them were being replaced by accountants and salesmen and money managers. By the middle 1960s Mayor Richard Daley of Chicago was the last of the big-city bosses, and when he died in 1976, no one could take over his once awesome machine. City leaders had all they could do to hold onto their own jobs, let alone command the reins of the city as in years past. By 1970, there were lots of fingers on the buttons of industry, entertainment and politics.

The changes in the culture and economy generally preceded and foreshadowed the changes in the political arena. As has been noted, the trend toward Presidential primaries accentuated the hold of party activists and extremists. The process of fragmentation was nowhere clearer than in Congress. The committee chairmen died off or had their wings clipped by backbenchers demanding more power and possessing the votes to make their demands stick. The assertion of Congressional authority against the President was followed rapidly by individual legislators establishing their own authority outside the committee structure. Instead of a few committee chairmen, Presidents had to consult dozens of different legislators on hundreds of different issues in order to build a coalition to get a bill enacted or a foreign initiative sustained.

With these changes in society and politics generally came the new Professional Elite in foreign policy. With Vietnam, with the growing importance of economic issues, with the domesticization of foreign affairs, politicians and press needed to know more and say more about international events. The political stakes in foreign policy were high, and so was the demand for foreign-policy expertise. And so the old Establishment was thus infiltrated, transformed and subsumed by the new broader grouping, a compound of professors, lawyers, think-tank experts, foundation executives, businessmen, Congressional aides and journalists. At their top is a smaller group of a few hundred wielders of power and ideas, jockeying to influence policy and to obtain the senior positions of government.

The seventies and eighties thus brought a demand for advocates not adjudicators, experts not generalists, full-time professionals not persons looking for an avocation, ideological loyalists and not simply good party men, and people who could operate in the public domain with words and symbols and not just the insider with committee skills. And these qualities, with all their advantages and disadvantages, were what the new class had to offer.

The Elite, like the Establishment, still came mostly from the best schools—Harvard, Yale, Princeton—but now also from places like Tufts' Fletcher School of Law and Diplomacy, the University of Chicago and the University of Virginia. They still came mostly from the Northeast, but increasingly from elsewhere. Many of the new breed did not come from the wealthy and privileged backgrounds of their predecessors either.

But what differentiated the Elite most from the Establishment was that they were full-time foreign-policy professionals. Their rise has altered the rules of the game for seeking power, and even the way the government operates in managing our foreign affairs. Most of them chose not to join businesses and law firms to go home to after government. If they were not in government, they would mostly be outside in the think tanks and universities or, even if in business, still at conferences working on foreign policy, writing about foreign policy, and talking to journalists about foreign policy. And all the while, they would be waiting to return to government, in a higher position than last time.

As full-timers, they were also experts. Modern foreign policy was highly complex and technical. The government had become deeply involved in trade and international monetary policy, and a specialized background was needed for an understanding of these fields. Arms control called for a certain amount of scientific knowledge and a keen grasp of concepts. Everything was connected with everything else, and everything seemed to have a domestic angle or a domestic impact. Trade issues affected jobs, arms control affected the military budget, and grain sales abroad to friendly and unfriendly nations helped to set the profit margins of American farmers. Efforts to prevent the spread of nuclear capabilities necessitated technical knowledge of nuclear energy, international trade and domestic energy needs. The part-time cadre of Establishmentarians could not stay on top of such issues. They were quickly outpaced by the full-timers and came to depend on them for advice.

The Establishment had sought power in Congress and the Executive Branch—but quietly, in the back rooms. The Elite sought influence more openly and over a wide range of foreign-affairs issues, courting the news media, and vice versa. Its members were sought by newsmen and legislators for the ideas they had to offer in challenging administrations. When a new party came to power, they were available to oppose.

It was not only ambition, of course, that drove them to write on and debate the issues. Ideas matter, and the views of most of the experts were deeply and sincerely held. Some, like Stanley Hoffmann, showed little inclination to parlay a luminous academic reputation into a job in Washington. But many more denizens of the Elite prepared and positioned themselves for official jobs during the whole of their professional careers. It was done through timing—knowing when to speak at a meeting, when to look for a new job, when to turn down a job that might be too visible, perhaps, or one that might type its holder too much. It was done by having former government service as a badge to point to, and by proving oneself on the outside by running a foundation, chairing a meeting, making the circuit of conferences, being among those in the "little groups" that were assembled to advise the candidates, having thoughtful articles printed in *Foreign Affairs, Foreign Policy, Commentary,* and the op-ed pages of *The Washington Post* and *The New York Times,* helping Senators and Congressmen write their speeches, and operating through the social connections known in Washington as "friends."

The writing game was itself revolutionary. With rare exceptions, Establishmentarians did not put their ideas down on paper, even in *Foreign Affairs.* It was totally against their ethos, a kind of intellectual indulgence of doubtful taste. Gentlefolk appeared in the newspapers only three times: at birth, marriage (once), and death. Much like that of the Foreign Service officer, their attitude was that foreign policy was less a matter of ratiocination and planning than getting in there and seeing what the problems were, of flexibility. But to the Professional Elite, words and books and articles were the very currency of their lives. An article was the way of announcing one's existence and showing the colors, of being talked about and asked to meetings and conferences.

Words and writings were also the link between the Professional Elite and the politicians. Politicians had become full-time performers and needed endless lines to deliver on a variety of complex subjects. And they needed respectability too. Reporters always wanted to know whom a politician had talked to in preparing his opus. Who were his authorities? His own staff aides were not sufficient; recognized authors and former government officials had to be named.

And politicians were the ticket to power for the Professional Elite. Getting top jobs in an administration was no longer a matter of someone thumbing through the membership list of the Council on Foreign Relations. One of the best ways was to have the backing of a politician whose support was needed by the new President.

This, in turn, made the Professional Elite more partisan than their Establishment predecessors. To be sure, Establishmentarians were Democrats and Republicans. But in as many cases as not, the party label had been secondary, and they were ready to serve Republicans and Democrats alike. Now nonpartisanship was a sign not of objectivity, but of lack of commitment. Partisans came first when rewards were distributed, and so many stood in line that little was left for people who saw both good and bad in what was going on.

The ink wars and partisan battles led to an atmosphere of highly competitive unfriendliness within the Professional Elite, as compared to the gentlemanly forms of disagreement within the Establishment. Grudges were bound to emerge in the Elite. Its members were putting their egos on the line with every page they wrote, and when they were attacked, arguments inevitably ensued. Not only did they criticize one another, but it became common practice to caricature an adversary's view. Professional politicians might have been able to shrug off such things as just business, but not intellectuals. Thus, personal animosities added a bitter edge to everything else. Motives were always being questioned, and no one in the opposing camp was to be given the benefit of the doubt. For those out of power, it meant getting back in. It meant not giving the President an inch.

The Establishment was in the main willing to go along with the President, whatever his political affiliation, and even if his views differed in some measure from their own, but the Professional Elite were unwilling to lend their support to an administration unless its policies agreed in nearly full measure with their own views. Even when in power, it was not easy for many of the Elite to compromise with their ideological cousins. For all of its ideological homogeneity as seen from the outside, internecine warfare within the Reagan Administration was every bit as intense as in the Carter Administration. In part, this had to do with the traditionalist tug of the Foreign Service officers who held key positions in the Reagan State Department. But the deeper reason had to do with the new breed of foreign-policy experts. Precisely because they were more ideologically committed than their predecessors, they were far less tolerant of differences even among their confreres.

In general, the Establishmentarians were used to adjusting conflicting opinions and beliefs, and they were experienced at it. It was a natural thing to do, among those for whom, by philosophical temperament, one view was essentially as good as another as long as it was somewhere near the center. In contrast, members of the Professional Elite were not so comfortable with compromise and adjustment, because they felt more passionately the "truth" of their views. And unlike their predecessors, who had been part of organizations, partnerships and systems for their entire careers, many of the Elite had been intellectual loners, working essentially by themselves.

The net effect was to make American foreign policy much more rigid and riddled with contradictions than before. Once in power, Presidents and their acolytes from the Elite neither wanted to walk away from their rhetoric as challengers nor found it easy to do so. True believers were always there to hold their feet to the fire. And when Presidents did alter untenable policies because of the press of realities and politics, they left a large residue of contradiction. For example, Reagan was never able to successfully explain to America's allies why it was unacceptable for them to sell industrial goods to the Soviet Union, while it was permissible for the United States to sell Moscow grain.

The net result of the transformation from the Establishment to the Professional Elite was the destruction of the foreign-policy center. It was the center that served as the sea anchor against the tides of popular passion, as a wall against extreme views and sharp breaks and lurches in the conduct of American foreign policy. With its demise, there was little to prevent wild swings in policy. And a President or Presidential candidate who might want to stay somewhere in the middle of the debate found it harder to mobilize support.

Traditionally, power in the politics of foreign-policy making resided in the center. As on a chessboard, whoever controlled the middle squares won the game, and the main battles in American politics were for the center squares. But where there was once power, there was now closer to a void. The extremes were dominating on issues such as human rights or relations with the Soviet Union or military spending or the handling of nuclear nonproliferation. The strength was at or near the extremes, and the Presidents and the Professional Elite who had led in those directions had to go there to find support.

III Congress and Press: The New Irresponsibility

WHILE the new Professional Elite was displacing the Establishment, related transformations were taking place in two much more visible American institutions—Congress and the press. Two searing national events, Vietnam and Watergate, moved legislators and reporters from instinctive support of Presidential policy to aggressive skepticism, from acquiescence to activism. On Capitol Hill, the new taste for foreign-policy engagement was buttressed by the staff explosion, a tripling of the number of policy aides serving Senators and Representatives. In the media, the more critical tone of print reporting was accompanied by the rise of television, which simplified and amplified overseas events and governmental foreign-policy actions.

In the early seventies, it seemed to many that these changes could only prove salutory. On Vietnam, decisions by successive Presidents had trapped the United States into a central involvement in a peripheral area. Responding to growing public discontent, reporters were now questioning the logic—and the veracity—of official explanations. Legislators were declaring that there had to be limits to how far we would go in defending interests that were distant from our primary alliances. Would not the new pressure from Congress and the media make future American foreign policy more pragmatic, more prudent, more realistic and responsible?

The answer is becoming clear. While the Congress and the press have provided important brakes and balance, in the end they have also helped to make the policy debate *more* ideological and unreal. For both of these institutions displayed a new form of irresponsibility. The now-critical press oversimplified issues and inflated personality conflicts. Legislators pressed unreal policy goals—condemning arms-control agreements if they failed to achieve all American objectives, insisting on the pure pursuit of human rights—and denounced Presidents for failure to achieve these goals. Members of Congress developed new ways of exploiting issues for personal and political gain, while ducking responsibility for policy consequences. In so doing, they tightened the political trap for Presidents, and for American foreign policy.

Irresponsibility took a very different form in the two decades after World War II. What were golden years for the foreign-policy Establishment and for the Executive Branch were for the legislative branch years of deference if not abstinence, particularly on the fundamental issues of war and peace. Individual members might use their chamber as a platform for critical speeches—Senator Henry M. Jackson about how we were "losing the Cold War," or Senator John F. Kennedy about the folly of France's colonial war in Algeria. It was one way to get recognition as a budding statesman; some serious-sounding talk about foreign policy was, after all, almost indispensable in buttressing a Presidential candidacy. But on the big issues, our national legislature was nearly supine.

Congress let President Truman decide to dispatch troops to Korea, not even protecting its prerogatives with a resolution endorsing the action. Legislators were content to be briefed by deputy assistant secretaries of State, four layers down in the bureaucracy, as Truman's senior advisers deliberated at Blair House. It was left to "isolationists" like Robert A. Taft to complain that the Constitution required something more. But his colleagues never challenged, as a body, Truman's right to engage Americans in what became, at the time, our fourth-bloodiest war. The result was that members of Congress, absent at the takeoff, were free to criticize Truman's handling of the controls as he sought, unsuccessfully, to find a safe landing. He became saddled with sole responsibility for an unpopular, frustrating conflict.

Dwight Eisenhower did not repeat Truman's political mistake of risking war without Congressional sanction; he used Congress to reinforce his policies. In 1954 he consulted with Congressional leaders about Indochina and used their reluctance to reinforce, and provide political cover for, his own reservations. In 1955, as the Taiwan straits crisis developed, he sought advance authority to use troops, not conceding that he "lacked constitutional authority to act," but in order to "make clear the unified and serious intentions" of the American people. The House of Representatives said yes within a day, by 410 to 3. The Senate, taking three days longer, voted 83 to 3. On the Middle East resolution two years later, the going was a bit harder—19 Senators and 61 Representatives voted no. But still, Congress went along.

The peak of accommodation came in 1964, when Congress gave President Lyndon B. Johnson a blank check on Vietnam. Not only did it accept with little question the Administration's description of what had happened at the Gulf of Tonkin; it went on to declare the United States "prepared, as the President determines, to take all necessary steps, including the use of armed force, to assist any protocol or member state of the Southeast Asia Collective Defense Treaty requesting assistance in defense of its freedom." This time the House was unanimous, and in the Senate only Wayne Morse and Ernest Gruening, two men known for idiosyncratic ways, stood in opposition.

Even members who had strong reservations went along, giving the President his due. Freshman Senator George McGovern, for example, had declared in the fall of 1963, "The U.S. position in Vietnam has deteriorated so drastically that it is in our national interest to withdraw." Ten and a half months later, after raising one marginal concern, McGovern joined 97 of his colleagues in supporting Lyndon Johnson. Helping to quiet his doubts was J. William Fulbright, who as Chairman of the Foreign Relations Committee was the Senate floor manager of the Tonkin Gulf resolution.

There was plenty of debate about foreign policy, criticism in editorials, eloquent rhetoric in the Congressional chambers. There was plenty of politics, but everyone understood the basic rules and played by them. If the President declared something was "vital to the national security interests of the U.S.," he could be attacked for letting the situation go too far, but in the end, he had to be supported. It was thought wiser, of course, if he consulted with a handful of senior legislators—the majority and minority leaders, the chairman of Senate Armed Services and perhaps Foreign Relations also. And if things didn't turn out well in the end, the President was vulnerable to blistering attack, as Truman discovered. But at the point of decision, Congress went along on the big matters. Politics never stopped at the water's edge. It was considered good politics, however, to stop short of actually blocking the actions of the man in the White House. Congress would complain loudly about foreign aid, sometimes cut it deeply. But on matters of peace and war, it opted out—and formal declarations of war seemed obsolete anyway.

This deference certainly made things easier for Presidents. And for the postwar internationalist generation, particularly the Establishment which had witnessed how Congressional resistance had made Franklin Roosevelt so slow and hesitant in his response to the Nazi challenge, this was unmitigated good. But it was also a matter of Congress avoiding the ultimate responsibility. Let Harry Truman be the man with the sign on his desk, "The buck stops here!" The world was a complicated place, American stakes in it were greater than ever, and the Establishment never tired of reminding legislators that others outside Congress knew much more about it than they. Better to leave foreign policy to the experts—diplomatic, military, intelligence—and to the President who had them on call. He "had all the facts"; Congress did not. And to try to learn them could be dangerous, for with knowledge might come the responsibility to share in tough and unpopular decisions.

It was J. William Fulbright, chairman of the Senate Committee on Foreign Relations, who gave one of the most thoughtful, sophisticated rationales for Congressional restraint. Even in 1961 he found Congressional influence excessive—and malign. He found it "highly unlikely that we can successfully execute a long-range program for the taming, or containing, of today's aggressive and revolutionary forces by continuing to leave vast and vital decision-making powers in the hands of a decentralized, independent-minded, and largely parochial-minded body of legislators."

Fulbright never really changed his view; he remained one of his institution's severest critics even as he moved to engage Congressional powers against the Vietnam War. What changed was his view of the Presidency, his concern for damage he saw wrought by "the misuse of power." In 1965 he entered a lonely dissent against Lyndon Johnson's dispatch of Marines to the Dominican Republic. In 1966 he began challenging Vietnam policy with televised hearings. And growing numbers of colleagues joined him.

But for years thereafter Congress limited itself to symbolic action, to Fulbright's growing frustration. The Senate expressed in 1969 its (nonbinding) view that "a national commitment" required joint Executive-Congressional action through "a treaty, statute, or concurrent resolution," a cautious counter to the Presidential practice of establishing obligations through secret pledges, or declarations that a country was "vital." Congress repealed the Gulf of Tonkin resolution in 1970, after the Nixon Administration declared it had no need of such legislative authority. It passed marginal restrictions, like a prohibition on sending United States military "advisers" to Cambodia. But with all of this said and done, the essential fact was this: not until the summer of 1973, after all American troops were withdrawn from Vietnam and the POWs returned home, did Congress actually take a firm stand by denying funds for American military operations in and over Indochina. Only then was it willing to exercise the power that it had possessed all along—to limit the war.

For Henry Kissinger, this was still too much too soon. He would later argue in his memoirs that this Congressional action torpedoed an admittedly "tenuous" diplomatic effort to build peace in Cambodia around a China-sponsored regime under exiled Prince Norodom Sihanouk. He saw his long-shot effort spoiled by a national legislature "no longer prepared to listen to arguments about the complexities of diplomacy."

But what was in fact being challenged was much more basic: the view that United States "national security" was really being advanced by the Presidential free hand that Kissinger—and Richard Nixon—thought so necessary. To the liberal and moderate critics who energized the revolt, a key "lesson" of Vietnam was that it was precisely this executive flexibility that had gotten us deeper and deeper into the quagmire.

In retrospect, it is clear that both sides were wrong. The war was lost by the time Congress acted to limit Kissinger's flexibility. And in the years before, Congress had lacked not the capacity to restrain the President, but the political will. The prime cause of Vietnam was not institutional imbalance. It was a failure of policy, reinforced by our domestic political imperatives, which would allow no President to declare Vietnam to be beyond our vital interests.

But neither Presidents nor the Congress saw things that way. Presidents saw the problem as legislative encroachments on their prerogatives and resisted all such encroachments. Congress saw the problem as Presidential freedom of action and set out to curtail it, not just on warmaking but on a broad range of policy instruments, such as arms sales and secret CIA operations. Since the President and the Secretary of State were determined to keep employing these instruments, the only way to enforce them was to enact binding statutes.

Beginning in 1973, Congress did just that. In the fall the War Powers Resolution was passed, over the veto of a Nixon weakened by Watergate. This established a time limit of sixty days for Presidential deployment of troops in combat without Congressional authorization. A year later, Congress added multiple new constraints: an embargo on arms sales to Turkey in retaliation for its invasion of Cyprus; a requirement that all major arms sales be reported to Congress and subject to its veto; a requirement that covert CIA operations be reported to responsible committees; the Jackson-Vanik amendment conditioning trade concessions to Russia on her openness to Jewish emigration; a requirement that food aid be allocated primarily to the neediest countries, instead of being used mainly to support political clients. In 1975 and 1976 there came the Tunney and Clark amendments barring covert CIA involvement in Angola, and the Harkin amendment prohibiting aid to "any country which engages in a consistent pattern of gross violations of internationally recognized human rights." Congress also required that the State Department report annually on the human-rights situation in all aid-recipient countries.

Most of these new laws were Vietnam-driven. Congress had spent years mustering the majorities, and the courage, to end our combat involvement there. But by the time Congress got itself pumped up over Vietnam the American boys were back home. So it sought other outlets for its new-found energy, and targeted policy situations or instruments—Angola, arms sales—that could be labeled as steps toward "another Vietnam."

The Congressional resurgence also had roots beyond the war, for a broader Congressional reform movement was peaking in the early seventies as well. Ever since the 1958 election, which brought liberal Northern Democrats to the Hill in large numbers unknown since the New Deal, these "new boys" were chafing at the bit, unhappy with the tradition of apprenticeship in the Senate, restive over what cynical House members called the "race between seniority and senility."

Increasing numbers of them were not products of established party machines, but media-sensitive, issue-oriented, ambitious men and women, political entrepreneurs who had raised their own money, run their own campaigns, and won. Domination of Congress by conservative Southern committee chairmen was an affront to their convictions. Equally important, it was a blight on their careers. More and more, these entrepreneurs asserted themselves. In the Senate change came gradually through the sixties and early seventies. In the House, entrenched barons like Wilbur Mills at Ways and Means held on longer, meaning that the power shift was more sudden and wrenching when it came. But come it did.

> The power differences between senior and junior members diminished, sometimes even vanished. Experience, expertise and political craftsmanship still brought influence, but tenure in office brought fewer rewards.
>
> Committee chairmen were forced to create subcommittees, with elected subcommittee chairmen, separate staffs and a central role in drafting legislation.
>
> Committee and subcommittee meetings were opened to the public, and bills were opened to amendment on the floor by roll-call vote.
>
> Finally, several particularly unpopular committee chairmen were overthrown by the House Democratic Caucus in 1975.

There was, in both houses, more procedural flexibility, more chance for aggressive members to develop and exploit their own power bases. When the agreeable John Sparkman succeeded Fulbright as Chairman of the Foreign Relations Committee, Hubert Humphrey seized day-to-day leadership on the committee's main legislation through the foreign-assistance subcommittee he chaired. Capable junior members like Iowa's Dick Clark could become leaders in a sphere like Africa policy.

Serving as both cause and effect of the revolution on Capitol Hill was the staff explosion.

Beginning in the late sixties, a growing number of talented middle-level Foreign Service officers began leaving the State Department, moving to Capitol Hill "where the action was." They came mainly to work for individual Senators, with Richard Moose joining Fulbright and Foreign Relations, Peter Lakeland serving Jacob Javits. Others came from universities or think tanks. They brought new knowledge and skills; they were a corps of foreign-policy professionals who could challenge an administration, not just on politics but on policy substance. They were there because suddenly Senators and Representatives found that they needed this expertise, the capability to match facts and arguments. They needed to demolish the presumption that had so weakened Congress in the past, that the Executive Branch had the facts and the knowledge and the legislative branch did not. Staff gave Congress credibility: in the Executive Branch, in the news media, and at least equally important, to itself. Staff gave members the confidence to act.

One early, impressive example of what staff support made possible came in November 1973. That month, a special committee of the United States Senate declared that most Americans had "lived all their lives under emergency rule," that Presidential declarations in effect since March 9, 1933, gave force to no less than 470 laws granting the Chief Executive powers to "seize property; organize and control the means of production; seize commodities; assign military forces abroad; institute martial law; seize and control all transportation and communication; regulate the operation of private enterprise; restrict travel; and, in a plethora of particular ways, control the lives of all American citizens." And behind this declaration was a 583-page committee report, pinpointing all 470 statutes and placing them in broader context. The report was followed, in due course, by enactment of Public Law 94-412, which terminated existing emergency declarations and established new Congressional checks on future ones.

The well-known names on the report were those of Frank Church and Charles McC. Mathias, Jr., Cochairmen of the Special Committee on the Termination of the National Emergency. The two men who made it possible were listed in smaller type. William G. Miller was a former Foreign Service officer who had moved to Capitol Hill to oppose the war in Vietnam and had become, at age forty-two, one of the most respected of Senate staff aides. Thomas A. Dine, nine years younger, had been a Peace Corps volunteer and an assistant to Ambassador Chester Bowles in India. Both were members of the emerging Professional Elite. Together they reached into the institutional expertise of the United States government: the departments of Justice and Defense; the General Accounting Office, and the Library of Congress. In less than a year, they put together a report so comprehensive that it led to fundamental statutory change.

Special Senate committees were nothing new. What was new—and significant—was this sort of activist, energizing staff entrepreneurship. Aside from a few aides in the White House, no one at the staff level of the Executive Branch could have this sort of opportunity, the running room in which to put something of this magnitude together.

In the early and middle seventies, the number of Bill Millers and Tom Dines would multiply. They would come to constitute what seemed almost like a new branch of government, a Congressional bureaucracy. A few of them would come to exercise enormous power, something a Foreign Service officer could only dream of—at least before he reached age forty or forty-five.

The numbers tell part of the story. From 1947 to 1976, the membership of Congress rose from 531 to 535, to make room for Senators from the new states of Alaska and Hawaii. But the number of people on their personal staffs rose from 2,030 to 10,190. Even greater was the proportionate increase in policy experts, aides working on substantive issues. In 1966, only a handful of Senators had foreign-policy specialists on their personal staffs. Now almost every Senator has one, and some have several. As for committee staffs, that of Senate Foreign Relations expanded from 25 in 1960 to 31 in 1970 to 62 in 1975. For the House Foreign Affairs Committee, the rise was from 14 to 21 to 54.

The Hill opened up a new shortcut for foreign-policy career advancement. Moose served the Congressional opposition to Nixon, Ford and Kissinger, then moved to senior State Department posts under Carter. So did Brian Atwood, a former Foreign Service officer involved (as aide to Senator Tom Eagleton) in rebuffing Kissinger on Vietnam and Turkey. He joined the State Department's Congressional Relations bureau, where his job was to protect Carter and Vance from similar treatment. He worked there initially for Douglas Bennet, who had previously been the first staff director of the Senate Budget Committee, and then succeeded him as assistant secretary.

Paula Stern, who as Gaylord Nelson's staff aide had managed his successful Congressional veto amendment on arms sales, was appointed by Carter to the U.S. International Trade Commission.

And if it was the liberal Senators who were the first to see the uses of such staff aides for policy and sheer publicity, conservatives caught on quickly. During the Carter years, the ubiquitous John Carbaugh, who served Jesse Helms, worked aggressively to overturn the combined British-American effort to bring peace in Zimbabwe-Rhodesia, even flying to London in September 1979 to urge white supremacist Ian Smith to hold firm against pressure from the British Foreign Secretary Lord Carrington.

Most aides still labored in anonymity, their reputations limited to the circle of Washington insiders. But some became publicly prominent. Larry K. Smith and Richard Perle, assistants to Gary Hart and Henry Jackson, debated the SALT II treaty between the covers of *Time* magazine. Perle, who managed Jackson's Jewish-emigration amendment as well as his formidable assaults on Executive Branch arms-control efforts, was perhaps the best-known and most feared of the lot, before he moved to the Pentagon to press his anti-Soviet cause from within the Reagan administration.

Now the Executive Branch had to deal not only with the elected legislators, but with these staffers. And unlike the legislators, the staffers worked on foreign and defense policy full time. Their power was further magnified by the fact that some of them could work full time on one or two issues. The time and capacity to concentrate, in a city where top officials are always being pulled in multiple directions, is an enormous advantage.

Aides formed competing coalitions. The "Madison Group" of conservatives was determined to reverse all policies of détente with the Soviet Union. Its rival was the aides to the "Cranston group" of Senators, who labored to keep SALT II's political prospects alive if not well. But what they did above all, by their numbers, their aggressiveness, their connections, was to make Capitol Hill a more creative and chaotic place. And they made foreign policy a much more visible, political issue. They tended to strengthen individuals at the expense of committees, in contrast to the times when the services of veteran aides like Carl Marcy and Pat Holt gave Chairman Fulbright substantive resources that his Foreign Relations colleagues could not match. Staff made it possible for a Nelson or a Tunney or a Helms to appeal a negative committee decision on the Senate floor, or to bypass the committee entirely. Sometimes everyone was surprised—in 1978 members only learned from reading the papers that they had adopted a Helms amendment which made it impossible for the United States to pay its dues to UN specialized agencies! Only in the following year was that statute straightened out.

There was a certain irony. Many staff aides joined the Hill because they cared deeply not about politics but about policy, its substance. Yet they would have impact—if at all—through their bosses, who were ambitious, publicity-seeking *politicians.* To get press, a proposal had to be different, sexy, even extreme. So the drafting of amendments bearing their bosses' names became a cottage industry. Thus, staff ended up contributing to polarization, to contention, to unpredictability. Congress had always been home to a member opposition—Robert Taft, John Kennedy, George McGovern, people who sought personally to replace an administration of the other party. But now it was home to a large, polemical staff opposition as well, mixing party with ideology, aspiring to positions of power at the other end of Pennsylvania Avenue. And, in turn, partisan and ideological staff battles deepened the divisions among the Senators and Representatives and made *their* fights more ferocious.

With this sudden Congressional emergence came parallel changes in the other key "adversary" institution, the news media.

In the twenty "golden years" after World War II reporters and their news organizations were, like Congress, basically in the President's camp. Not that they didn't cause their share of trouble, with those stories that were "off the mark," or just "not helpful." But on the big matters they were manageable.

President Kennedy couldn't keep *The New York Times* from learning key facts about preparations for the Bay of Pigs, but he did persuade the paper to delete some specifics and downplay the story. Two weeks thereafter, he wondered whether this had served America's interests: "Maybe if you had printed more about the operation," he told the *Times*'s executive editor, "you would have saved us from a colossal mistake." But he was nonetheless grateful to be able to phone publishers Orvil Dryfoos and Philip Graham eighteen months later and get the *Times* and the *Washington Post* to hold off on revealing the Cuban missile crisis until the President could announce his response.

The news media were generally more than manageable; they were useful. The leading newspapers could be expected—not always, but usually—to accept the government's definition of events, the White House or State Department version of truth. The media had few alternative sources. The foreign-policy Establishment had not yet been supplanted by the outspoken Professional Elite with its taste for public spats. Nor were there hundreds of Congressional staff aides available to offer—or exchange—"inside" foreign-policy information.

The government-press relationship was mutually supportive, even cozy. As James Reston put it, the Executive Branch was "the only known vessel that leaks from the top." Presidents, Cabinet secretaries, and White House aides used favored reporters and columnists to make their versions of reality public, send messages to audiences at home and abroad, shape perceptions of other participants in the Washington policy game. And on the big issues, the press followed the flag, with news stories and editorials that summoned citizens to sacrifice for America's causes rather than examining their necessity.

The treatment of the U-2 incident of 1960 was typical. Journalists like Reston and Chalmers Roberts of *The Washington Post* had long known that the United States was sending regular photographic reconnaissance flights over Soviet territory, but, deferring to what they considered the national interest, they denied themselves this scoop. Even when the Eisenhower Administration claimed that the downed plane was merely flying a weather mission for NASA, the press went along—until Nikita Khrushchev broke the real story in Moscow with the live, confessing pilot as evidence.

But by 1965, as the United States was plunging into Vietnam, such press trust in our government had begun to erode. In December of that year, Murrey Marder of *The Washington Post* coined a new phrase, "credibility gap." He defined it cautiously as "a perceptibly growing disquiet, misgiving or skepticism about the candor or validity of official declarations." Others began to use phrases like "official lying." As confidence eroded, so did the readiness to follow the flag. By December 1966, Reston, perhaps the most adroit operator within the cozy old system, was issuing a call for changing it. The press needed to be more aggressive, using its "artillery" to check and balance a too-powerful presidency. "Our job in this age, as I see it, is not to serve as cheerleaders for our side in the present world struggle but to help the largest possible number of people see the realities of the changing and convulsive world in which American policy must operate."

The press, for the most part, had pulled its punches as United States troops poured into Vietnam, hundred thousand by hundred thousand. Then step by step, it moved—like the Congress—toward a declaration of independence.

In early 1968, Walter Cronkite paid a visit to the scene of the suffering. Television had been bringing the Vietnam War nightly into Americans' living rooms. Reporters in the field had long been pessimistic, but their front offices had been less so. Now the man who was the embodiment of the news tradition of objectivity and restraint, of deference to Presidential responsibility and official truth, returned from Saigon and Hue to declare on a special February 27 news report that we were not succeeding in Vietnam, and had no reasonable prospect of succeeding. "It seems now more certain than ever that the bloody experience of Vietnam is to end in a stalemate . . . the only rational way out then will be to negotiate, not as victors, but as an honorable people who lived up to their pledge to defend democracy, and did the best they could." In making this declaration, Cronkite gave sudden legitimacy to all the reporters who had been fighting to report independently and critically on the war and on the government policies behind it.

Three years later, breaking with the Nixon Administration and beating it in court, Neil Sheehan and his *Times* colleagues published volumes of documents from the "Pentagon Papers." *The Washington Post* did so as well, and this decision to confront the government represented, in David Halberstam's view, the *Post*'s "coming of age" as an independent national institution.

The Papers case produced, as one notable by-product, an affidavit by *Times* correspondent Max Frankel explaining the "cooperative, competitive, antagonistic and arcane relationship" through which "a small and specialized corps of reporters and a few hundred American officials regularly make use of so-called classified, secret and top-secret information and documentation."

> Presidents make "secret" decisions only to reveal them for the purposes of frightening an adversary nation, wooing a friendly electorate, pro-

> tecting their reputations. The military services conduct "secret" research in weaponry only to reveal it for the purpose of enhancing their budgets, appearing superior or inferior to a foreign army, gaining the vote of a Congressman or the favor of a contractor. High officials of the Government reveal secrets in the search for support of their policies, or to sabotage the plans and policies of rival departments. Middle-rank officials of government reveal secrets so as to attract the attention of their superiors or to lobby against the orders of those superiors. Though not the only vehicle for this traffic in secrets—the Congress is always eager to provide a forum—the press is probably the most important.

Frankel was describing the old system of press-government relations; his going public about it was a harbinger of the new system. The reward system was changing. Up to the middle sixties, reporters who would rock the boat were usually excluded from foreign-policy reporting. But after men like David Halberstam and Seymour Hersh made their reputations by exposing official lying and cover-ups, editors began encouraging more. They began to share the assumption that the government not only exercised its right not to tell the truth, but also was all too likely to violate the precept of telling nothing but the truth. Even before the triumph of Woodward and Bernstein, the press began to see itself as a kind of "truth squad" holding officials to account.

The press, like other major American institutions, was opening up, becoming more competitive, more infused with the "adversary culture" that burgeoned in the sixties and dominated the decade thereafter.

The media and Congressional transformations were exciting. While they were unfolding, they also offered hope that balance and reason would be restored to foreign policy. And Watergate reminded Americans that Presidents needed to be kept honest, not to mention legal.

But along with these good effects came a new form of irresponsibility. In the years up to the Vietnam debacle, Congress had ducked responsibility by lying low, playing silent partner in a game called "President knows best." Now Congress was anything but silent. But the noisy position-taking and the frequent legislating did not mean that Congress was now ready to take on serious, continuing policy responsibility itself. Too often, rather than define issues and choices more clearly, legislators simply exploited them—while the media amplified their exaggerations. Rather than enforce an alternative policy when unwilling to follow the Presidential lead, Congress would simply increase the political cost of what the Executive Branch wanted to do. This happened to both Carter and Reagan on Central America. Legislators adopted half measures, chopping funds for Presidential programs and attaching strings to them. They ducked the harder choice of either sharing responsibility for the President's policy or imposing a coherent alternative. Thus, the United States ended up without *any* consistent, sustained course of action on an issue of growing importance.

The problem was not in the general laws that gave Congress new hooks on Presidential policy. The major ones struck sensible, pragmatic balances. The War Powers Resolution sought to enforce the principle of shared responsibility for committing American troops to foreign combat. It allowed the President some leeway in deploying them, but drew a time line—troops could not stay beyond sixty days without explicit Congressional approval. Thus legislators reclaimed at least some of their Constitutional power to declare war, without depriving the President of all leeway to respond to crises. If he worked with legislative leaders, he had a good shot at combining strong overseas action with visible Congressional backing. Similarly, on intelligence and covert CIA operations it was reasonable for the Congress to establish special monitoring committees and mandate executive consultation with these committees, in secret, about specific operations. Again, this allowed Executive Branch flexibility but brought legislators at least marginally into the game. They could ask hard questions about operations they felt were wrong or simply stupid.

It also made sense for Congress to institute a legislative veto over large arms sales. Such sales are sometimes major acts of foreign policy. Yet, Congressional insistence on approving each one explicitly, in advance, would not only tie the President's hands; it would inflict gratuitous public insults on all the specific countries whose arms requests Congress denied or cut back. By establishing a veto power (which in fact it never employed and seldom even threatened), our national legislature created pressure for an administration to consult on the large sales in advance, to test the political waters before its prestige—and that of the recipient—were tied to a specific, detailed arms package. Seen in this light, the summer 1983 Supreme Court decisions rendering such legislative vetoes unconstitutional could prove to have bad policy consequences. For they mean that Congress must either give up authority over all individual arms sales, or move to assert its influence by direct, country-specific statutory action.

Another constructive example was the work of the Special Committee on the Termination of the National Emergency. Its report led to a reasonable Congressional action that could win overwhelming endorsement in both houses. It was our national legislature not only defining and delimiting Presidential emergency powers in a way not heretofore achieved, but accepting the political responsibility for doing so.

Congress also played an important role in the definition of national policy goals. It was concern on Capitol Hill that increased the priority given to human rights and nuclear nonproliferation. And later in the 1970s legislators led the way in channeling more resources into national defense.

The problem was not with these general laws, or with Congressional efforts to share in defining national policy objectives. The problem was rather that Congress repeatedly ducked the responsibility for making the laws work. Until the deployment of Marines to Lebanon—discussed later in this chapter—there was no clear test of the War Powers Resolution. But Senators seemed as determined as Presidents to minimize its relevance by treating marginal cases as outside its scope. On Carter's attempt to rescue American hostages in Iran in 1980, for example, the Senate Foreign Relations Committee posed no serious objection to the lack of any prior consultation as urged (though not required) by the Resolution.

So it was with other laws too. Did Congress really mean for the President to terminate aid to country X if it failed to meet American human-rights standards, or to give the President leverage to use on country X? Or was the prime purpose to give legislators publicity on a "motherhood" issue? Did Congress really want all those reports it requested—on arms sales, on the "arms control impact" of weapons systems, on human rights, or any of dozens of other subjects when they were required? Were these statutes serious efforts to improve

Congressional information, or the brain children of ambitious staffers, or consolation prizes for Congressmen unable to legislate actual changes but wanting something to claim credit for? If they were serious—and they took hundreds of man-hours for executive officials to complete—why did Congress usually ignore them? Why did legislators so seldom hold hearings to expose the bureaucratic compromises buried in the committee-drafted prose of these reports? Why did even Senator Gaylord Nelson later admit to a reporter that he seldom if ever examined the arms-sales reports his amendment had mandated? Why, after legislators had exerted enormous efforts to win the right to know about the CIA budget and the operations it supported, could *The New York Times* report on October 19, 1983, that as of that date, "only two members of the House [had] traveled to the committee offices to examine [classified documents concerning] the intelligence activities and operations that Congress [was] about to authorize."

Another form of Congressional irresponsibility was to avoid direct action on a proposal from the President and employ it instead as a political punching bag. Such was the fate of the SALT II treaty that Carter completed in 1979. The limits on strategic arms that it contained would have modest immediate impact, but they were useful in stabilizing the nuclear competition, reducing uncertainty in defense planning, and establishing a framework for future talks. And SALT II would have forced dismantlement of certain Russian systems, while it constrained the United States hardly at all.

But rather than ratify this as a modest but useful step toward further arms-control efforts, Senate conservatives used it as ammunition in a broader campaign to discredit Carter defense and foreign policies. Senator Howard Baker saw the opportunity to mend fences with the Republican right, which he had alienated by supporting Carter on the Panama Canal. Democratic Senator Sam Nunn conditioned his support of SALT II on large, across-the-board increases in the defense budget. Some liberals got scared and joined the hard-line bandwagon, as when Senator Frank Church tried to use his revelation of a 2,600-man Soviet "brigade" in Cuba to score political points at home, declaring that the arms treaty could not be ratified without the brigade's withdrawal. Other liberals attacked SALT II for not cutting arms enough. The invasion of Afghanistan sealed its fate.

After a year of effort to gain its ratification, Carter pulled back. Congress never bit the SALT II bullet, and the United States entered the Reagan period having to rely on informal Soviet commitments to arms restraint.

Another pattern of irresponsibility was Congress surging into a specific issue but framing the choice in grossly exaggerated, ideological terms. Here a prime example was the rebuff of Kissinger's 1975 program for "covert" CIA involvement in the Angolan civil war. At stake was who would hold power in a country of, at most, moderate importance, and a respectable case could be made either way—for seeking to counter Soviet support of one of the factions contending for power or for abstaining on grounds of limited United States interest or the poor prospects for success or the damage to American interests elsewhere in Africa. It was not, as liberal critics claimed, anything remotely like a repeat of Vietnam—no United States troop commitment was in prospect. But neither was Angola, as Henry Kissinger would have it, a crucial test of Soviet fidelity to the "principles of détente"—the Soviets had never pledged to stay out of "wars of national liberation," and Kissinger knew it. Pretending that they had damaged United States–Soviet relations with no compensating foreign gain. But in years to come, hard-liners would find Angola a useful club to use against liberals, blaming United States "softness" there for future Soviet actions in Ethiopia, Yemen and Afghanistan. Thus, both sides reinforced the President's political trap. One saw "another Vietnam." The other saw "another Munich." It was neither one.

Why had Congressional reform turned sour? Why had a movement aimed at redirecting and reforming American foreign policy produced such mixed results? Why did what began as a move to reassert responsibility end up generating new forms of irresponsibility? Why were legislators so often acting like political snipers, taking pot shots at issues, ducking responsibility for real-world foreign-policy results?

One important answer was a change in how Presidents were playing the foreign-policy game. Vietnam had shattered the consensus on which executive leadership had been founded. Presidents, beginning with Lyndon Johnson, tried to maintain their power not by changing the policy but by scaring Congress into submission. With persuasion less effective, they turned to the bludgeon, raw

Presidential power. Johnson wrapped himself in the flag, with an obvious political message for Vietnam-policy adversaries. Nixon went much further: with his White House "enemies list" loaded with Vietnam critics; with the political tactics that Spiro Agnew called "positive polarization" to link those critics with those unpopular, long-haired antiwar demonstrators; with the identification of opposition to Presidential policy with endangering the lives of "American boys" on the battlefield. He used the political arena not to respond to the critics substantively, but to frighten them. The message was that the game was political hardball and they would get hurt, by fair means or foul, if they didn't back off.

In the short run, such tactics worked. They bought time. The critics did back off. Over the long run they created enormous resentment, a desire to get even. And they demeaned the President, brought him down from his pedestal. He lost trust—for his person and his office. So, when the political tables were turned, his policies were defenseless. And just as he had used international issues to bludgeon his political adversaries, they did likewise. There was in summer 1973, for example, a policy case for retaining the option of renewed Indochina bombing, as a means of enforcing the Paris peace accord. But by then the majority of Congress simply did not trust the President with such a power. And if driving the final nail into our Vietnam coffin involved also the humiliation of Richard M. Nixon, that was icing on the cake.

Another contributor to Congressional irresponsibility was, ironically, some of the procedural reforms adopted in responsibility's name. The new "sunshine" regulations had been adopted to make members more accountable for their actions. Committees were required to draft most legislation in sessions open to the public, and it became far easier for members to insist on recorded votes on amendments presented on the House floor. The aim was to insure that organized interests did not quietly attach amendments they favored and scuttle proposals they opposed.

But as former Congressman Charles W. Whalen, Jr., (Republican, Ohio) has written, these increased the "potential for electoral damage" as opponents exploited individual floor votes in misleading ways—a vote against an impractical restriction on World Bank lending could become, in an adversary's TV spot, a vote in favor of aid to Cuba. Or as discovered by a veteran Ohio Democrat defeated for reelection in 1980, a minor vote against a foreign-aid cut could be distorted to label him a "big spender." Similarly, an Alabama Republican was defeated in his 1980 renomination primary, with charges that he had supported "Communist Marxist African Dictatorships" playing a significant role. It is hardly surprising that many of their colleagues indulged in what Whalen labels a "damage limitation exercise," taking the politically safe side and, in order to reduce their political vulnerability, voting for proposals that they knew were irresponsible. And for those who didn't there was yet another reminder in August 1983. Democrats who had, in support of the Reagan Administration, stood against an amendment requiring the United States representative to the International Monetary Fund to oppose all loans to (undefined) "communist dictatorships" discovered that the Republican Congressional Committee was mailing news releases to their districts the next day asserting that they "voted . . . to loan U. S. taxpayers' money to communist nations."

If open practices worked badly, closed processes sometimes worked better. On trade in 1979, Congress was able to employ something resembling the discredited smoke-filled room—closed meetings of Senate Finance and House Ways and Means developed the implementing legislation for the multilateral trade agreements. The result: Congress got a significant say in, and shared responsibility with the executive for, a jointly developed American trade policy. And special-interest amendments were avoided.

But in general, the new Congress was one where organized special interests were more active and influential on foreign policy, with weakened committee chairmen less able to act as counterweights. And the growing power of these interests was also a major contributor to irresponsibility. The embargo imposed on arms sales to Turkey in early 1975, for example, may have had a broader rationale—contrary to bilateral agreement and United States law, Turkey had used American arms to intervene in Cyprus, drastically altering the balance between its Greek and Turkish communities. But Congress applied the principle selectively, under pressure from the Greek-American lobby. Nobody would have dreamed of applying the same principle, say, to arms sales to Israel.

The pattern of special-interest influence held on arms sales more generally. The Nelson amendment gave the Congress power to veto any large sale (excepting those made to allies). But with one exception, the only proposals to which legislators mounted serious objections were sales to Middle East countries posing current or potential threats to Israel, like hawk missiles to Jordan, or F-15 fighter planes to Saudi Arabia. The most dramatic episode came in 1981, when the American Israel Public Affairs Committee (AIPAC) lined up fifty-four Senators against the Reagan Administration's proposal to sell the Saudis advanced radar warning aircraft (AWACS). In so doing, it stole a march on the White House, which was preoccupied with selling Congress on the President's economic program. AIPAC forced Reagan to mount an enormous personal lobbying effort, with the time he devoted out of all proportion to the sale's intrinsic importance, in order to get enough Senators to change sides to avert a humiliating defeat. And the battle weakened United States credibility with Arabs and Israelis alike. (Active on the Saudi side of the issue was former Kennedy aide Fred Dutton, whose law firm circulated, on behalf of its foreign client, a slick, multicolor brochure glorifying United States relations with that desert kingdom.)

A more open foreign-policy process meant more points of access for special interests, and thus more opportunity for policy impact. Interest groups that could provide or withhold campaign money, through their Political Action Committees (PACs), or which were well organized in individual members' districts or states, could clearly sway votes on those issues that most mattered to them.

This did not mean, of course, that lobbies dominated Congressional foreign-policy making. For one thing, their focus is relatively narrow; they concentrate mainly on government decisions that concern them very directly. Defense contractors can move legislators to back their particular weapons systems, but not on arms-control policy. AIPAC targets United States military dealings with crucial Mideast nations, but not overall energy policy, notwithstanding its important general effect on these dealings. Similarly, the textile industry has greatest influence in defending or extending *its* import quotas, and will stay on the sidelines on general trade policy if it gets its specific way.

Even so, a lobby seldom wins unless it can align its interest with an argument that has broader appeal. The "Greek lobby" could not have prevailed on the partial arms embargo for Turkey without the evident fact, in the second year of Watergate, that that government had broken United States law and Henry Kissinger's State Department was acquiescing. AIPAC needed disillusionment with détente to win broad support for the Jackson amendment on Soviet trade and Jewish emigration in 1973–74. It needed concern about transfer of sensitive military technology to build a near-winning coalition against selling AWACS in 1981. And interests sympathetic to Rhodesia needed a national-security argument in 1971 to win enactment of the Byrd amendment, which exempted that outlaw nation's chrome from the United States trade embargo; they found one in the fact that the Soviet Union was the only other major exporter of that scarce commodity. Nor were the special interests, once successful, impossible to turn back later. Carter obtained reversal of both the Turkish embargo and the Byrd amendment early in his administration. Yet even when lobbies are beaten, they can levy a substantial tax on the time and energy of executive and legislative leaders. And they contribute no little to vacillation and uncertainty in United States policy stances.

Congressional participation in foreign policy has had, of course, a brighter side as well. There have been many cases of individual legislators like Dante Fascell or Lee Hamilton or Stephen Solarz making constructive policy contributions on issues from Latin America to the Middle East to southern Africa. They have repaired or refined draft legislation; they have played critical roles in coalition building to get it enacted. And in late 1983, whatever one thought of the substance of their position, one had to recognize that representatives like Les Aspin and Albert Gore, Jr., and Senators like William Cohen and Sam Nunn, were providing much of the force pushing the Reagan Administration toward realism on arms control as they linked their crucial support of the MX missile to reformulation of the United States negotiating position in the strategic-arms-reduction talks (START) with the Soviet Union.

What was far more evident in the decade after 1973, however, was a Congress with almost infinite means for checking, constraining, questioning—means it employed intermittently and not always predictably—but with little capacity or taste for making responsible decisions and accepting their consequences.

The American press joined with Congress and interest groups in contributing to our "collective irresponsibility," as Thomas L. Hughes has labeled it. One reason was that conflict on an issue like AWACS was news, especially when it could be personalized. Would the Senate follow the House, which had voted 301–111 to veto the sale? Or would Ronald Reagan's personal magic work as it had on budget and tax cuts the previous summer? And the story was not so much the substance—was the sale wise policy?—it was the politics, Reagan or Begin? Israeli versus Saudi lobbyists! President versus Congress!

Why did the press overstress the politics angle? One reason was that it was something just about all reporters, and their audiences, could understand. For every Murrey Marder who has made himself expert on diplomatic history and strategy there are a hundred reporters who are political experts, or who see themselves that way.

When Edmund Muskie criticized Nixon's Vietnam policy early in the 1972 Presidential primary season, press people inundated his staff with questions, as well they should have. But they were not questions about substance. They were about politics. Why was the Senator issuing this statement now? How did it fit into his campaign strategy? Which of his advisers were for it and which were against? What mattered was not who was right, but who was winning and how this statement might affect the game.

When Jimmy Carter responded to Afghanistan by cutting wheat sales to Russia, the key question was not whether it would hurt Moscow. It was how it would play in Dubuque, in the Iowa Presidential caucuses later that month. (This was, of course, a big thing inside government as well. At one post-Afghanistan meeting, Vice-President Walter Mondale reportedly turned to Secretary of Defense Brown and asked, "Got that rapid deployment force ready yet, Harold? I'm going to Iowa and I could use some protection!")

There was nothing new, of course, about press interest in politics, or conflict. Nor was there anything peculiar to the seventies and eighties about the attention paid to individual American citizens (like the Teheran hostages) in hard situations far from home, or about the moral relativism which allotted far less print space or air time to foreigners in similar plights. After all, it was before World War II that E. H. Carr cited the rule of "an American newspaper correspondent in Europe . . . that an accident was worth reporting if it involved the death of one American, five Englishmen, or ten Europeans."

What was new, and absolutely crucial, was the central role of television. Since 1959, the Roper organization has been asking people, "Where do you usually get most of your news about what's going on in the world today?" In 1963, Roper reported that television passed newspapers as "the source of most news." By 1981, 64 percent of Americans were saying they got their major information from this source, either alone or in combination with another.

This does not mean that the print media do not remain very important. In fact, national newspapers like *The New York Times* and *The Washington Post* have grown in circulation and influence, and they, together with the newsweeklies, give international events very substantial coverage. Indeed, television reporters themselves, less able to specialize or investigate, draw much of their sense of what's happening from what they read in the papers or *Time* or *Newsweek.* And one scholar, Lawrence Lichty, argues persuasively that the people who tell pollsters they learn primarily from TV must be wrong, since other surveys indicate that Americans just don't watch television news that regularly. But even he acknowledges that the perceived dominance of TV is crucial, since "Presidents, Senators, and other politicians . . . have come to act on the assumption that it *is* true."

The central impact of television, real *and* perceived, has several very important effects on foreign-policy making. First, it gives enormous—and apparently increasing—emphasis to national political issues. A recent study by Richard L. Rubin concludes:

> . . . only 60 percent of all lead stories on network television had political topics in 1963, [but] by 1975 about 80 percent of all top news stories reaching the air were "political." In contrast, the newspapers' lead headline stories were political (either local or national) in only a little over 25 percent of the cases, and the trend between 1963 and 1975 indicates, if anything, no increase in political news stories.

Second, when political candidates succumb to the long-standing, almost irresistible temptation to use foreign-policy issues to gain national press attention, they are now driven to do it with a pithy telegenic statement, one that the evening news might pick up as a twenty- or thirty-second segment of a two- or three-minute news report. This is not an ideal way for candidates to plumb the depths of complicated international issues. It is no wonder that a Presidential candidate without much prior international experience can come to office with a collection of half-minute clichés in his head masquerading as foreign policies. And Senators may think they have "solved" a foreign-policy problem when they develop an answer that meets the thirty-second test.

Third, once our leaders make it to high office, the intensity of television coverage reduces their flexibility in determining which foreign-policy issues are crucial and which they can downplay. James Reston had called in 1966 for a "redefinition of what is 'news,' with more attention to the causes rather than merely the effects of international strife." But TV's impact is the opposite; it amplifies the conflicts of the here and now. Iran becomes news when there is revolution, and it dominates our living rooms when American diplomats are held captive. Jimmy Carter certainly inflated the hostage issue and milked it for partisan gain, using the Rose Garden for cover against Teddy Kennedy. But even if he had behaved more responsibly, it is anything but clear that he could have kept things in proportion when the networks brought chanting demonstrators to us nightly and Walter Cronkite began counting the days.

Fourth, the intensity of the TV spotlight increases the risk of the monumental blunder that can haunt a political leader thereafter. Gerald Ford's epic misstatement about "no Soviet domination of Eastern Europe," which could not have been intended the way it sounded, would not have been epic had it not been made live, to the enormous nationwide audience watching his second debate with challenger Jimmy Carter. And who would remember Alexander Haig's self-destructive declaration, "I am in control here," if he had not spoken to a nation alarmed at the Presidential assassination attempt of March 1981 and turning to TV for information and reassurance? For those who missed it live that afternoon, Haig's disastrous moment would be replayed over and over that evening. Dwight Eisenhower, by contrast, could avoid live television coverage of news conferences. Franklin Roosevelt dealt, in the main, with captive

White House reporters, under ground rules giving him a second chance—to clarify and correct, or deny direct responsibility. On live television there is no second chance.

Finally, there is evidence that the types of news that TV chooses to bring into viewers' homes, combined with the skeptical aggressiveness that reporters frequently display toward national leaders and institutions, have made the public more cynical about United States international involvement and about their leaders' motives in advocating it. Thus the medium of television reinforces, and renders harder to reverse or balance, that mood of cynicism and skepticism among reporters and their audiences that Vietnam and Watergate understandably produced.

Taken together, the rise of Congress and the press has increased the force of "disintegrative" institutions in our society, those that highlight differences, promote controversy, reinforce the episodic nature of public policy concerns. Both tend to surge into issues. There is "pack journalism," the product of a large number of correspondents drawing their cues from one another. Thus we get what Eugene McCarthy likened to "blackbirds on the telephone wire—one flies away, they all fly away; one comes back, they all come back." So also with Congress. Panama negotiator Sol Linowitz found it hard to get Senators to focus when he was consulting on the treaties in the spring of 1977. But twelve months later everyone was obsessed with Panama, fashioning his own reservations and amendments.

Congress and press have a symbiotic relationship. Senators and Representatives need reporters to achieve the publicity, the name recognition, they require for reelection at home and influence in Washington. Reporters find Capitol Hill a major source for stories not just about Congress but about Executive Branch actions. And both are nourished by the intense combat within the executive branch among members of the new Professional Elite.

Richard Rovere, in his semiserious spoof of twenty years ago, insisted that Congress was outside the "American establishment." But today members with a taste for policy or senior Congressional staff aides are active members of the new Elite. So are Washington journalists, whose numbers, sophistication and social status have risen sharply in the postwar period. The Council on Foreign Relations membership roster includes—to select a few names in alphabetical order—Elie Abel, John Chancellor, Elizabeth Drew, Max Frankel, Meg Greenfield, Joseph Kraft, Murrey Marder, Don Oberdorfer, James Reston, Harrison Salisbury and Sanford Ungar. And it includes such current members of Congress as Les Aspin, Howard Baker, Charles Mathias and Stephen Solarz, and such staff aides (of current or recent vintage) as Miller, Perle, Smith and Jan Kalicki, chief foreign-policy aide to Senator Edward Kennedy.

The Congress and the press have very different formal roles, the former as part of the government and the latter as recorder and critic of its actions. But in their impact on foreign-policy making they have much in common. Both make the public better informed through hearings or investigative reporting, through the charges and countercharges that they make or record. Their contribution to opening up our policy processes, particularly since 1970, increases the likelihood that a particular issue or governmental action will receive the skeptical scrutiny it surely deserves.

But there is a serious problem of balance. For we want two "good" things that conflict in practice. We want exposure of issues and alternatives by the press and by the Congress, that governmental body most representative of national sentiment. But at times like the present, when the public and experts alike are deeply divided about the substance of policy, their activism makes very much more complicated the attainment of another "good" that we badly need and want—sensible, persistent, reasonably coherent foreign policy. That requires that Congress and press and public be prepared to deal constructively with the President and his top aides, even grant them a certain leeway. The patterns of Congressional irresponsibility recounted in this chapter, amplified by press reporting, have worked against this. The President often cannot do what he wants, but leaderless Congress does not make clear what it wants him to do instead. It seldom bargains effectively to produce a sensible compromise. It doesn't enforce a practical alternative policy. Nor does it supply the sort of consistent political and policy constraint that would allow an administration to make reliable calculations about which policies might fly and which the Congress will shoot down.

What can be done? Some critics have suggested that the answer lies in turning back the clock. Senator John Tower (Republican,

Texas) has explicitly proposed "a return to the situation that prevailed in the 1950s and 1960s," through repeal of the major legislation enacted thereafter. But it is neither possible nor desirable to return to the "golden years" of Congressional and press deference, the extreme form of "my President right or wrong."

Of the legitimacy of Congressional participation in foreign-policy making there can be no doubt. Presidential advisers like to think otherwise; as recently as April 1983, Edwin Meese was insisting that "it is the responsibility of the President to conduct foreign policy; limitations on that by the Congress are improper as far as I'm concerned." Unfortunately for Meese and his associates, the Constitutional Convention of 1787 decided the matter otherwise. It ordains Congressional involvement by giving the legislative branch important foreign-policy powers—confirming ambassadors, ratifying treaties, declaring war—as well as the general authorities to legislate and appropriate—authorities that spill over from the domestic to the international realm. Congress cannot, of course, claim *primary* jurisdiction (except in specific realms such as foreign commerce), for the President has major Constitutional authorities also. And the practical need, in Alexander Hamilton's words, for the executive qualities of "decision, activity, secrecy, and dispatch," gives his branch the initiative most of the time. But neither can the executive claim, under our system, that it has the right to dominate foreign policy.

This means, in Edwin Corwin's classic formulation, "an invitation to struggle for the privilege of directing American foreign policy," a bipolar policy process featuring, in Richard Neustadt's apt words, "separated institutions sharing powers." In today's world, the President and his courtiers and barons will inevitably be taking the lead on most issues, most of the time. And when Congress is serious about influencing foreign policy, matters will inevitably be complicated for the executive, since even the most statesmanlike struggle over competing policy courses will, until resolved, prevent persistent and effective pursuit of any one of them. But this is the necessary price we pay for having an independent legislature, our type of political system. And it has clear advantages—in checking excesses, in generating innovation—as the early seventies demonstrated.

We pay a higher price, unfortunately, when Congress behaves irresponsibly, committing errors either of omission or of commission.

We pay when Congress plays the silent partner. We pay when loud position taking and political and ideological point scoring substitutes for willingness to act and share or bear the consequences.

If Congressmen and their constituents are dissatisfied—and many were in the early seventies, as many are today—with major aspects of recent United States foreign policy, then they have a duty to define and debate the large issues and realistic choices, to take clear action on them, and be visibly accountable to the voters for the consequences. That is the highest obligation of legislators as representatives of the country at large.

How can the odds for responsible Congressional policy making be improved? On this, as on other subjects, we will leave specific recommendations to our concluding chapter. But we can shed further light on the malady with a final look at three disparate cases: one where Congress behaved responsibly, one where its contribution has been largely irresponsible, and a "mixed case" with its own particular lessons to offer.

The good example lies in how Congress responded to the Carter Administration's summer 1977 proposal to sell AWACS aircraft to Iran. On July 7, the President sent the required formal notification to Capitol Hill. Critics protested, led by Iowa Senator John Culver. Not only might this upset the balance of power in the Persian Gulf region; it also would risk loss of United States technological secrets if, for example, the Soviet Union could induce an Iranian AWACS crew to defect. Senator Majority Leader Robert Byrd asked Carter to withdraw the sale proposal temporarily and consider modifications proposed by the Senate Foreign Relations Committee. When Carter initially refused, the House International Relations Committee voted in favor of a veto resolution.

With the Senate committee certain to do likewise, Carter reconsidered. He withdrew the notification on July 28, and when it was resubmitted the following September, it was with amendments which met the main Congressional objections. Specifically, it provided that highly secret coding and communications gear would be removed. Congress took no further action, allowing the revised sale to proceed.

As events unfolded, the Shah fell before any of the aircraft were actually delivered. But the episode nonetheless offers a model for constructive Congressional participation in an important, specific foreign-policy decision. Critics pinpointed a serious problem that the Administration had neglected. They proposed concrete ways of dealing with the problem. They used the veto threat to force reconsideration by the Executive Branch. And last but not least, they let the sale proceed once the main Congressional concerns had been addressed.

Standing in sharp contrast is the way in which Congress has dealt with United States policy toward Central America. With both Carter and Reagan, legislators have been vocal in their attack on Presidential policies, and have imposed restrictions that sharply reduced any chance that these policies might succeed. But in neither case did Congress develop and stand behind a specific alternative.

Carter sought expeditious action late in his term on an emergency bill to "assist in the reconstruction of the Nicaraguan economy" after the overthrow of the Somoza dictatorship. A key aim was to try to encourage moderate forces in the ruling Sandinista coalition, which had just come to power. But House conservatives delayed the bill and attached thoroughgoing restrictions, insulting to the new Nicaraguan government, which more than offset any political good that the aid might have done. Carter's approach was admittedly a gamble, but Congress in 1980 neither approved it nor substituted another approach to dealing with Nicaragua. It simply took away the timeliness and flexibility of Carter's approach, and without these, his policy was bound to fail.

On El Salvador, the Reagan Administration has received similar treatment. Many legislators have been legitimately upset about the "death squads" there and the inability of the government we are supporting to bring them under control. But to deny aid unless and until such control was achieved would have meant reversing the Reagan Administration. Congress would itself have had to take on responsibility for consequences, for a possible "loss" of El Salvador. But neither would it make political sense simply to go along with an unpopular foreign involvement. The former would violate the "containment" imperative of American politics; the latter, the "peace" imperative.

So, liberals and moderates found a way to straddle the issue. Congress attached to the aid-authorization bill a requirement that, as a precondition for further military assistance, the President certify every six months that the Salvadoran government was "achieving substantial control" of its armed forces in order to end "indiscriminate torture and murder," that it was "implementing essential economic and political reforms, including the land reform program," and that it was holding free elections and demonstrating a willingness to negotiate a political settlement.

Some members saw this as a sincere way to pressure the President to lean on El Salvador. Others were more cynical, seeing it as something with which to beat him on the head, to force him to lie, to make him vulnerable to political attack. Thus the expected Presidential certification (yes, El Salvador was making progress) could bring the anticipated Congressional denunciation. "Fraud, pure and simple," said one senior representative. He was referring to the Administration's case for going forward. But the phrase could equally be applied to the certification requirement itself. It provided Congressmen a good soapbox, but left the President to wrestle with the dilemma and take responsibility for any costs in either direction. And as if to make sure that the Reagan approach would not have a chance to work, Congress also cut back sharply on the amount of aid the President requested.

The point is not that the Reagan approach was necessarily right or realistic, or that Carter's effort to woo the Sandinistas would necessarily have worked. It is that Congress, in both cases, made it very much harder for the President to succeed with his policies, without offering any serious alternative. What it amounted to was a kind of fake activism, playing to the media grandstands, complicating United States foreign policy without establishing clear control or giving serious direction.

In 1984, interestingly, Congress became more responsible—by our definition—in its Central America policy role. On El Salvador, responding to the election of Napoleón Duarte as President, Congress increased aid and relaxed strings. On Nicaragua, responding to the hardening of Administration rhetoric and CIA actions, legislators drew a clear line against further support of the *contras* seeking to overthrow the Sandinista regime. The Administration, of course, welcomed the first and denounced the second, but both represented clear, responsible Congressional choices about the substance of American foreign policy.

Finally, there was the mixed case of the deployment of U. S. Marines in Lebanon. This was ordered by President Reagan in 1982, as part of a multinational peace-keeping force. He reported the action to Congress, but not under the subsection of the War Powers Resolution which requires Congressional authorization if the forces were to stay beyond sixty days. The applicability of this provision was unclear at the time of initial deployment, for it covered situations where "imminent involvement in hostilities is clearly indicated by the circumstances," and such involvement was neither desired nor planned for the Marines in Lebanon.

But not only did Senators and Representatives acquiesce in this defensible interpretation; they backed away from any serious review of the rationale for the deployment or the broader Mideast policies to which it related. Legislators were worried about both, but they were uncertain about how the politics would play at home or how events would unfold abroad. It was safer to let the burden rest on Administration shoulders.

They could no longer leave it this way after August 29, 1983, when two Marines were killed and United States forces began to take some limited combat initiative. Now the War Powers language clearly applied. But the White House refused to make the notification of "involvement in hostilities" that the law now plainly mandated. None of Reagan's predecessors had invoked this provision, or even conceded its constitutionality. He wished neither to tie his hands nor to set a legal precedent. Yet Reagan badly needed Congress to share responsibility for a chancy and unpopular use of American troops.

So, the White House entered negotiations with Senate Majority Leader Howard Baker and House Speaker Thomas P. O'Neill, and they reached a curious compromise. Congress would itself declare that the Marines were now in hostilities. *It* would invoke the War Powers Resolution, as part of a bill authorizing the forces to remain for eighteen months (moving the matter conveniently beyond the 1984 election). The President would sign this bill, but state separately at the same time his reservations about the constitutionality of War Powers. Senate Democrats found this insufficient. They wanted Reagan to comply explicitly with the War Powers Resolution, and many also thought eighteen months too long a time period. So the vote in their Republican-controlled body was 54–46, almost entirely along party lines. (The margin in the House was greater, 253–156.)

This outcome was tolerable for foreign policy. Congress did move, albeit reluctantly, to take a share of responsibility. And it was not a repeat of the Gulf of Tonkin Resolution, for the legislation had some bite: it limited the size and mission of the forces, and Reagan promised, by letter, that he would comply with these limits (or seek a new, broader Congressional authorization if circumstances changed). So the War Powers Resolution worked, though hardly in the straightforward way its drafters intended. But Congress did not use the opportunity to extract from the Administration any clear explanation of what the deployment was expected to achieve. Nor did it succeed in gaining the President's explicit adherence to what was, after all, the law of the land.

The ink was hardly dry on the Lebanon compromise when Congress undercut its own work through inaction on Grenada. When President Reagan ordered the invasion of that tiny Caribbean island in late October, he again dodged formal compliance with the law by reporting this action to Capitol Hill leaders in "accordance with my desire that the Congress be informed on this matter, and *consistent with* the War Powers Resolution" (emphasis added). The immediate Congressional impulse was to follow the Lebanon pattern, and separate motions invoking the War Powers Resolution for Grenada won strong majorities in the House and Senate. But once the public began to cheer, Congress backed off, adjourning for the year without completing any legislative action on the subject. And there was a ready legal excuse, for the troops' "involvement in hostilities" had lasted only a few days, and U.S. combat forces were brought home less than sixty days after they were dispatched.

Every war-powers case will differ in its specifics; few will fit the Vietnam model that dominated Congressional minds when the resolution was enacted. Nevertheless, our system would work a lot better if both branches approached each new case by accepting the law and using it to clarify policy goals and build political support. On Lebanon, for example, how much better it would have been had the Reagan Administration sought Congressional action when it all began, in the second half of 1982. The President might have noted that experts differed on the applicability of War Powers in this particular case, but he did not want his deployment action undermined by either legal doubts or lack of broad, bipartisan support. Congress would certainly have given him the authorizing legislation he wanted. And legislators could also have used this opportunity, *before* American blood had been shed, to press Administration officials to spell out the military and political assumptions behind the deployment. In this way, leaders in both branches would have been using our political process as it should be used—to clarify our choices and set a policy course that has the support necessary to be credible and sustained over time. Raising these hard questions earlier might have helped avert the debacles which were to follow: the terror-bombing of the Marine compound in October 1983, and the hooking of American prestige to an army and government which came apart early in 1984.

But as this final example suggests, responsible Congressional policy making requires more than political will and courage in the Congress; the President and his top aides must be skillful in blending the development of international strategy with the building of domestic support, in including the Congress at the early stages of issues that may later prove divisive.

Recent administrations have failed badly in this task. Top Presidential aides have spent more and more time fighting one another, diverting them from concentration on the world beyond. It is in these battles between our Presidential courtiers and barons that we find another major element in the unraveling of postwar American foreign policy.

IV

Courtiers and Barons: The "Inside" Politics of Foreign Policy

JAMES FORRESTAL was one of the first to see the need. As Secretary of the Navy in 1945, he recognized that preserving the dearly bought peace would require sustained, comprehensive United States engagement in the world. For this our country would need far stronger institutions for policy making, policy integration, and policy execution. We would need to link military and economic instruments to diplomatic objectives, incorporating a high standard of information, analysis and interagency deliberation.

Only the President could take the lead in creating such institutions and making them work. Yet Forrestal was nervous about Presidents as people. He was personally close to neither Roosevelt nor his Missouri successor. He saw the former as an idiosyncratic, even chaotic foreign-policy manager and he worried about the latter's will to make the necessary hard decisions to maintain and use American power. And both men, in Forrestal's view, were too sensitive to short-run political pressures to be relied on to do what was best for the nation. What was needed was a way for national-security managers to plug into Presidential power but curb Presidential whim.

So Forrestal proposed an organizational fix, a "National Security Council." Modeled on the British War Cabinet, this committee of the most exalted United States officials, chaired by the President, would review issues in their broadest perspective and offer authoritative advice to the chief executive, advice he would be constrained to follow. Policy would be integrated, and Presidential power would serve the highest national need.

Forrestal had, understandably, some narrower personal and organizational goals also. He initially pressed the council proposal as an alternative to a unified defense establishment, which his service, the Navy, strongly resisted. And as a strong-willed man with global-policy interests, he wanted to be sure that he (and other service representatives) would be in on the crucial foreign-policy deliberations—a National Security Council could help here as well. Still, there is no reason to doubt that this brilliant, driven man was sincerely pressing the national interest as he saw it.

In both personal and policy terms, Forrestal's initiative was, in the end, a failure.

A National Security Council was, of course, created by statute in 1947, charged "to advise the President with respect to the integration of domestic, foreign and military politics relating to the national security." The NSC still exists today, bringing a note of formal continuity to postwar foreign-policy making. But the same National Security Act that brought it into being also took the first step toward incorporating the Navy within a Department of Defense, which Forrestal had resisted. He did receive the consolation prize of being named the first Defense Secretary in July 1947, after Secretary of War Robert Patterson (Truman's initial choice) turned the job down. But when Forrestal then tried to have the NSC staffed from the Pentagon and treated as "an integral part of the national defense setup," Truman rebuffed him. Instead, the President followed Budget Director James Webb's recommendation to employ the NSC as a means to "further enlargement of the presidential staff," with its executive secretary the equivalent of a new administrative assistant. And Truman asked Secretary of State George Marshall, not Forrestal, to preside over Council meetings in the President's absence.

Forrestal also failed in his larger goal—to use the NSC to envelop the President within a broader, collegial process of making decisions. Truman, again following Budget Bureau advice, stayed away from early NSC meetings to preserve his independence. Eisenhower, who strengthened and used the Council, was much less dependent on its deliberations than he pretended to be. And beginning with Kennedy, Presidents began to turn Forrestal's idea on its head, to use the Council as a cover for a White House foreign-policy staff which would give them greater independence from their senior statutory advisers.

Forrestal was a "baron," a senior official in formal charge of an important domain within the Presidential realm. He was neither the first nor the last baron to get at cross-purposes with his chief. Abraham Lincoln had to squelch Secretary of State William Seward, subordinate him to Presidential authority, before he could trust him and use him effectively. Woodrow Wilson's Secretary of State, Robert Lansing, "seems to have spent most of the time" at the Paris Peace Conference which followed World War I "writing caustic but anxious comments in his private memoranda book . . . embittered by Wilson's repeated slights and his publicly displayed preference for [Colonel E. M.] House's counsel and aid." Franklin Roosevelt used Harry Hopkins and circumvented Cordell Hull; Richard Nixon would employ Henry Kissinger to exclude and humiliate Secretary of State William P. Rogers. Alexander Haig would style himself Ronald Reagan's foreign-policy "vicar," and ultimately drive the President (who entered office determined to strengthen the Secretary) to accept his resignation with profound relief.

As a baron, Forrestal saw the President as the national policy leader who should make hard choices and give his Cabinet subordinates the backing and the resources to carry them out. But Presidents are not just policy leaders. They are also idiosyncratic individuals and national politicians. As individuals, they have personal styles, preferences, some relationships with which they are comfortable and others with which they are not. All of these personal things shape their policy making. As politicians, Presidents must be sensitive (as national-security Cabinet members and their bureaucracies often are not) to broad public sentiment, and also to their partisan and electoral interests. Like kings in the Middle Ages, Presidents have "courtiers" in the White House who gain influence by responding to both their personal needs and their political priorities. And these courtiers come inevitably into conflict with the barons.

The inside story of American foreign-policy making since World War II is the story of Presidents, courtiers, and barons and how they worked with and against one another as they coped with matters international. This type of conflict was as old as organized society. What was new was that these relationships were playing themselves out in a period of global United States engagement, on top of foreign-policy bureaucracies of unprecedented size and scope.

And entwined with the ebb and flow of people and relationships was a longer-term trend. Increasingly, the courtiers—the people and institutions tied to the President as person and politician—were winning out over the barons and their institutions and processes. In foreign policy, this meant in particular the White House over the

State Department, the national-security assistant contesting and often supplanting the secretary of state, "in-and-outer" policy aides overshadowing the established Foreign Service.

The story unfolded in three stages. In the Truman–Eisenhower period, Presidents in general supported their preferred barons and encouraged development of formal interagency processes, even as they guarded their personal flexibility. In the Kennedy–Johnson period, free-wheeling White House foreign-policy-staff courtiers emerged in uneasy coexistence with senior Cabinet members and the standing departments. Then, beginning in 1969, the personal-political Presidency circumvented and supplanted the barons and their institutions. Accomplished policy courtiers Henry Kissinger and Zbigniew Brzezinski became national media figures. The political genie, which Forrestal had feared and sought to bottle up in the National Security Council, had escaped.

Reacting to Roosevelt: 1945–1960

Many Presidents talk about wanting a strong State Department. Harry S. Truman really meant it. Franklin Roosevelt had worked above and around Secretary of State Cordell Hull, even as he permitted him to set the all-time record for tenure in that office. John F. Kennedy would talk of State as "agent of coordination" while strengthening the White House; Richard Nixon would label William P. Rogers "the chief foreign policy adviser" even as he humiliated him by his obvious reliance on Kissinger. But Truman was simple and direct. He wanted a strong secretary of state with whom he could share, intimately, overall foreign-policy responsibility. When his first appointment did not work out, he would try again.

Truman's initial choice was James Byrnes, FDR's wartime economic czar. Byrnes had sought the 1944 Vice-Presidential nomination, and Truman (once Byrnes's admiring Senate junior) had supported him until Roosevelt signaled his preference for the less experienced man from Missouri. Truman offered Byrnes the senior Cabinet job just four days after Roosevelt's death; by early 1946 he was making plans for Byrnes's departure. Health was the ostensible reason. More important was Byrnes's inability to adjust to the fact that the man who had followed him in the Senate was now his boss. In Dean Acheson's apt formulation, it was necessary "that from first to last both parties to the relationship understand which is the President." Neither man understood when Truman appointed Byrnes, but the President proved the faster learner.

Truman turned quickly to an even more accomplished baron, George C. Marshall, organizer of military victory in World War II. While Marshall was on Presidential assignment in China, seeking to mediate between Chiang Kai-shek and Mao Tse-tung, Truman employed General of the Army Dwight D. Eisenhower as an emissary to learn whether he would agree to be Byrnes's successor. The return message was affirmative. When the China mission ended and Marshall prepared to return, the President confirmed this agreement through an indirectly worded exchange of cables, and announced it in January 1947.

Behind this seemingly impersonal procedure was enormous respect, even awe. While a Senator, Truman had called Marshall "the greatest living American." Truman had enormous confidence in Marshall's judgment, and he needed the general's prestige to bolster a sagging Administration. Yet Truman was not repeating his mistake with Byrnes. For the President knew also that his new Secretary of State would be sensitive and scrupulous in return. Byrnes had hardly communicated with Truman during a critical Moscow conference: as he explained it to Ambassador Averell Harriman, "I can't trust the White House to prevent leaks." Marshall would send "long cable report[s]" from China, "sometimes two and three times a week," enabling the President "to follow every step as the story unfolded."

Truman was a simple man, ready to make hard decisions—sometimes too ready. He governed neither by manipulation nor by seizing direct operational control. Instead he sought out barons he could trust, insisted on being the ultimate decision-maker, but generally followed their counsel. When Marshall, pleading health, retired at the end of 1948, it was former Under Secretary (and close Truman confidant) Dean Acheson who succeeded him. When war in Korea brought need for a new Secretary of Defense, Truman brought back Marshall. A particularly adroit aide, like Presidential Counsel Clark Clifford, could involve himself intermittently in international issues—providing an independent analysis of the Soviet threat in

1946, making connections between foreign policy and the 1948 Presidential campaign. But with the partial exception of policy toward Palestine—especially the decision to recognize Israel—it was Marshall's (and later Acheson's) counsel that prevailed.

So when Forrestal lost out in 1947 it was not to a courtier but to a competing baron, one who felt—perhaps even more deeply than Forrestal—that foreign policy should be above domestic partisanship. Marshall had made it a point never even to vote in national elections. Truman's respect for Marshall's priorities was painfully demonstrated in October 1948, when two speech writers sold him on a proposal to send Chief Justice Fred Vinson on a peace mission to Moscow (and thus undercut dissident leftist Presidential candidate Henry Wallace). Truman had already booked radio time to announce the mission, and he phoned Paris (where Marshall was engaged in negotiations) to give him advance notice. When the Secretary put his foot down, Truman reversed himself, accepting humiliation when, inevitably, the story leaked and made him look as if grasping at political straws.

This "above politics" approach extended to the new National Security Council and its staff. Truman firmly rejected Forrestal's efforts to make it into a "war cabinet" which would compromise his Presidential decision-making prerogative. To protect his independence, he presided over the first NSC meeting but stayed away for the next ten months, returning only to coordinate specifics of the Berlin airlift after he decided (*not* at a Council meeting) to proceed with it. Two years later, he decided outside the NSC to resist North Korean aggression, then met regularly with the Council to help implement this decision and develop its global implications.

Truman also insisted that the Council staff be brought within the Executive Office of the President. But he made it a career staff, intended to "serve as a continuing organization regardless of what Administration was in power." Its first head, Executive Secretary (and reserve Admiral) Sidney Souers, held scrupulously to the policy-neutral, anonymous role called for in ascendant public-administration doctrine. A Missouri insurance executive with experience in wartime intelligence, Souers saw himself as a "non-political confidant of the President," who was to "forego publicity and personal aggrandizement." He stayed away from the morning meetings of Truman's regular political staff, seeing the President privately thereafter; he limited those working for him to a small secretariat, with the main NSC policy studies and preparation for Council meetings handled by committees of departmental officials.

The Truman period was one of unprecedented organizational change. The Department of Defense was created, as well as the Central Intelligence Agency and the Economic Cooperation Administration, the first of a series of foreign-aid agencies. The fact that this organizational growth took place mainly outside the State Department sowed the seeds of future department weakness. But State itself also underwent substantial internal reform. Upon assuming office, Marshall established an Executive Secretariat to coordinate department-wide communication. He asked George Kennan to organize and head a new Policy Planning Staff, charged with broad policy analysis. This staff played a key role in the development of the European Recovery Program.

In 1949, after Congress enacted the needed legislation, Dean Acheson implemented a broader restructuring that established, for the first time, assistant secretaries of state for the geographic regions. Such reforms made the department more responsive to secretarial leadership. And because he both listened to career officers and defended them—most of the time—against McCarthyism, Acheson won from them a personal affection and loyalty not equaled under any of his successors. But what made him dominant, and Marshall before him, was the Truman connection. And this connection remained solid, despite the incredibly vitriolic partisan attacks that Acheson was sustaining from the Republican right.

With Truman committed to direct dealing and with Marshall and Acheson insisting upon it, and with both men loyal to him as President (and Acheson assiduously responsive to him as person), there was no opening for a White House courtier. Souers proved a useful coordinator, with his low profile and deference to Marshall and Acheson, and with his good personal connection to Truman. James Lay, who succeeded Souers as NSC executive secretary in 1950, had a weaker Presidential account and had to work more through Truman's aides. But as Richard Neustadt later put it, "The gap between the White House staff, as a politically oriented, totally Presidential entity, and the neutral secretariat of NSC was never bridged in Truman's time on any systematic basis."

Dwight Eisenhower, the most organizationally minded of Presidents, closed this gap in a formal sense by creating a new position, Special Assistant to the President for National Security Affairs. He placed in this job an energetic Boston banker (and campaign adviser), Robert Cutler. He charged Cutler with infusing a broad, Presidential perspective in the work of the policy-neutral, career NSC staff which Lay, as executive secretary, continued to head.

This was part of an intensive effort to use—and publicize—the National Security Council. In the 1952 Presidential campaign Eisenhower had denounced Truman's reluctance to let it become more than a "shadow agency." In office he embraced it, encouraging Cutler and his successors to organize and administer a system of comprehensive policy planning the likes of which this country has not seen before or since. The Council held 346 regular meetings in eight years, about one each week, compared to 128 meetings in 5¼ years under Truman. Two and a half hours was a typical duration, with Eisenhower himself presiding about 90 percent of the time, whenever he was well and in town. The NSC typically considered policy papers carefully prepared by the NSC Planning Board, an interagency committee, chaired by the Special Assistant, which developed comprehensive drafts setting forth "basic national security policy," area policies, and functional policies. A total of 187 serially numbered NSC policy documents were approved, 67 of them still current on January 20, 1961. There was also an Operations Coordinating Board to oversee policy implementation.

Cutler made it all sound mechanical, a bit boring. He wrote in *Foreign Affairs:*

> Assume that the National Security Council sits at the top of policy hill. On one side of this hill, policy recommendations travel upward through the Planning Board to the Council, where they are thrashed out and submitted to the President. When the President has approved a policy recommendation, it travels down the other side of policy hill to the departments and agencies responsible for its execution. Each department or agency with a function to perform under such approved policy must prepare its program to carry out its responsibility. Part way down this side of the hill is the Operations Coordinating Board, to which the President refers an approved national security policy as its authority to advise with the relevant departments and agencies as to their detailed operational planning and as to coordinating the interdepartmental aspects of their respective programs.

To critics, all this sounded overorganized, bloodless. They felt that such a committee-dominated process could only produce mushy prose and overcompromised policy. In fact, Cutler's description was deeply misleading. It implied that the NSC was the predominant means through which the President received policy advice and arrived at policy decisions. In fact, it was just one of several means. Dwight Eisenhower was far more sophisticated than contemporary detractors believed. He balanced his use of the Council with heavy reliance on Secretary of State John Foster Dulles. And he balanced the planning-oriented NSC staff by employing, for day-to-day issues, a "staff secretary" based in the White House.

John Foster Dulles, who turned sixty-five years old in 1953, had long yearned to be Secretary of State. He had anticipated fulfillment in a Dewey Presidency; Eisenhower was his last chance. His maternal grandfather, John Foster, had held the office for eight months in 1892–93. His uncle, Robert Lansing, had been Secretary a quarter century later. As a junior member of the American delegation at Versailles, Dulles had observed at first hand how isolated and ineffectual Lansing became without the confidence of his President.

But Dulles was close to Dewey, not Eisenhower. The latter had appointed him without any great personal enthusiasm—because of his standing as the ranking Republican foreign-policy statesman; because the New York lawyer's ties with Robert Taft and other conservative Republicans offered protection against the party's right (sometimes isolationist) flank. In their early encounters Eisenhower apparently found Dulles long-winded and boring, and he did not disguise his impatience.

Dulles understood this weakness, realized that it could quickly become fatal, and worked assiduously to overcome it. Like Acheson, he had no doubt "which was the President." He saw Eisenhower regularly at the White House, alone whenever possible; he consulted by telephone several times in a typical day. He was clearly the junior partner in a much-misunderstood relationship. But the President did defer to him, increasingly, on matters of both policy and prerogative, making him Secretary of State in fact as well as in name. In return, Dulles took enormous personal heat for things that went wrong, like the short-lived British-French invasion of Suez in 1956. This allowed Eisenhower to attach his reputation to more positive enterprises and outcomes.

Dulles was relentless in defending his prerogatives. Efforts by White House aides Nelson Rockefeller and Harold Stassen to establish themselves as independent substantive advisers "led to showdowns and their resignations." He lived well, however, with Eisenhower's national-security assistants, who held—in the main—to policy-neutral, process management roles.

Dulles was the only postwar Secretary of State who consistently took a harder foreign-policy line than the President he served. He did so, in all probability, out of devout anti-Communist conviction, but he was fully aware of the political protection his hard line offered. He had watched Dean Acheson come under withering attack from the Republicans on the right. He was determined to avoid such a fate, and if the price was to allow the State Department loyalty program to be administered by a virulent McCarthyite, Scott McLeod, he was fully prepared to pay it. Foreign Service officers like John Carter Vincent and John Paton Davies had reported, accurately, that Chiang Kai-shek led a corrupt, discredited government likely to lose the Chinese civil war. Dulles did not accept McLeod's view that they should therefore be fired for disloyalty or suspicion thereof. But once the new secretary had overruled his security chief by affirming their patriotism, he found rationales for dismissing them anyway—Vincent had failed "to meet the standard which is demanded of a Foreign Service officer of his experience"; Davies had shown "disregard of proper forbearance and caution." Even George Kennan was forced into retirement. Thus were promising government careers prematurely terminated. Thus was the message sent to the diplomatic service that analytic clarity and frankness could prove fatal, particularly if the subject were Communism in East Asia.

For Dulles, the need for "positive loyalty" among career officials was intertwined with his determination to lead the United States to major policy change—or at least appear to be doing so. Eisenhower was more cautious, seeing his own role as that of confirming American internationalism. He forced Dulles to drop any thought of abandoning the nomination of distinguished Soviet specialist Charles E. Bohlen as ambassador to Moscow, even though Bohlen had been a translator and adviser at Yalta and refused to endorse Republican party platform charges (drafted by Dulles) that Roosevelt had sold out Chinese interests there. (After Bohlen was confirmed, Dulles—in a suggestion that says much about his anxiety and the Washington mood—urged him not to travel alone to Moscow, a week or two ahead of his wife and family, lest he open himself to suspicions of homosexuality.)

And in the elaborate, NSC-managed "solarium" policy-review exercise of summer 1953, Kennan was invited back in to argue at length, before the President and his senior advisers, the case for a "containment" approach to Soviet relations, in opposition to the "liberation" strategy with which Dulles was at least rhetorically identified. The exercise resulted in a general Eisenhower decision to pursue, in the main, a containment line. This line was tragically confirmed when the Administration saw no way to impede the Soviet invasion of Hungary three years later.

As the solarium exercise illustrated, Eisenhower balanced Dulles' advice by seeking, quietly but persistently, alternative views, and by making it clear—inside government—that he was the one in command. Dulles could and did play the role of prime diplomat, spokesman, and Presidential counselor. But Eisenhower would allow him no monopoly. This was one major purpose of all of those Thursday morning NSC meetings: Eisenhower could allow Dulles to take the foreign-policy lead there, but also hear challenges from men like Admiral Radford or Treasury Secretary George Humphrey or the always-willing Harold Stassen. In the words of his last special assistant for national security affairs, Gordon Gray, Ike could thereby play the role of "President in Council," giving his senior aides continuing exposure to him and to one another, encouraging development of the sense of a senior national-security team, with a regular process for reviewing issues and with no doubt, at least inside the government, as to whose personal responsibility it was to resolve them.

There is evidence that Eisenhower himself grew bored with discussion of planning documents. To Cutler on April 2, 1958, he "expressed a strong preference that future Council meetings should focus *less* on discussion of papers and *more* on discussion of issues." But he seems to have recognized how the process helped to hold his government together. In the words of one NSC staff member of that time, regular meetings and (re)drafting of policy papers contributed to "the process of coordination, planning, discussing, educating, and creating a network of [interagency] relationships which constituted a national security community."

But the NSC was, of course, far too cumbersome and structured a system to use for fast-moving, day-to-day decision-making. So, on issues like Indochina in 1954, Suez in 1956, and Lebanon in 1958, Eisenhower made his major policy choices as all other Presidents have made them—after informally organized Oval Office consultations with those members of his Administration he trusted or needed. Managing these meetings, and the telephone and paper traffic surrounding them, was not the national-security assistant but the White House staff secretary. He handled an invisible, but absolutely central, foreign-policy process in the Eisenhower Administration.

The staff-secretary position had its origins in an incident during the settling-in period, in 1953. As General Andrew Goodpaster tells the story, it was a time

> when some paperwork got crossed up—someone had done something unaware that another line of activity had begun. [Eisenhower] said, "I look to my staff to keep such things straightened out. I should not have to be my own sergeant major . . ."

The audience of White House staff civilians was uncertain as to exactly what a sergeant major was or did, so they went to Brigadier General Paul "Pete" Carroll, Eisenhower's aide for national security and intelligence liaison, for enlightenment, which he supplied.

> About ten days later the same thing happened again, and [Eisenhower] called the chief people of the staff and said, "I told you I don't plan to be my own sergeant major, and I don't. I want to have a staff secretary, and General Paul Carroll, you're going to be the staff secretary now."

A year later, when Carroll suffered a fatal heart attack, Goodpaster, who had worked for Eisenhower in Europe, was called in to succeed him.

Officially, the staff secretary was the White House superclerk. His job was to be sure that paperwork was complete and properly circulated, the staff kept in proper administrative order. He had to be down the hall from the Oval Office, on call when the President wished to learn about, or reach into, a matter of detail. But because Carroll was first given the job, it became joined with national security and intelligence liaison, including the management of top-secret communications to and from the President. And Goodpaster found this national-security function taking up most of his time. Eisenhower made it clear that he was absolutely to stay out of "the political side of things." But he became not just an information channel but an operational coordinator who watched over, for example, the supersecret U-2 spy-plane operations. He organized and took notes for Eisenhower's many Oval Office foreign-policy meetings, and he initiated follow-up action as appropriate. "Tending the door and handling urgent messages silently—a wise and good man"; that is how McGeorge Bundy described Goodpaster and his role in a January 24, 1961, memo to John F. Kennedy. But it went well beyond passing messages. Eisenhower's national-security assistants managed the formal planning system; Goodpaster served the President on the here-and-now.

And the role grew. In 1954 Andrew Goodpaster was a distinctly junior participant in the process, scrupulously anonymous, and deferential to Dulles ("Mr. Secretary," not "Foster"). This contrasted with Special Assistant Cutler, who enjoyed senior status from the start. By 1960 "Andy" was clearly a senior player in fact if not form. Dulles began by insisting on having his meetings with Eisenhower alone, which helped to establish his unique status but caused problems for everybody else. As his trust in Goodpaster grew, Dulles began asking him from time to time to join them, or even raise a matter with Eisenhower directly and save Dulles a phone call or a trip from Foggy Bottom. After Christian Herter became Secretary in the spring of 1959, when Dulles was stricken with cancer, Goodpaster and his deputy, John Eisenhower, "began monitoring all meetings between Herter and the Boss, even private ones." Herter acquiesced. In fact, he found it very useful since he was hard of hearing and he didn't like asking the President to repeat things. With a reliable third party present, he could ask Goodpaster, after the meeting, what Eisenhower had actually said or meant.

Inside his government, then, Eisenhower had, for most of his term, three major resources for foreign-policy management: the Secretary of State, the National Security Council, and the White House Staff Secretary. He had in addition scores of relationships with leading Americans and Europeans, developed during his years of service in and after the war. He used these facilities and relationships to get information and—when it suited him—to assert control. On the big decisions, emerging documents suggest that, contrary to the caricatures of the fifties, he knew what was happening, knew what he wanted, and prevailed. He kept the United States out of Indochina and forced the British and French out of Suez.

But he also kept himself out of many issues, at least publicly, practicing what Fred Greenstein has labeled "hidden hand" leadership. Even on matters where he cared deeply he would sometimes stand aloof, questioning here, prodding there, but never forcing the issue. He regularly sought an easing of the Cold War, a more manageable relationship with the Soviet Union. Yet, despite a number of initiatives—atoms for peace, the Geneva summit of 1955, the Khrushchev visit in 1959, a suspension of nuclear testing—no enduring breakthroughs resulted. Through most of his term, Eisenhower seemed to stand semidetached as aide after aide—Emmet John Hughes, C. D. Jackson, Nelson Rockefeller, Harold Stassen—waged a losing battle with the skeptical John Foster Dulles, each encouraged by Eisenhower to search for means to ease Cold War tensions, each unable to get decisive action. Only after Dulles died did the Administration seem truly liberated for "waging peace."

One episode, recounted by Goodpaster, illustrates the unique Eisenhower combination of strong policy conviction and lack of follow-through. The President, alone with his staff secretary, repeated his oft-expressed view that we should begin reducing our troops stationed in Europe, and said that this was the established policy of the United States government. The Staff Secretary replied that this was the policy objective, but with the proviso that the action be implemented only when the situation in Europe permitted—and specifically when the Europeans could take over. The response was vintage Ike: "Andy, our policy is clear—it is to start to get our troops out! Foster Dulles is coming over here this afternoon and we'll straighten this out once and for all!"

When the Secretary came over, Eisenhower began by saying, "Foster, tell Andy about our policy to remove some of our troops from Europe!" Dulles responded, "Mr. President, it isn't quite that way." We were committed to the goal of reduction, but only on the condition that a suitable balance of forces be maintained. Eisenhower responded, "Foster, I've lost my last friend." But he didn't insist on his view, and the American troops remained in Europe.

Eisenhower's practices avoided the squandering of Presidential capital and the loss of popular esteem. It was hardly a coincidence that as policy after policy lost public and Congressional support, the President himself did not. Pushing his Cabinet officers into the limelight was good management for the government, and good politics for Ike as well, offering him insulation without sacrifice of his ability to intervene in a specific matter when he so desired.

But there were serious costs, to policy and process alike. When defense experts found a "missile gap" and Democrats began to exploit the charge, Eisenhower knew their alarms were exaggerated, if not completely mistaken—photos taken from the U-2 spy plane had shown him that—but he never found a way to make his assessment prevail in the public arena. So, our President with the greatest expertise in military matters, whom the American people trusted on national security more than any other before or since, found his defense policies under bipartisan attack in 1960, from not only John F. Kennedy but Nelson Rockefeller as well.

Eisenhower's policy processes became a campaign issue as well. He had developed, in fact, a sophisticated and balanced system. But its public face exaggerated the influence of Dulles and the importance of the formal NSC, while minimizing precisely those things—the daily private conversations, the role of Goodpaster—that kept Eisenhower in the central position, continuously engaged.

From the way the Administration presented itself, it was easy to believe that Eisenhower was a sincere but slow pupil of John Foster Dulles, a benign chief executive with nothing better to do than preside over long, formal meetings of the NSC. If one looked only at the NSC planning process, it was easy to conclude that it was a cumbersome, frequently irrelevant paper mill. And Eisenhower Administration foreign-policy making was characterized precisely this way by two overlapping groups of critics—experts fearful that our policy was being mismanaged and our security was being endangered, and Democrats hungry to populate the White House with one of their own.

Senator Henry Jackson belonged to both groups. In 1959, in the initial months of his second term, he won Senate consent to establish a Government Operations Subcommittee on National Policy Machinery, which would make, in his words, "a nonpartisan study of how well our Government is now organized to develop, coordinate, and execute foreign and defense policy." The problem was how well we were responding to our "most serious challenge since the founding of the Republic . . . the relentlessly growing overall strength of world communism."

Nor was Jackson reluctant to announce his personal verdict before conducting the trial. The United States, he declared in April 1959, was "losing the cold war"; the NSC under Eisenhower was a "dangerously misleading façade," fuzzing issues it should be sharpening, he told a National War College audience. As a result, "our governmental processes do not produce clearly defined and purposeful strategy for the cold war." And as he began his hearings early the following year, an all-star galaxy of former officials and current academics joined in the attack—Dean Acheson, George Kennan, Henry Kissinger, Robert Lovett, Hans Morgenthau, Walt W. Rostow, and a former Eisenhower aide who was now Governor of New York, Nelson Rockefeller. They varied in detailed diagnoses and prescriptions, but one theme kept coming back—policy making had to be rescued from those cumbersome, compromise-prone committees. In the words of Lovett, the Wall Street Republican who had served Truman, "The authority of the individual executive must be restored."

The Administration response to this attack was curiously counterproductive, in part because it was left to the NSC system managers to reply. Grasping too well the partial truth that the assault was "politically motivated," they did not take the critique seriously and failed to make a credible response. Confronted by testimony about overcrowded meetings, too much paper, often-sterile discussion, the Eisenhower NSC people did not acknowledge that these were problems inherent to government, and that they had been persistently working to resolve them. Still less did they put the formal system in broader context by explaining the informal means that Eisenhower regularly employed. After all, it was *their* procedures that were under assault; their natural response was to reiterate the formal system's logic and importance.

So, they took refuge in almost-loving description of the NSC committee apparatus and how it operated, interrupted only briefly by some *pro forma* recognition that (to select from one Cutler statement) "the President may—and does—use from time to time other procedures and mechanisms for particular national security matters." In the end, through their overemphasis on the formal NSC, Eisenhower's aides unwittingly "supported the conclusions of their critics," as George Washington University historian Anna Nelson has perceptively observed. For these critics "knew" that government couldn't work this formally. What they didn't know was that Eisenhower knew it too.

So on January 13, 1961, Eisenhower's final special assistant for national-security affairs, Gordon Gray, wrote him a long letter of resignation and summation. In it he followed three proud pages of rather sterile bureaucratic history—about 366 "regular and special" NSC meetings, the various reorganizations undergone by its staff—with a proud conclusion: "Thanks to your strong participation there is in existence a well-established organizational structure readily adaptable to the particular needs of the next President."

The conclusion was essentially correct, though the "organizational structure" was broader and more fluid than the one Gray described. The Eisenhower system offered balance between careerist expertise and political leadership, between the White House and the State Department, between capacity for planning and for operational command. It offered, most importantly, a balance between barons and courtiers—the barons could be strong and visible leaders, without the President being deprived of staff protection. In the sixties and seventies this balance would be lost.

But by distorting the Eisenhower system (through exaggeration of the formal), Gray and his associates discredited it. The distortion was mostly inadvertent; probably only Eisenhower (and to some extent Goodpaster) had a clear sense of how all the pieces of this system fit together. But it was nonetheless fatal, for how could John F. Kennedy and his "new generation of Americans" accept institutions that seemed to cast the President in a passive role, with little leeway for leadership? Thus policy process joined policy substance as a rewarding (if subordinate) campaign target, something a new President would have to streamline if he were to "get this country moving again."

The Eisenhower people had unwittingly misrepresented their system. Partly for this reason, the Kennedy people misunderstood it. The old administration paid for this error in 1960. Now it was Kennedy's turn.

Activism in the White House Basement: 1961–1968

John F. Kennedy came to office with no prior experience as political executive. Unlike Eisenhower, he had no clear strategy for managing foreign policy. Ironically, his personal engagement generated an organizational innovation, the activist White House staff, which was to endure in a way in which his predecessor's system had not endured. It was in this period that the courtiers began to get the upper hand.

One man who was thinking organizationally in 1960 was Henry Jackson. He and Kennedy had entered the Senate together in 1953, and had been House colleagues over the six years before. Jackson had had hopes that Kennedy might choose him as Vice-Presidential running mate and had won instead the consolation prize of being named chairman of the Democratic National Committee. In September 1960, Jackson suggested to Columbia Professor Richard Neustadt, consultant to his subcommittee and author of a new book, *Presidential Power,* that he prepare an advance memo on what needed doing during the hoped-for Eisenhower-Kennedy transition.

Neustadt had never met Kennedy, but he wrote the memo and brought it to Jackson. The Senator liked it and took it and the Professor to the Georgetown home of the candidate. Kennedy read the memo immediately and liked it also—"Will you keep on it, will you do more?" The answer was, of course, affirmative. Neustadt presented one set of papers to Kennedy in the campaign plane a week before the election, and he worked intensively in Washington for the two transition months thereafter.

It was a brief period of excitement and "dangerous influence," Neustadt recalled more than twenty years later. "Everybody thought I must have been an old friend of Jack's," even though the President-elect was just learning to pronounce his name. In fact, Neustadt brought to this opportunity the discipline and the political insight that he had gained as a junior aide in the Truman White House. To minimize the threat he might pose to longtime Kennedy associates like Kenneth O'Donnell and Theodore Sorensen, he insisted that he had no interest in a permanent position, and he cited as evidence his plan to leave for England on a sabbatical the following summer. He produced hundreds of pages of concise, polished memos on personnel and organizational issues, most of them addressed to Kennedy directly, but some to official transition representative Clark Clifford or to Sorensen or O'Donnell.

On national security, Neustadt reflected the Jackson subcommittee approach that he had helped to shape. Sidestepping the efforts of outgoing officials to sell their organizational structure, he wrote to Kennedy that the post of special assistant for national-security affairs "should be avoided by all means until you have sized up your needs *and* got a feel for your new secretaries of state and defense." His hope, in fact, was that the position could be eliminated, with a return to the Truman model of an NSC executive secretary like Sidney Souers, possessing direct Presidential access and supported by a career staff like that of the Bureau of the Budget. He urged repeatedly, however, that Kennedy designate "a Personal Assistant to the Commander-in-Chief-Elect" to bring him rapidly up to speed on sensitive military and intelligence matters, to handle duties that "roughly correspond to (and expand upon) the work now being done for Eisenhower by General Goodpaster."

Kennedy did not adopt this recommendation per se, but when he met the retiring President on December 6 he won his reluctant consent to Goodpaster's staying on a month after the Inauguration, deferring Goodpaster's transfer to the active-duty post that Eisenhower had been helping to hold open. And when Kennedy did name a national-security assistant, Neustadt wrote a memo to Clifford, entitled "Introducing McGeorge Bundy to General Persons," declaring that Bundy would be doing the jobs of no fewer than five senior Eisenhower national-security-staff aides. This summary dismissal of the elaborate Eisenhower structure anticipated the very different Kennedy pattern to follow.

Neustadt's coolness toward formal procedures was matched—indeed, exceeded—by the President-elect himself. And Kennedy's use of a transition consultant he had barely met signaled his broader operating style; he thought in terms of people, not processes or structures—if a man seemed useful, he would bring him in and give him a mandate, leaving it up to him to work out his connections and conflicts with other aides, and withdrawing confidence if he messed things up. Thus, his senior foreign-policy team was a collection of ad hoc choices: Robert McNamara the supermanager at Defense, with whom Kennedy got on famously; Dean Rusk, "everybody's second choice" at State, with whom he didn't; Chester Bowles, Rusk's deputy selected before Rusk in payment for his early campaign commitment (and who clicked with neither the President nor the Secretary); Adlai Stevenson, whose entitlement to a prestigious post was met, barely, through the UN Ambassadorship; McGeorge Bundy (the dean of the faculty who had impressed Kennedy at meetings of the Harvard Overseers) as national-security assistant after Rusk and Stevenson both resisted Bundy's placement at State; Walt Rostow as national-security deputy after Rusk vetoed him for head of State Department Policy Planning.

With this mixed team, replete with personal incompatibilities, the President set out on January 21 to "get the country moving again" in foreign policy—coping with crises in Laos and the Congo, jousting with Khrushchev over Berlin, developing new approaches to Latin America and Africa. White House aides joined in the fray: Ralph Dungan, Arthur Schlesinger, Jr., Dick Goodwin. So did senior outsiders like Dean Acheson. Rusk, who valued clear-cut roles and procedures, found it hard to function when "people with no responsibility" kept moving into issues. When he brought in Lucius Battle to be executive secretary of the department, he urged, "For God's sake try to get the White House under control. They are all over this building, at every level." Kennedy in turn found the Secretary's lack of initiative disappointing, and the State Department's cautious responses even more so.

By contrast, Bundy flourished. He was a crisp, terse intellectual operator, accustomed to the chaos of a university faculty. He was close to an aggressive, pragmatic President whose style meshed well with his own. He began to recruit a small but impressive senior staff: Carl Kaysen, who agreed to take leave from Harvard to handle defense and international economics after his longtime friend phoned him—"We're having a lot of fun down here; why don't you join us"; Robert Komer, whom brother Bill Bundy deemed the best operator in the open part of the CIA. But aside from the business of managing formal NSC meetings—and Kennedy had only three of these in his first three months—Bundy's role and mandate were surprisingly unclear. He was to support the President on foreign-policy matters, but others were doing this also. And Eisenhower's interagency-committee system had been dismantled with a haste that surprised even Neustadt.

It might be right to abolish the Operations Coordinating Board, and scores of less exalted interagency committees. But one needed to substitute some alternative procedures and responsibilities, not simply to say in a press release that they would henceforth be performed by the Secretary of State. By late February, however, Neustadt was no longer involved in NSC matters. Goodpaster was disengaging from his transition service, as his national-security functions were passed on to Kennedy officials—Bundy above all. And organizationally, Bundy's priority was dismantlement, ending the NSC staff as a "continuing organization" by halving the number of staff positions and transferring dozens of career aides to other government positions.

Neustadt later suggested that the Jackson subcommittee critiques had "aimed at Eisenhower and hit Kennedy." And they did—at the Bay of Pigs. The Eisenhower system, it should be emphasized, had hardly achieved full and effective control over CIA covert operations. But, for Kennedy in early 1961, there was hardly any control at all.

One reason was that the Cuban operation's prime entrepreneur and expert was a man known and admired socially and professionally by almost every new appointee in the Administration, Richard Bissell, the Deputy CIA Director for Plans. As a Yale economist he had taught McGeorge Bundy as well as Walt Rostow; before that, he had been columnist Joseph Alsop's Groton classmate. As Allen Dulles' special assistant he had been centrally involved in the overthrow of the Arbenz regime in Guatemala. He was seen as the best of intellectual operators: brilliant, tough, pragmatic. Bundy and Bowles, usually on differing wavelengths, agreed that Bissell should be named Deputy Under Secretary of State for Political Affairs; he was the sort of man who could really energize the department. The President had a better idea. He wanted Bissell to succeed Dulles as Director of Central Intelligence.

Bissell was well organized and knew what he wanted; on the Cuba operation, Kennedy and his administration had neither characteristic. Thus, no one above the CIA deputy seems to have had a comprehensive fix on the invasion plan—what decisions had been made, what the strategy was, what its operational assumptions were. Kennedy had as yet, unlike Eisenhower, no single aide like Goodpaster to serve as his prime intelligence channel. Bundy, who would so serve later, seems to have played, by available accounts, just an intermittent role—he did not take the initiative in pulling the information and the options together for hard analysis. Nor did anybody else. Nor did Kennedy ask them to.

Uncertain about the venture but feeling personally vulnerable, worried about secrecy, the President took several cautionary steps: he asked the JCS to review the plan; he encouraged Senator Fulbright to voice his doubts; he insisted on reducing direct United States involvement. But neither he nor anybody else pulled these things together, so Kennedy's impact on the plan was to force changes that eliminated its very slight chances for success without achieving their purpose of concealing United States responsibility.

In the immediate aftermath of that April fiasco, Bundy was among those whose standing suffered. One visitor to the Oval Office in early May heard the President talk of bringing General Maxwell Taylor into the White House, as special military adviser. He concluded that Bundy had lost perhaps 50 percent of his Presidential credit: "Mac's OK for foreign affairs, but I have to have somebody who knows these military people and can deal with them." It was also apparently around this time that Bundy penned a note of resignation to the President, an artful mix of form and substance. As a general principle, he wrote Kennedy, "you ought to have in hand [your associates'] resignations. Here is mine. . . . You know that I wish I had served you better in the Cuban episode. . . . If my departure can assist you in any way, I hope you will send me off."

But in the months that followed, the Bay of Pigs led in fact to a strengthening of Bundy's role. This triggered, in turn, a broader transformation of Presidential foreign-policy making that has continued to the present.

It was not a matter of an explicit Presidential decision. There was no formal declaration that to improve policy coordination and Presidential control, all information and analysis would henceforth be channeled through the special assistant for national-security affairs. Insofar as any reorganization scheme issued directly from the brigade fiasco, it was one propounded by Taylor and endorsed by Robert

Kennedy, providing for elaborate interagency machinery to wage comprehensive Cold War. But the President rejected this; it didn't fit his style. What actually happened was less planned but more interesting. The aftermath of the Cuba fiasco put new pressures on Bundy, and he responded in a way that pulled foreign-policy power to him and his national-security staff.

There was, first of all, the matter of the office in the White House basement. Bundy had originally inherited not Goodpaster's West Wing office but Gordon Gray's spacious quarters in the Executive Office Building across the street. But the Bay of Pigs aftermath meant more foreign-policy meetings, more carefully organized, and thus more direct Presidential business. Even the formal NSC sprang back to temporary life, with no less than seven meetings in the month after Castro crushed the brigade. Bundy had an operational need to be in the White House, within a minute's walk of the Oval Office; otherwise he had either to waste time hanging around to see Kennedy or to be stuck too far away. He managed to wangle some cramped, low-priority basement space, adjacent to where records were stored, space that Goodpaster had occasionally used as a hideaway.

Eisenhower holdover Bromley Smith learned of the move one day in May or June when Bundy summoned him: "Come on. We're going across the street." Smith thought Bundy meant to a White House meeting, only to discover that his chief had something more permanent in mind. And once he gained his tiny toehold in the White House, Bundy moved to expand his quarters, to make them more habitable and to provide the space needed for his growing information-management operation. By January 1962 he was pressing O'Donnell for more room—"The President called it [Bundy's quarters] a pig pen, and my pride is hurt." Then, moving to the punchline: "In the olden days of Eisenhower, the NSC people all stayed on the other side—but I can't do my job from over there, and all this trouble follows from that. It all comes from having a President who has taken charge of foreign affairs." Next to Bundy was an area used to store White House records; these were moved elsewhere, and the Bundy basement space grew.

This meant that Bundy could be "at the end of the buzzer," where Gordon Gray advised him in January that he would need to be. It meant closeness not just to the President but to the other key Kennedy staff members. It meant absorbing the feel of the White House. And it gave Bundy enough space to run the communications-management operation that he and Bromley Smith were putting into place: The White House Situation Room.

The following chapter will describe how this was constructed and what it meant politically and operationally, not just in Kennedy's time, but as a powerful instrument for White House dominance thereafter. But unlike Cutler under Eisenhower, Bundy was not seeking to implement some grand organizational scheme. He was coping, incrementally, with the needs and demands of an activist President, seeking to connect him with his appointees in the permanent government—especially State—and working to win the action the President clearly wanted. In so doing, Bundy was serving his larger goal—to staff Presidential foreign-policy making directly and personally, and keep himself at the center of the action. Activism blended with caution—Kennedy felt constrained by his thin electoral margin, humiliated by the Bay of Pigs, and challenged by Khrushchev at their June 1961 meeting in Vienna. But he wanted to be the one who decided whether or not to move on policy, not to succumb to the built-in lethargy of the State Department.

Kennedy's frustrations with State continued; complaining about its disorganization, he dictated a note to Rusk in August 1961 requesting "a memorandum on the present assignment of responsibility within the Department of State." Interestingly, some saw this sort of memo as reflecting White House disorganization, for Kennedy would dictate messages which his secretary Evelyn Lincoln would then transmit, typos and all, without the responsible Presidential aide seeing it. But Kennedy's problems with Rusk were real enough. There was the unhappy contrast of his caution with the aggressiveness of McNamara, who was moving forward with Defense initiatives that the President supported and admired. There was, as one senior associate remembers it, Rusk's failure to "understand the telephone," to realize that phone communications with the White House were secure, which reinforced his reluctance to engage in the verbal shorthand through which much Kennedy business was communicated. Rusk's model was Marshall serving Truman, a scrupulously loyal Secretary whose responsibility the President accepted without question.

Rusk was certainly not, by either background or temperament, one of the "happy few" intellectual-operational insiders who were truly at home in the Kennedy regime.

It was, in many ways, a curiously elitist administration. Having grown up in an important family and attended the "right" schools, the President thought it normal to assume that he had some personal connection—direct or one step removed—to individuals who entered his service. The Ivy League staffing pattern reinforced this. Thus, late in 1962, Bundy would reidentify senior aide Robert Komer to the President as a man who was "at Harvard with you." When Kaysen proposed William Roth for an important trade negotiator position, Kennedy wondered what his college grades had been and inquired whether he had been checked out with Sargent Shriver, who was in the same Yale class.

Nonetheless, the internal style was open and fluid. It proved a bit too fluid for one Henry Kissinger, an early NSC staff consultant, who never came on full time and departed in mid-1962—to what he later labeled as his and Kennedy's "mutual relief"—after publishing a lead article in *Foreign Affairs* critical of the Administration's European defense policies. (In signing off on a short extension of his consultancy, Bundy noted the President's political wariness: "JFK agrees—he doesn't want to put him out in a way which would suggest pique at FA article.")

The Kennedy touch was nicely reflected in the recruitment of another aide, Michael Forrestal, son of James, a young New York lawyer whom Kennedy had known socially. They had talked privately, at Kennedy's postelection request, at a luncheon meeting at the home of Averell Harriman. Forrestal was somewhat let down when the President-elect's main request was for help in getting the sixty-nine-year-old past-and-future statesman to wear a hearing aide. But seemingly as an afterthought Kennedy inquired about Forrestal's availability, and when the reply was that he could not leave his firm (where he had just become a partner) before 1962, Kennedy seems to have remembered it. For he phoned again a year later, saying that he remembered Forrestal's promise and that he really needed him now. Only thereafter did Bundy contact him, and only after Forrestal came to Washington did he learn—from Kennedy—that he was slated to work on the Far East, for which Harriman had just become

Assistant Secretary, and about which region Forrestal knew next to nothing.

Bundy was less threatened by this sort of recruitment, and the direct staff access to Kennedy that it created, than most others in his position would have been. For one thing, he was by now confident of his place with Kennedy. Secondly, he preferred to concentrate his substantive energies. As one aide later put it, "For Mac Bundy, the world was Europe, and Europe was the United Kingdom, Germany, France and Russia." So, it was in his interest to have congenial associates brief Kennedy on other areas—Forrestal on East Asia, Ralph Dungan on Latin America and sometimes Africa, Arthur Schlesinger, Jr., on Latin America and Italy, Carl Kaysen on technical economic and military issues. Initially, deputy special assistant Walt Rostow dealt with Kennedy on most non-European issues. But when he proved too discursive and ideological for Kennedy's taste ("Walt uses a lot of words"), he was moved to the State Department in the 1961 "Thanksgiving Day massacre," which saw George Ball replace Chester Bowles as Under Secretary of State. Bundy was responsive to Kaysen's request that he be given Rostow's formal place. When Kennedy kept asking Bundy for briefings about the war in Yemen, the Special Assistant would respond, "Don't ask me, ask Komer." Eventually, Kennedy did request Komer's presence when he was phoning Prime Minister Harold Macmillan about the issue, and handed him the phone to respond to Macmillan's specific questions. When the result was that Macmillan overruled his Foreign Office in favor of Kennedy's position, Komer became "a person" to Kennedy, the man who "really cleaned up on the Prime Minister" and henceforth on the list of those with whom JFK dealt directly.

As Komer described the system in a 1964 oral-history interview for the John F. Kennedy library,

> The manner and style of the President's use of the Bundy operation, particularly of Mac and Walt and Carl Kaysen, but the rest of us, too, was never to have more than five or six people in the thing. We had maybe twenty people in all, but a lot of them were just normal liaison types of one kind or another, or doing security jobs, or special details. The inner group was four, five or six, seldom more.
>
> [The NSC label was] merely a budgetary device. Since NSC already

> had its own budget, it was sacrosanct. So instead of adding people to the White House staff, Bundy carried them all over here. But in fact, Kennedy made very clear we were his men, we operated for him, we had direct contact with him. This gave us the power to command the kind of results that he wanted—a fascinating exercise in a presidential staff technique, which, insofar as I know, has been unique in the history of the Presidency.

As Komer described it further, the staff acted as the "eyes and ears" of the President, who wanted "a complete flow of raw information over here." It was also a "shadow network which clued the President on what bidding was before a formal, inter-departmentally cleared recommendation that got to him." Thus "the President had sources of independent judgment and recommendation on what each issue was all about, what ought to be done about it, from a little group of people in whom he had confidence—in other words, sort of a double check." Finally, it provided "follow-through," working "to keep tabs on things and see that the cables went out and the responses were satisfactory, and that when the policy wasn't being executed, the President knew about it and he could give it another prod."

This type of staff could not help putting the slower-moving State Department (or *any* established organization) somewhat in the shade. And although an internal memo stressed that the staff was "*not*—though this is a hard rule—a place meant for men trying to peddle their own remedies without presidential backing," particular members of the staff, like Kaysen and Komer, did become identified with strong policy preferences that they worked to advance. But these were preferences generally encouraged by the President, even when he felt unable to fully support them.

Bundy channeled an enormous volume of information and advocacy to the President, generally seeking to pinpoint and balance others' biases rather than to press his own. In transmitting an early report by Dean Acheson on strengthening West European defenses, he cautioned:

> A quick look at the front page—a proposed statement of National Security Policy—suggests to me that there may be more here than we

> should swallow quickly. Acheson is so strong a partisan of NATO that at a number of points he suggests a balance of policy that you may not wish to accept.
>
> In spite of these reservations, I think the main body of the report is an extraordinarily useful document.

He also played the role of Presidential enforcer. When a September 1962 speech by Chester Bowles created something of a furor, Bundy reported to Kennedy: "Clearance of the Bowles Cuba speech turns out to be a semi-comedy of low-level errors." After describing pithily how various offices had failed to focus on the matter, he added:

> I have spread enough terror so that I doubt if this particular mistake will occur again, and I have sent a message to Bowles (who is still out of town) that he should not add a syllable to what he has said on the subject of Cuba. When he gets back, I am sure he will call me in an apologetic mood and explain that he was only trying to back up your press conference statement. I will then tell him again what I have told him by message: that in matters of this kind, when you have spoken clearly on a sensitive matter, it is generally best to leave things where you have left them.

All this involved, one should emphasize again, working with the established agencies, facilitating the policy rather than dominating it as Kissinger later did. In regions like East Asia and Africa, strong assistant secretaries of state teamed harmoniously with White House aides. On a crucial negotiation like the limited-test-ban treaty of 1963, Under Secretary of State Harriman—a rising star in Camelot—was Kennedy's hand-picked negotiator, and communications between the White House and the Moscow negotiating team—which included Kaysen—were controlled not from the Situation Room but by Benjamin Read, State's executive secretary.

Nonetheless, the vigor and activism of the Bundy staff operation served to pull power into the White House. As Bromley Smith put it,

> It is true that although State officers had the authority, they did not exercise it. They did not exert leadership at the various levels. Therefore, when the President had to have something done, it was almost easier for McGeorge Bundy to call a meeting in the Situation Room, bang all the

heads together and get things going. The tendency was to do it that way.

Kennedy had replaced Eisenhower's balanced, cumbersome-looking policy-making system with one that was overtly and aggressively informal, personal, fluid, focused on the here-and-now. Bundy had brought to the position of special assistant for national security affairs the personal, day-to-day staffing tasks that Goodpaster had performed in the fifties. The old NSC policy papers were supplanted by National Security Action Memoranda (signed by the President or by Bundy) which were issue-specific and operational.

Bundy became "more than a Goodpaster," a senior policy adviser in his own right. He transformed NSC staffing. His predecessors had brought in career officials expected to provide continuity between administrations. Under Bundy the tone of the staff was set by what became known as "in-and-outers," people like Kaysen and Forrestal, activist intellectuals from the broader policy community who would be identified with the current President and his administration. Bundy cut the NSC staff sharply in numbers. At the same time, he shifted its focus sharply from serving the Presidency as institution to serving the President as person.

The "here-and-now" emphasis sometimes purchased flexibility at the cost of care and comprehensiveness. Vietnam policy was mainly a series of *ad hoc* responses to short-term threats. And even with the greater order that Bundy and Smith had brought to the communications flow, it was possible, on an August 1963 weekend during which not a single policy principal was in town, for a cable to be dispatched to Saigon flashing a green light for a coup against embattled leader Ngo Binh Diem.

The focus on serving the President as a person also meant, of course, sensitivity to the President's political interests and episodic involvement in them. Thus, for example, in the spring of 1963 Kennedy sent Bundy at least three separate memos about the "missile gap" issue and the President's need for political protection. One dated May 15 read, in its entirety:

1. What progress are we making on the analysis of the missile gap. The report that we got was too superficial. I want to be able to demonstrate

that there was a military and intelligence lag in the previous administration that started the missile gap.

2. What progress are we making on our analysis of information to us prior to 1958 that Castro was a communist.

Still, Bundy and his associates had no strong partisan identity—in fact, the special assistant himself remained a registered Republican throughout the Kennedy Administration. Nor was it their style to conduct foreign policy in-house, as Kissinger would later. Bundy took care—usually—to respect the Secretary of State and his formal prerogatives. Kennedy was, by a number of accounts, looking toward following the example of Truman with Byrnes, toward replacing Rusk with someone he found more congenial. But by removing the Eisenhower structure, by personalizing the process, Kennedy created greater leeway not just for himself, but for his successors.

As 1963 moved toward its conclusion, the President and his key associates, given new life by their Cuban missile success a year earlier, were looking forward to the 1964 election where they might, finally, receive a liberating mandate. Foreign policy was becoming less confrontational and was beginning to show results—like the limited-test-ban treaty—though de Gaulle's rebuff in Europe and the quagmire in Vietnam were items on the debit side. Operationally, Bundy and his staff officers were very deep into departmental business—clearing a wide range of cables, drafting or redrafting many themselves, using the new communications-monitoring system to be sure they were involved everywhere they wished to be. State Department officials frequently found this useful, but they also resented it as an infringement on what they saw as their prerogatives, and because it made their jobs more difficult. Thus things stood on November 22.

Johnson. Looked at retrospectively, the Johnson Administration's foreign-policy making has much of the surface appearance of its predecessor's. The President achieved control—when he achieved it—through direct operational management. There was no Eisenhower-style planning process; the National Security Council played the same peripheral role that it had played under Kennedy. The operational NSC staff was maintained, as was the Situation Room, and they survived Bundy's replacement by Walt W. Rostow in 1966. Secretaries Rusk and McNamara served Johnson longer than they had served Kennedy, and key deputies George Ball and Cyrus Vance stayed on after the transition and the 1964 election.

Such continuity was anything but a foregone conclusion in the harrowing days and weeks that followed the assassination. When a leader is suddenly replaced by another who did not work closely with him, everything is up for grabs. No one knows what people, relationships, and processes he will continue, create or discard. But urgent business must be transacted; the new leader must somehow be reached and engaged. In that fearful November, McGeorge Bundy demonstrated his allegiance to the Presidential office as well as the man, eliciting a comment from the surprised Rusk about how faithfully he was serving the new President, and some resentment from the slain leader's personal entourage. But by all accounts, Johnson did not immediately reciprocate—Bundy was both part of, and symbol of, that smug Cambridge intellectual group that seemed, to the proud but anxious Texan, unable to mask its sense of Eastern superiority.

So in the remaining weeks of 1963 there was a certain chaos. George Ball and the State Department's secretariat began using other channels to reach the new President—notably a Foreign Service officer named Lee Stull, who had been on detail as an aide to Vice-President Johnson. Bromley Smith noted a sharp drop-off in the volume of traffic crossing his desk, and countered by using his White House connections to block end runs.

Bundy's immediate future was secured, it appears, when he took a vacation in early 1964 and Johnson noticed the sharp drop in the quality of staff service. But he and his associates soon faced another problem—Johnson just didn't seem very interested in foreign policy. If Kennedy's vice was to engage too readily, to pick up a phone or dictate a memo on impulse without calculating his effect on the ongoing process, Johnson was hard to involve at all. His mind was largely elsewhere—on handling his transition, pressing his domestic agenda, winning the 1964 election. His love of the telephone notwithstanding, aides learned quickly of his dislike of *incoming* foreign-policy calls—they put him on the spot, requiring actions or reactions he was not prepared to undertake. (On this he was similar to Ike, who encouraged the false notion that he hated the telephone, in order to discourage people from calling *him.*)

Johnson pressed second-echelon aides like Kaysen, Komer, Dungan, and Forrestal to remain, insisting that he needed them much more than Kennedy did. An impromptu lunch he hosted one day in December laid bare the awkwardness on all sides. It began with a nude swim during which Komer lost his glasses diving into the White House pool. This was followed by a meal in the President's living quarters (to which Dungan, a long-time Kennedy aide, had never before been invited). A further false note, particularly repellent to Kaysen, was sounded when the new President insistently pointed out the places where he and Lady Bird had redecorated.

Oversolicitousness about keeping the Kennedy men on board was joined with indifference to the substance of their work. Forrestal was struck by the sterility of an NSC staff meeting, a sort of show-and-tell session apparently called to show the value Johnson attached to the staff's work, but where his attention quickly drifted away. And some of the staff members drifted away too, when they saw no prospect of developing the sort of Presidential-policy connections they had had with JFK. Others, like Komer, stayed—he had gotten on well with *Vice-President* Johnson.

On Latin America policy, Johnson did move quickly, on both process and substance. Kennedy had never been satisfied with his staffing pattern for this region, and in November 1963 he had made the tentative decision to create a new position, Under Secretary of State for Inter-American Affairs. The problem was that Kennedy didn't have a clear candidate in mind to fill such a job. Johnson did, though his organizational solution was a bit different—in December he named Thomas C. Mann, a conservative Foreign Service officer from Laredo, Texas, to three posts—Assistant Secretary of State, Coordinator of the Alliance for Progress, and Special Assistant to the President.

On selected issues, Johnson would leap personally into the fray—responding to Panama riots in 1964, sending over 20,000 troops to the Dominican Republic a year later, escalating (reluctantly) the war in Vietnam. But the Mann appointment illustrated his preferred way of running foreign policy. He liked to delegate, to give broad grants of authority. At the Cabinet level he leaned immediately on Robert McNamara, with whom he was enormously impressed. He delegated increasingly to Dean Rusk, a fellow Southerner who had shared Johnson's exclusion from Kennedy's happy few. He relied on their advice, and shared their resentment of staff kibitzing; when he wanted to get other views, he would go not to bright young aides but to senior Washington personages like Dean Acheson and Clark Clifford and Abe Fortas. He valued the weight of their judgment, and the political support and protection that came from reliance on men with their public stature.

This approach had some impact on Vietnam policy. Officials inclined to be Vietnam skeptics—Forrestal, Roger Hilsman, and, above all, Averell Harriman—had had influence because of their Kennedy connections. With his death they lost their Presidential access, and hence their ability to keep issues open, to keep raising questions. Hilsman was driven from government in early 1964. Harriman remained, but he now bore the burden of known intimacy with Robert Kennedy, not to mention the growing enmity of Dean Rusk. As a man who thrived on inside influence, he found the fall from grace particularly painful. He was less and less disposed to engage on Vietnam issues, something that Forrestal attributed to lack of a clear Presidential market. After the 1964 election, Harriman wrote Johnson an almost-pleading memo, seeking the sort of connection that he had made with Roosevelt, Truman and Kennedy, complaining that he had "not been consulted on many of the major issues" in the past year and citing the respect in which he was held by leaders in Russia, Britain, Germany and Latin America. But Johnson was unmoved—only after March 1968 would he give Harriman a prime assignment, the Vietnam peace negotiations. More important, the fading of the skeptics meant that when Johnson finally did focus on Vietnam in early 1965, the advice he received would be heavily weighted toward the option of military escalation.

The Johnson approach also meant a muting of policy-activist, entrepreneurial activity by Bundy's staff associates. On Latin America, for example, the Mann appointment made Dungan's broad role unsustainable, so Bundy brought in a more junior man, Foreign Service officer Robert Sayre, and Dungan became, in due course, Ambassador to Chile. Still, the core responsibilities of the staff and the special assistant continued, surviving the curious transition from Bundy to Walt W. Rostow in March 1966.

Part of Rostow's attraction to Johnson seems to have been that nobody else saw him as appropriate for the White House national-security job. Thus he could be "my goddam intellectual," beholden to the President alone. Bundy was very important to Johnson in 1964 and 1965, but the President simultaneously resented his dependence. And in the latter half of 1965, Bundy's unhappiness grew, partly for Vietnam-related reasons. It was not that Bundy opposed escalation—he supported it forcefully as the least-bad option, though he was skeptical (as was Rusk) about its short-run effectiveness and would pose hard questions to McNamara about the expansion of our ground-troop commitment in July. But Bundy felt that a major war required a strong, sustained campaign to sell it publicly—something that Johnson resisted doing. Bundy was also unhappy about what he saw as Johnson's increasing tendency to give the military all it wanted. He broke step with the President when he agreed to debate Hans Morgenthau. Johnson didn't want to dignify his Vietnam opponents with such debates; he preferred to defend the policy by wrapping himself in military colors.

So, Bundy was inclined to leave, Johnson wasn't resisting, and the Ford Foundation was offering its Presidency. Bundy saw the ideal successor as Johnson press secretary Bill Moyers, a Vietnam dove who was a superb staff man. As a longtime LBJ aide, Moyers would have, Bundy thought, a much easier personal relationship with the President. McNamara favored Moyers also. No senior foreign-policy person short of the President—not Rusk, not Ball—supported the person who finally got the job.

Walt Rostow had been an odd man out in Kennedy foreign-policy making. Though considered a valued professorial adviser when Kennedy was Senator, once he joined the Administration he was quickly tabbed as too verbose, too ideological, too wrapped up in large conceptual constructions of uncertain utility. He had never meshed as Bundy's deputy during his 1961 NSC tenure. In fact, his biggest enterprise that year was in domestic economics, pressing union and management leaders to link wage hikes to productivity increases, and thus dampen inflation. Kennedy moved him to the directorship of State's Policy Planning Council in November. One of his projects there was to develop broad, Eisenhoweresque policy documents for which he vainly sought Kennedy's endorsement. Another was the infamous MLF, the proposal for a joint United States–European multilateral nuclear force, which Johnson finally vetoed in December 1964 when Bundy and others exposed its illogic.

He was nonetheless personally a very decent man—direct, considerate, irrepressible, perhaps too insensitive to be put down. He continued to communicate directly with Kennedy and, with the help of White House aide Jack Valenti, developed a modest link with President Johnson in 1964 and 1965. He was not an important player in the Vietnam escalation decisions in 1965; in fact, his State planning-staff colleague, Robert H. Johnson, had led a study exposing some of the perils of this course the year before. But Rostow supported the war passionately; in fact, he had been pushing the idea of bombing the north since 1961.

The Bundy–Rostow transition was handled in typical Johnsonian style. In early February, shortly after Bundy's departure plans became public, the President summoned Rostow from the eastern slopes of the Andes (where he was negotiating a sensitive expropriation issue with the Peruvian president) to Honolulu (where Johnson was meeting with Vietnamese leaders). LBJ told Rostow he wanted him to join the White House staff, but to keep the matter absolutely secret. When Bundy departed three weeks later, the President minimized the event's significance and asked *Komer* to take over Bundy's tasks but not tell anybody he was doing it. Then Johnson watched as others maneuvered, and Rostow thought that perhaps he had changed his mind. Then, at the end of March, the President phoned Rostow and said he was announcing the appointment the following day. He did not give Rostow the full Bundy title, but described him simply as a "Special Assistant to the President" who would "work principally, but not necessarily exclusively, in the field of foreign policy." When a reporter asked, "Could it be said that . . . Mr. Rostow will take over all or many of the duties and assignments handled by McGeorge Bundy?" Johnson responded, "It could be, but that would be inaccurate." (This inevitably created confusion in the foreign-policy bureaucracy, forcing NSC aides to counter with the message that officials should ignore these Presidential words and deal with the staff as they had done before!)

Johnson's purpose, presumably, was to put down Bundy, not Rostow. Nonetheless, though Rostow developed and maintained a much closer personal relationship with the President and did in fact play the general national-security-coordinator role, he had less overall policy influence than his predecessor. Johnson continued to rely primarily on his Cabinet officers, above all the ever-loyal and indefatigable Dean Rusk. And while Bundy had been generally regarded as a reliable channel, an honest broker if a demanding one, Rostow was quickly viewed as an ideologue, screening out information inconsistent with his preconceptions, reinforcing the President's will to believe we were winning the war in Vietnam. Thus, departmental officials were far less likely to bring issues to him for resolution. He was a courtier in the pejorative sense, making sweet music for Presidential ears. Had Johnson been more of an initiator on international issues, and less inclined to lean on his barons for political protection, Rostow's creativity and strong views might have dominated and distorted American foreign policy, as did those of certain successors. But since Johnson's involvement was selective and defensive in his final three years, the Rostow effect was far less.

Despite Johnson's ties with Rusk, there remained considerable dissatisfaction with the State Department and its failure to assert foreign-policy leadership. One result was the so-called "SIG-IRG system." Maxwell Taylor, back in Washington after service as Ambassador to Vietnam, was pushing a return to the comprehensiveness of the fifties, the sort of broad, formal, NSC-based restructuring that he had failed to sell to Kennedy after the Bay of Pigs. Unable to win support for this, he teamed with Deputy Under Secretary of State U. Alexis Johnson to put forth an alternative plan. This would strengthen State Department authority by establishing interagency committees chaired by its Under and Assistant Secretaries—the Senior Interdepartmental Group (SIG) and Interdepartmental Regional Groups (IRGs)—to review and resolve policy issues.

With NSC staff cooperation, this system was decreed by President Johnson in National Security Action Memorandum 341 of March 6, 1966. It was timed to coincide with Bundy's departure, since the vacuum this created would make it easier for new policy-leadership patterns to take hold. But this timing meant that the key role in implementing the SIG-IRG system fell to Under Secretary of State George Ball, who was less than enthusiastic about this reorganization and was about to leave government anyway. Hence it never really got going. Ball's successor, Nicholas Katzenbach, was able to make use of the SIG in limited ways. But most assistant secretaries did not use their IRGs to seize power. Nor did Rusk press them to do so.

More revealing was an internal Administration report kept secret at the time—that of the seven-man foreign-affairs subgroup of an advisory body called The President's Task Force on Government Organization. Chaired by Chicago business executive Ben W. Heineman, its members included such Kennedy-Johnson luminaries as McNamara, Bundy, and LBJ's first two Budget Directors, Kermit Gordon and Charles Schultze. After a series of weekend meetings in the spring and summer of 1967, the group conveyed its findings to the President on October 1. "Neither the formal arrangements of the 1950s nor the informal approaches of the 1960s have yet met our fundamental organizational needs." What was required was "a transformation of the State Department" and a redefinition of the role of its Secretary, who "must become not primarily a diplomat, a defender of policy, or an international negotiator (although he will on occasion be all of these) but preeminently the director and coordinator, for and on behalf of the President, of all U.S. foreign and national security policy." It was, in short, a call to turn back the tide of the sixties, by reinforcing the primary baron of foreign policy.

Dean Rusk was not mentioned in the report. But this thinly veiled critique of his stewardship, by men who might hope to succeed him, would certainly have been front-page news had its words reached the contemporary press. Since—by Johnsonian edict—even the existence of the Task Force was secret, this did not happen. The report reflected, however, a consensus of continued frustration, in and outside high government, with America's foreign-policy-making apparatus and the procedures and structures within it. Johnson was reportedly impressed with this (and with other Heineman Task Force reports on domestic organizational issues), but he took no immediate action. Instead, he forbade their further circulation and put them in his desk drawer, for priority action—it was said—by the Johnson Administration in 1969!

This was, of course, not to be. In 1967 and 1968 the President, beset by Vietnam, huddled regularly with his "Tuesday Lunch" group of senior advisers—Rusk, McNamara, Rostow—seemingly determined to tough it out until the Tet Offensive shattered what domestic consensus remained. Then Johnson, urged on by his new Secretary of Defense, Clark Clifford, called a halt to escalation as he withdrew, politically embattled, from the 1968 reelection campaign. And just as the Heineman Task Force had drawn organizational lessons from LBJ's foreign-policy experience, about the need to strengthen State and its Secretary, now-departed aide Bill D. Moyers would draw political ones. "The reaction to the war has been so fierce and sustained," he wrote in the July 1968 *Foreign Affairs*, "that I cannot see future decisions involving similar consequences being made without asking the people to share more fully in the responsibility."

Both conclusions had broad support in a foreign-policy community caught up in the anguish of Vietnam. But the administration that followed Johnson's would have other ideas.

From 1945 until 1969, the policy process within the Executive Branch remained relatively open. The State Department might frustrate Presidents by its frequent lethargy, but the department was a regular player in the interagency policy game. On closely held issues, the Secretary of State himself was almost always an important Presidential adviser. The next chief executive would change all this, using the activist NSC staff in a way in which Kennedy and Johnson had not—to supplant and exclude State (and Defense) on the issues the White House cared about most. As Vietnam drove foreign policy more and more into domestic politics, as leading Democratic Establishment figures began to assail a Republican President, he would withdraw more and more within an inner circle of White House aides.

The White House Ascendant: 1969–1980

"From the outset of my Administration . . . I planned to direct foreign policy from the White House." So says Richard M. Nixon in his memoirs, and the credibility of that particular sentence is high. So is that of the one that follows it: "Therefore, I regarded my choice of a National Security Adviser as crucial." If Bundy's rise under Kennedy had been largely unplanned, the result of his capacity to fill evolving Presidential needs, it seems clear that Richard Nixon desired from the start that Henry Kissinger be dominant among his advisers, albeit not as prominent as Kissinger eventually became. Kissinger's appointment was announced a week before that of Secretary of State William P. Rogers. He was to build on the considerable clout that Bundy had brought to the national-security-assistant position, adding brilliance in the age-old role of courtier, and a passion for secrecy and manipulation that fully matched Nixon's own. Rogers, Attorney General under Eisenhower and a longtime Nixon friend and counselor, proved no match. His exclusion from Presidential foreign-policy making brought to mind Robert Lansing and Cordell Hull, except that on the crucial issues it was even more complete.

While Nixon was putting his system in place, he explained his approach as a return to the orderliness of the fifties. In an October campaign speech entitled "The security gap," Nixon went so far as to call the Eisenhower National Security Council meetings "the controlling element in *our* success in keeping the peace throughout *our* eight White House years" (emphasis added). These had been replaced by "catch-as-catch-can talkfests between the President, his staff assistants and various others. I attribute most of our serious reverses abroad since 1960 to the inability or disinclination of President Eisenhower's successors to make effective use of this important Council." Nixon promised to "restore the National Security Council to its preeminent role in national-security planning." And as he named Kissinger, he emphasized the role he was to play in developing a process that would accomplish this goal.

In fact, however, Nixon was not rejecting the Kennedy-Johnson legacy so much as he was building upon it. The Bundy and Rostow precedents made it natural to place an academic intellectual in the White House national-security post. The changes they had brought to NSC staffing made it seem like business almost as usual, when Kissinger immediately replaced all but two Council staff officers with his own group of activist foreign-policy analysts and bureaucrats. This gave Nixon the means to turn James Forrestal's NSC on its head, to employ it as a means to *exclude* the established advisers and agencies more systematically than Franklin Roosevelt had ever done.

This was not apparently his initial intention. The original plan was to have a carefully structured formal system guaranteeing State and Defense a regular, if subordinate role. Nixon asked Kissinger to devise "an Eisenhower system, but without the concurrences," one designed to present him with options rather than consensus recommendations, but designed also to assure "all Departments concerned with a problem . . . that their positions will reach the Council without dilution, along with the other alternatives." And while the White House would manage the "planning" process, State was to lead in implementation.

To flesh out the proposal that Nixon requested, Kissinger turned to two quickly recruited staff aides whose future lives would take very different paths—Lawrence Eagleburger and Morton Halperin. He turned also, at Nixon's urging, to Andrew Goodpaster. On December 27 he presented Nixon with a memorandum drafted by Halperin and Eagleburger following his instructions, entitled "Proposal for a New National Security Council System." It set forth a structure and procedure calling for comprehensive national-security studies, to be conducted by interagency committees, screened by a review group, which Kissinger would chair, and then brought before the National Security Council for discussion and Presidential decision. Kissinger has outlined in his memoirs the curious process by which Nixon first retreated from, then overrode, the objections of Rogers and Under Secretary-designate U. Alexis Johnson to the central role Kissinger was given. The overriding point is that the new system was ordered into effect promptly on January 20, 1969. This signaled to all concerned that the new President was behind it.

In Nixon's early months the system seemed to function as designed—a wide range of studies was completed, the National Security Council met regularly to consider them, and the President was following these meetings with decisions on a range of issues—Vietnam policy, chemical and biological weapons, the return of Okinawa to Japan. But simultaneously there was emerging a separate, almost private Nixon-Kissinger track. Rogers was excluded from Nixon's first meeting with Soviet Ambassador Anatoly Dobrynin, and when the Secretary himself discussed Vietnam with Dobrynin later, Nixon instructed Kissinger to inform him that Rogers had gone beyond the President's views on the subject. To quote Kissinger, he and Nixon "came to deal increasingly with key foreign leaders through channels that directly linked the White House Situation Room to the field without going through the State Department—the so-called back-channels." The Kennedy-Bundy innovations, designed originally to inform and engage the President and to oversee the permanent government, became now a means of circumventing it.

This tendency was reinforced by changes in the national-security staff. Most noticed was its expansion in size—from fewer than a dozen substantive officers serving Kennedy and Bundy and a peak of eighteen under Rostow, to twenty-eight under Kissinger initially, reaching fifty-two by early 1971. More important was a subtle shift in its character. The types of people Kissinger brought on were quite similar to those who served Bundy and Rostow—operationally oriented intellectuals (or intellectually oriented operators) from the foreign-policy community inside and outside government, people without overriding partisan ties to either the President or his political party, and without any career attachment to the NSC as an institution. But the tradition of professional, impartial process management, which remained an important if occasionally subordinate feature of the Kennedy and Johnson years, departed. Executive Secretary Bromley Smith moved on, and his position was never filled. Instead there was a lower-ranking staff secretary, former Rockefeller associate William Watts for a year until his resignation and Jeanne Davis thereafter. But unlike Smith the staff secretary sat in the old Executive Office building, not the White House. The real management of NSC business rested with Kissinger's staff-within-a-staff in the White House, labeled the "Office of the Assistant to the President for National Security Affairs." And the emerging figure there was Colonel, soon-to-become Brigadier General, Alexander Haig, who started as Kissinger's military aide but rose to become his deputy. (In so doing he supplanted the quick-to-depart Richard Allen, Nixon's campaign national-security adviser, who had reason to think he had been offered the deputy position but was in fact pushed aside early as a right-wing ideologue.)

It took some time for senior NSC staff members housed in old EOB to perceive the degree to which Kissinger was cutting them out of the substantive action. Halperin found that Kissinger would repeatedly promise him full access to information, then exclude him. Economic aide C. Fred Bergsten did not learn until much later that Kissinger was negotiating intensively (and unsuccessfully) to resolve the bitter textile dispute with Japan. Watts learned about, and became marginally involved in, this venture when he went across West Executive Avenue to sit in Haig's White House office during the latter's travels. There Watts would get access to matters he simply wasn't informed about when he was in his spacious EOB office across the street. Associates would watch with amusement the efforts of longtime Kissinger friend Helmut Sonnenfeldt, the staff's senior Europe and Soviet Union expert, to keep track of his boss's meetings with Dobrynin. And Sonnenfeldt was more successful in such enterprises than most.

Middle East expert Harold Saunders, one of the two Rostow staff holdovers, risked Kissinger's periodic wrath when he played the classic staff role of including, not excluding, key officials like Assistant Secretary Joseph Sisco at State. He survived and eventually prospered, due in part to the low priority Kissinger gave most Mideast matters in Nixon's first term. Less fortunate was Latin American aide Viron (Pete) Vaky, whose efforts to play the broker went unappreciated by both Kissinger and Rogers. The latter was, by 1971, inclined to strike back at the White House by punishing Foreign Service officers who were serving on NSC details when their names came up for follow-on assignments.

The Nixon-Kissinger penchant for private management, rooted in their personalities, was strongly reinforced by the continuing national unrest over Vietnam. Alone among Nixon's senior advisers, Kissinger supported the April 1970 incursion into Cambodia. College campuses exploded in protest, three NSC staff members resigned, and two hundred Foreign Service officers signed a petition in opposition. Nixon took this petition very personally—phoning Undersecretary of State U. Alexis Johnson at 1:30 A.M. the night of his Cambodia speech demanding that he fire all two hundred by morning, and after this proved obviously infeasible, ringing Johnson every month or two thereafter to insist that none be promoted.

This was, of course, an extension of earlier Nixon reactions to critics of his Southeast Asia policy—wiretapping of aides in response to press leaks about the secret bombing of Cambodia; ostentatiously ignoring or even provoking antiwar demonstrators; and appealing to the "great silent majority" of Americans to rise up against them. What was later labeled a "domestic" issue, Watergate, issued directly from the bitter Vietnam policy struggle. And former Kissinger aides became actively involved in the Muskie and McGovern Presidential campaigns of 1972. Even more joined the Carter bandwagon in 1976. From 1970 on, White House national-security staffs began to take on partisan coloration, with their members carefully screened for political loyalty.

To liberal and academic friends, Kissinger would represent himself as a man caught in the middle, sympathetic to their views but required to defend Presidential policy. Anguished he may well have been, but his internal posture was clear—he stood with Nixon. On policy, it was hard to tell where Kissinger left off and Nixon began, though far too much journalistic ink was spent on this question. They were basically in accord on the main policy questions, and both were disposed to distrust the bureaucracy and cut it out of the action. Exclusion extended to the senior Cabinet, exacerbated by Nixon's visceral inability to tell any senior aide what he didn't want to hear. It was better just to avoid them, keep them out of things. The National Security Council met less and less. Interagency coordination was managed at the subcabinet level, by Kissinger-chaired committees on crisis management, covert operations, and arms control. State and Defense were excluded as secret talks were inaugurated on Vietnam. Breakthroughs on SALT and China were negotiated without the Secretaries of State and Defense even aware of the back-channel negotiations that were bringing them about. Rogers was publicly and repeatedly humiliated. Melvin Laird, a savvy veteran of Congressional and political wars, fared better notwithstanding the Nixon-Kissinger tendency to see him as an enemy.

Unlike Bundy (and unlike Rostow, who screened ideas but not people), Kissinger built himself up by cutting others down. It was only he and a small number of inner-circle aides who would eat in the White House mess, he who should deal with the President and other senior foreign-policy principals. Until Haig maneuvered his way into a direct Nixon relationship, Kissinger's staff was hierarchical and dominated by him personally—there were no Kaysens or Komers. He drove relentlessly those aides whose work he valued, but they labored for him, not the President. When Haig did establish a Nixon connection, Kissinger saw it, not without reason in this case, as a direct threat. With the other senior aides in direct contact with

Nixon—H. R. Haldeman, John Ehrlichman—Kissinger's relations ranged from wariness to hostility. But the Nixon White House was much more compartmentalized than any postwar predecessor; so, if Kissinger stayed out of others' business, they would usually stay out of his. This is one reason for his curiously limited influence over national-security appointments outside the White House—they came across Haldeman's desk, not his own.

One area of inevitable conflict was public relations. There was constant suspicion among the Nixon loyalists that Kissinger was getting too large a share of the foreign-policy credit. The President himself felt this acutely—witness Kissinger's pleas to *Time* in December 1972, when he and Nixon were about to be jointly named "men of the year," that his face be taken off the cover lest his status with the President be destroyed. And such concern on Nixon's part was anything but groundless. Paralleling his unprecedented influence, Kissinger got far more publicity than any previous national-security assistant, though the peak did not come until his "back-channel" negotiating role became publicly known in 1971 and 1972.

Such visibility was unavoidable given Kissinger's power and personality. And as David K. Hall has noted, the Administration needed Kissinger the spokesman as much as it resented the need. "Given the improbable combination of a press-shy introvert as President, a foreign-affairs novice . . . as Secretary of State, and a twenty-nine-year-old advertising agent [Ronald Ziegler] as Press Secretary, the necessity of employing Kissinger—who was now discussing foreign policy with Nixon ninety minutes a day—soon became obvious." Still, the exposure of his name was limited by the convention of "background" briefings where the "senior official's" name was not to be employed by the reporters to whom he gave the authoritative word. In fact, not until late October 1972 was Kissinger to appear for the Administration on live national television, with his declaration that "Peace is at hand" in Vietnam.

Long before the first Nixon term was over, Kissinger was beyond question the President's primary policy adviser, spokesman and negotiator. His rise to preeminence was reflected and symbolized by his movement up from the Bundy basement quarters to a prestigious corner office on the White House main floor. If Bundy had intruded on the role of the Secretary of State, Kissinger obliterated it. In so doing, he became Nixon's chosen agent in significant policy achievements—a lasting breakthrough with Peking, a more fragile "détente" with Moscow, and a temporary resolution of the Vietnam conflict that brought home, at long last, all American troops. All of these issues were fully exploited in the 1972 election, allowing Nixon to play the role of a tough, constructive American statesman fighting the radical McGovernite tide.

Yet, as the second Nixon term began, Kissinger's tide was clearly receding. He had become the functional equivalent of a strong, prominent Secretary of State—the very thing that Nixon had never wanted. But his position as personal aide, totally dependent on Presidential confidence, made him especially vulnerable. It seemed only a matter of time before he would have to go. Kissinger could feel Nixon's dissatisfaction during the final stages of the Vietnam negotiations. Nor was there major positive incentive for him to try to hang on—there seemed no policy breakthroughs on the horizon comparable to those already accomplished. So Kissinger busied himself with righting imbalances in policy—declaring a "Year in Europe" for a continent he had been neglecting—and planned, by his account, to leave government sometime in 1973. And Nixon planned to replace Secretary Rogers with his Deputy, Kenneth Rush, who as Ambassador to Germany had played a key back-channel role in negotiating the Berlin agreements two years earlier. (Three decades earlier, Rush had been Nixon's law professor at Duke University.)

Then Watergate came to Kissinger's rescue. By summer 1973, the scandal had overturned Nixon's electoral mandate. He was transformed from a President coldly exploiting a 49-state election victory to an embattled, forlorn man seeking to salvage his office. He desperately needed any and all ornaments to his Administration, and Kissinger was one he could not afford to lose. This truth was recognized also by another with whom Kissinger had an alliance of convenience and mutual wariness—Alexander Haig, who had replaced H. R. Haldeman as White House chief of staff in the spring.

So, on August 22, 1973, Nixon announced the appointment of Henry A. Kissinger as Secretary of State. Over the next twelve months Kissinger fought to shelter American foreign policy from the ravages of Watergate. His success in this endeavor was substantial, and surprising, in view of the fact that the initial "Watergate" acts—wiretapping, the burglary of the office of Daniel Ellsberg's psychiatrist—were undertaken to combat the enemies of Nixon foreign policy, and in view of the further fact that Kissinger himself was a major participant in the wiretap affair. But Americans wanted to believe otherwise—that Watergate was the product of Nixon and his vulgar "domestic" aides. Kissinger played on this want, reinforced by his own genuine fear that, with the President's credibility demolished, the conduct of foreign policy would prove impossible.

As he moved up to and through his Senate confirmation hearings, Kissinger spoke of the need to "institutionalize" foreign-policy making and to develop broader public support. The time seemed opportune. Nixon had reluctantly brought "truth in packaging" to foreign-policy government, giving the title of Secretary of State to the man who was playing the role. Kissinger's position was buttressed by his simultaneous retention of the national-security-assistant position. Haig, who in other circumstances might have threatened his White House account, was spending full time on Watergate and domestic issues. And Watergate made it both possible and desirable for the new secretary to make the department, not the White House, his primary base of operation. He brought to State such key aides as Winston Lord, who became Director of the Policy Planning Staff; Lawrence Eagleburger, executive assistant to Kissinger and later Deputy Undersecretary for Management; Helmut Sonnenfeldt, Counselor; William Hyland, Director of Intelligence and Research. Lieutenant General Brent Scowcroft, who had replaced Haig as deputy national-security assistant at the start of 1973, remained in the White House, backstopping Kissinger and managing day-to-day coordination.

But Kissinger remained very much the solo operator. Politically, his approach to building consensus was not to engage key Senators and others in policy formulation, but to dazzle them with his brilliance and articulateness. This he accomplished with the Senate Foreign Relations Committee, which—with Vietnam over—was free to move, under chairman (and fellow intellectual) J. William Fulbright, into strong support of Kissinger and Administration foreign policy against the ravages of Watergate and antidétente Senator Henry Jackson. But because these and other Kissinger allies were giving little positive political energy to the foreign-policy task and getting little credit for it, they added no real political weight in support.

As for the Kissinger tendency to dominate matters within the executive, to do everything himself, there was speculation that this pattern might be somewhat altered now that he could operate more in the open at State, with an array of Deputy and Under and Assistant Secretaries and Ambassadors under his direct command. Since the courtier had now become a baron, might he not transfer some of his new strength to the institution he now headed? But the outbreak of a new Mideast war in October, less than two weeks after his Senate confirmation, drove him immediately into his accustomed pattern of personal negotiator, this time with Cairo, Jerusalem, and Moscow. What he accomplished was enormous—a cease-fire in which neither Israel nor Egypt was unambiguously defeated, and one which placed him in the position to mediate, for the United States, a step-by-step process of troop-withdrawal agreements that foreshadowed Carter's Camp David accords. It was, quite possibly, Kissinger's most substantial personal accomplishment in foreign policy—for, unlike his earlier achievements with Nixon, he did this one basically on his own with the President too weak and embattled to offer much besides trouble and complications. But the preemptive personal style meant a split-level State Department—the chosen few involved in the Secretary's enterprises, and everybody else.

It was during this period that Kissinger was winning remarkable public acclaim for a Secretary of State. He came in first in the national opinion sweepstakes as America's "most admired man" in 1973 and 1974. When charges arose again that he had not told the full story about his role in the wiretappings, he could demand—and receive—an affirmation of his innocence by the Senate Foreign Relations Committee as the price of his staying in office.

So when Gerald Ford assumed the Presidency, it was hardly a surprise that he would initially seek to identify himself with the Administration's greatest asset. His very first step, after Nixon confided his intention to resign, was to get the Secretary on the phone and say, "Henry, I need you." That evening, speaking from his front lawn in Alexandria, he moved quickly from the obligatory expression of sympathy for Nixon to the announcement that Kissinger, "a very great man," would "stay on and . . . be the Secretary of State under the new Administration."

When author John Hersey spent a week with the new President

seven months later, Kissinger's dominant influence remained, to Hersey's expressed alarm:

> I had seen endless meetings of six, eight, ten advisers sitting with the President to hammer out policy on the economy and energy and Congressional tactics and everything else under the sun . . . But foreign policy was apparently of a different order . . . this President, who had had a minimal exposure to foreign affairs before he came to office, heard, I was told, only one voice, and a mercurial voice it was, Henry Kissinger's. Yes, this was the most alarming thought I had had all week.

Nor, in the years that followed, did Kissinger lose Ford's basic confidence. In fact, when considering another Presidential run in the spring of 1980, Ford made the impolitic statement that he would, if nominated and elected, bring his old Secretary of State back into power with him, despite the fact that the man had become by then a primary target of the Republican right. Kissinger's preeminence as chief foreign-policy operator and spokesman continued until he left office on January 20, 1977; it was he who personally negotiated on SALT with the Soviet Union, and he who continued to shuttle between capitals in the Mideast. When Ford wrote his memoirs, his pride was evident—"I think we worked together as well as any President and Secretary of State have worked throughout our history."

Still, a new President meant a new cast of courtiers with whom Kissinger the baron had to joust. Ford's courtiers were a mix of long-time staff loyalists, such as speech-writer Robert Hartmann, and old House colleagues like Jack Marsh and—most important—Donald Rumsfeld. Ford had summoned Rumsfeld, a former Illinois Representative, home from Brussels, where he was serving as Ambassador to NATO, to head up his hastily assembled transition team. In September, he prevailed on "Rummy" to succeed Haig as White House chief of staff.

Rumsfeld was an ambitious, intense, politically attuned conservative who fought, frequently against Ford's good nature, to run a taut White House ship. With Kissinger determined to dominate the foreign-policy channel, tension was inevitable. The Secretary's style, as one Ford aide recalled later, was to throw tantrums when others encroached on his terrain, but not in front of Ford—who abhorred such infighting. One example was when the White House redrafted a statement about Eastern Europe, on the eve of Ford's departure to the Helsinki Conference, to make it more responsive to Americans of East European ancestry.

The national-security staff, however, remained under Kissinger's wing, as Ford initially rejected the transition team's recommendation that to avoid overconcentration of power, Kissinger should "wear only one hat." More important, Ford developed, beginning in his Vice-Presidency, a relationship of confidence and trust with Kissinger's low-profile NSC deputy, Lieutenant General Brent Scowcroft. This protected the Secretary of State, and simultaneously gave the President an additional staff aide and counselor who would play an increasingly important role.

One man whom Ford did not like was his Defense Secretary, James Schlesinger. He thought him condescending personally and maladroit in dealing with Capitol Hill, and considered his "hardline" defense reputation to be phony. So Ford decided, in the fall of 1975, to replace Schlesinger with Rumsfeld, and to package this with other changes: replacing William Colby with George Bush as CIA Director, and giving Scowcroft Kissinger's second "hat," the title of Assistant to the President for National Security Affairs. Rumsfeld's White House deputy, Richard Cheney, was elevated to chief of staff.

Each of these changes made operational sense; together they might have been interpreted as Ford's coming of age as President. But early leaks forced the President's hand and put him on the defensive when he explained the shuffle to the press. Moreover, it came the same week that Ford, bowing to right-wing pressure, got Vice-President Nelson Rockefeller to declare his nonavailability for renomination in 1976. So the whole package was dubbed the "Halloween massacre," and instead of reinforcing Ford's Presidential character, it made him look weak, embattled. Ronald Reagan rose in the polls and moved toward the decision to challenge Ford in the primaries of 1976.

A rewarding target throughout the campaign was the person and policies of Ford's Secretary of State. Ronald Reagan scored primary points by denouncing détente with Russia, the draft treaty "giving away" the Panama Canal, and Administration foreign policy in general. Jimmy Carter would charge that "as far as foreign policy goes,

Mr. Kissinger has been the President of this country." White House aides sought to protect Ford by separating him from the Secretary, and to penetrate Kissinger's veil of secrecy so that the President could reap more personal political gains from foreign policy. They pressed Scowcroft to play a larger public role to counter the notion of a Kissinger monopoly. But though the Air Force Lieutenant General dealt frequently with the press on "background," and did emerge as an important Ford adviser in his own right, he did so in the classic, anonymous staff mode of Sidney Souers or Andrew Goodpaster.

In challenging Kissinger, White House aides were driven by more than personal ambition. For, in Washington and across the nation, the right wing—its influence long dampened by the domestic reaction to Vietnam—was now on the rise. The first signal was the remarkable success of conservative Democrat Henry Jackson in scuttling the United States–Soviet trade agreement, a centerpiece of Administration détente policy, by conditioning the grant of "most favored nation" trade status on a public, on-the-record Soviet commitment to ease restraints on Jewish emigration. Jackson's legislative effort had the backing of a broad coalition of Jewish, human-rights, labor, and anti-Soviet organizations, and Senator Adlai Stevenson had added his own successful proposal to limit trade credits. It illustrated the domestic political weakness of the Nixon-Kissinger policies toward the Soviet Union. Conceived and executed in secrecy, exploited politically as the dramatic personal accomplishments of two lone individuals, they lacked a committed and engaged corps of political allies to whom the Administration might turn in time to challenge.

For the Ford White House, the most troubling challenge was from right-wing Republicans. Kissinger was rapidly joining Nelson Rockefeller in their pantheon of *bêtes noires*. Ronald Reagan challenged Ford for his party's 1976 nomination and began to score rhetorical ten-strikes among "true believer" party audiences by his attacks on SALT and Panama.

And if the Republican right saw Kissinger as too soft, liberals were attacking his policies as too hard, too obsessed with military and paramilitary instruments—arms sales, covert operations, threats to use the American troops. Under Ford, they won enactment of a

In his publicly proclaimed management doctrine, Carter was committed to Cabinet government, openness, decentralization. Reacting against what he had denounced as Kissinger's one-man show, he would operate a "spokes of the wheel" advisory system, hearing a range of voices from his central vantage point. He himself would be "President of this country" for foreign policy.

Unlike Nixon, Carter announced his Secretary of State two weeks before his national-security assistant. Unlike Kennedy, he gave his secretary a free hand in selecting his State subordinates.

But Carter balanced what seemed a strong mandate for his new Secretary with creation of an interagency coordinating system that gave Brzezinski an important bureaucratic advantage, the chairmanship of the Cabinet-level Special Coordination Committee (SCC).

Following the Kissinger precedent of 1968–69, Carter's aides worked out the details with the President-elect first and brought the new State appointees into the game only minimally until the basic decision was made. David Aaron, Carter's NSC transition coordinator and future deputy national-security assistant, developed for Brzezinski a proposed NSC system of seven interagency committees. Brzezinski was to chair three: for arms control, covert operations, and crisis management. The assistant-designate took it to the President-elect, who rejected it: it was too complicated, and looked too much like the Nixon-Ford system. Carter and Brzezinski then worked out an alternative, which telescoped the committees into two: the SCC and the Policy Review Committee (PRC), which would coordinate policy reviews on subjects where one department had clear lead responsibility and be chaired by whichever department had primacy on the issue to be considered.

The SCC was given explicit responsibility for "oversight of sensitive intelligence activities," "arms control evaluation," and "crisis management"—everything that Brzezinski had originally sought. And according to Brzezinski, neither Vance nor Secretary of Defense Harold Brown saw anything on paper until they received Carter's signed Presidential Directive (PD-2) the afternoon of Inauguration Day. When Vance showed it to his aides, they protested vehemently—it would give the national-security assistant too much power. Even Kissinger had never chaired a Cabinet-level committee before he became Secretary of State. The SCC's responsibilities for SALT and crisis management were particularly threatening. If

Vance were not to be weakened at the start, he needed to get the directive modified, these aides felt, and they urged him to do so.

But the Secretary was reluctant to risk a State–White House fight that would almost surely become public. So, to his aides he was firm—Carter had endorsed the system, and it made no sense to fight the President on process, as Rogers had done. Instead, he would win foreign-policy leadership through substantive performance and scrupulous loyalty to Carter personally. Vance also, however, phoned Brzezinski, protested the lack of consultation and insisted that they discuss the matter further. But no changes in the system resulted.

Since the new system depended on close judgments about whether an issue was a "crisis," or whether one department had a primary interest, its smooth operation would depend on *collegiality*—the watchword of those early days. Vance feared that an initial fight over "turf" would destroy any possibility of achieving the needed rapport and mutual confidence among the President's aides.

But the national-security assistant was a man who thrived on polemics, on controversy, on acting first and consulting later. He seemed not to perceive how his combative style could disrupt a process he was charged with running smoothly, or how preemptive personal action could undercut his Cabinet associates. So, the system was a prescription for enhanced competition between the barons and the courtier.

In 1977 Vance seemed to be winning. Countering Brzezinski's proposal to begin the Administration's Soviet dealings with a broad dialogue on the principles of détente—one which Brzezinski, as global strategist and advocate of this approach, saw himself as conducting personally—Vance won adoption of his pragmatic approach: negotiating case-by-case, with arms control the priority. And while the unsuccessful March 1977 "deep cut" SALT proposal that the Secretary took to Moscow bore Brzezinski's stamp more than his own, State recouped with a pragmatic fall-back position that, pushed aggressively by chief negotiator Paul Warnke, made a final SALT II agreement appear imminent by early fall. On the Middle East, Brzezinski and his staff held the early initiative. But Vance took charge that summer, after his first Mideast trip, and he continued as Carter's primary man for this region through the achievement of the Camp David accords.

variety of restrictive laws, establishing a Congressional veto over arms sales, requiring notification of Hill committees when the CIA engaged in covert operations, banning any such activity in relation to the war in Angola, limiting military aid to South Vietnam in the months before Saigon's fall.

Thus, as 1976 came to a close and Jimmy Carter prepared, after a narrow election victory, to succeed Gerald Ford, American foreign policy had come to an ironic pass. Kissinger remained personally ascendant, and while he was publicly committed to departing at the end of the term, it is more than possible that Ford would have pressed him to remain had thirty additional electoral votes landed in the Republican column. Yet the main lines of his policy were in shambles. A framework for SALT II had been agreed on between Ford and Brezhnev at Vladivostok, but Defense Secretary Rumsfeld and the Joint Chiefs of Staff, aligned with Jackson and other antidétente conservatives, had persuaded Ford to reject the draft treaty that Kissinger was negotiating with Moscow. On other United States-Soviet matters, Congress was taking away both carrots and sticks—limiting trade, but limiting political-military engagement as well. Similarly, Kissinger was finding himself rebuffed by Treasury Secretary William E. Simon and Agriculture Secretary Earl Butz in his efforts, triggered by the 1973 oil crisis, to develop more forthcoming United States economic policies toward the Third World.

In form, and in control of day-to-day-policy practice, Kissinger had brought power back to the State Department. But in substance it was stalemate that Jimmy Carter inherited in January 1977 when he took power from the man who had done so much "to heal our land."

One of the minor surprises of early 1977 was how much time Jimmy Carter was devoting to foreign affairs. This preoccupation was foreshadowed neither by his background as Governor of Georgia nor by his campaign, which gave priority to the economy and domestic issues. Nor was it forced by world events. For 1977 was internationally a rather quiet year, in sharp contrast to previous transition years—1961 with Laos, Cuba and Berlin crises, or 1969 with the ongoing Vietnam conflict. Yet the new President was pressing initiative after initiative—promoting human rights, limiting arms sales, seeking to curb nuclear proliferation, proposing "deep cuts" in nuclear weapons, concluding a treaty on the Panama Canal.

Such personal engagement usually enhances the role of the President's policy staff. And just as Carter's determination to define his international agenda contrasted with Ford's willingness to address problems as his subordinates defined them for him, so his choice for national-security assistant was a man very different from his predecessor's anonymous "inside" manager Brent Scowcroft.

Zbigniew Brzezinski was an activist intellectual who had achieved prominence in both international-affairs writing and Presidential-advisory politics. He might even have been Hubert Humphrey's national-security assistant in 1969 had the votes added up differently. Like Kissinger, "Zbig" was a professorial entrepreneur of European origin. He had risen, however, despite the mixed reviews of his peers and the lack of a single long-standing patron such as Kissinger had possessed in Nelson Rockefeller. One modest symbol was the way he was elected to the Board of Directors of the Council on Foreign Relations in 1972. He got on the ballot not through the normal route of designation by its nominating committee, but by petition. This opportunity had been made available just that year by the Committee on Procedures under the chairmanship of one Cyrus R. Vance, who had become a Council Director four years earlier, one year after leaving the position of Deputy Secretary of Defense.

Vance was, by 1976, the liberal foreign-affairs community's consensus choice for Secretary of State. Having gotten his governmental training in the demanding McNamara school, he was operationally tested. And his peers liked him; he was bright, collegial, prudent, and, unlike Kissinger, a "team player." He lacked one thing, however, that the flashy, articulate, and controversial Brzezinski possessed—a substantial personal connection to President-elect Jimmy Carter. Vance too had been engaged in the advisory politics that surrounds Presidential candidates, and had quietly worked to position himself for the secretaryship. But if Vance had intermittently counseled Carter, "Zbig" had persistently tutored him. He had connected with Carter early in the Presidential quest and he continued, as one of us reported in October 1976, "to be the most influential figure in the Democratic nominee's stable of foreign policy advisers . . . the only person to whom Mr. Carter has publicly promised a top job if he is elected." He would shortly become the first national-security assistant who had actively, even relentlessly, campaigned for the position.

And Brzezinski appeared to be restraining himself. Upon his appointment he had described his job with words Goodpaster or Scowcroft might have used—"heading the operational staff of the President, helping him to facilitate the process of decision-making in which he will consult closely with his principal Cabinet members." Once in the White House he gave his staff a decentralized, collegial character that contrasted sharply, and not accidentally, with the stern Kissinger regime. The distinction between senior and junior staff was abolished. Aaron, a former aide to now-Vice-President Walter Mondale, functioned as a semi-autonomous Deputy. There was no Alexander Haig to impose discipline, no Bromley Smith to coordinate operationally. By cutting the number of professionals from over forty (under Scowcroft) to thirty-some, the new assistant shielded himself from assault by Carter's executive-office reorganizers, who had a strong mandate to press cuts in Presidential staff. And Brzezinski stressed the ease of his personal relationships with "Cy" and "Harold" (Brown), who generally did not assert himself on foreign-policy questions.

But the roots of conflict were there. Carter had minimized, in his public and intragovernmental utterances, the role of Brzezinski, out of deference to convention and to Vance, and because he didn't want himself overshadowed by "another Kissinger." But while the Secretary and his senior subordinates were determined to exploit what they saw as a strong leadership mandate, Carter had given a strong mandate also to an in-house aide whose prime goal was not to manage policy but to make it. And he *liked* Brzezinski. He would later write in his memoirs, "Next to members of my family, Zbig would be my favorite seatmate on a long-distance trip; we might argue, but I would never be bored."

Moreover, Carter's determination to make detailed decisions himself without reference to any overarching strategy—and his willingness to remake and remake them—meant that no single subordinate would have his constant backing. This too gave advantage to the aide who would personally staff out these decisions.

Tensions became public in a major way in early 1978; they centered on the conflicting Vance and Brzezinski approaches to the Soviet Union. The Assistant, alarmed at Soviet-Cuban inroads in southern Africa and Ethiopia, pressed for strong action in response, including a slow-down in the SALT talks. The Secretary, less alarmed by Russia's Africa gains, saw linkage as inappropriate for countering them; he favored quiet diplomacy (insisting that Ethiopian troops not invade Somalia, for example) and completion of SALT II on its own terms. Carter seemed unable or unwilling to choose either of the two alternative Soviet policies, or either of the two men. His ambivalence was nicely illustrated when, in a speech to the Naval Academy designed to end the confusion, he "stapled together" Vance and Brzezinski drafts in a hybrid formulation that raised confusion and criticism to new heights. At this same time, Brzezinski was beginning to preempt, through his pungent verbal assertiveness (and Vance's reticence), the Secretary of State's established role as the President's primary foreign-policy spokesman.

Brzezinski precipitated a climax of sorts when, after returning from a negotiating trip to Peking, he declared on *Meet the Press* that Soviet behavior in Africa was not "compatible with what was once called the code of détente," and that it "could produce consequences which may be inimical to them." Vance went privately to Carter protesting both the language—more threatening than either he or the President had employed—and the broader fact that Brzezinski's public policy statements were undercutting Vance's credibility as Secretary of State. Providing external support for the Vance position were fourteen members of the House Committee on International Relations, who wrote Carter in June expressing puzzlement as to "what is U.S. policy on such issues as Soviet-American relations and Africa," and asking which official in his administration could provide authoritative clarification.

Carter addressed the matter directly early that same month, at one of the ongoing series of weekly, "principals only" Friday breakfasts he held with Vance, Brzezinski, Brown, Mondale, and White House political aide Hamilton Jordan. Vance emerged the apparent winner. He would henceforth be the primary spokesman, with Brzezinski muting his public voice, playing the role of "inside" adviser and coordinator. And in the weeks ahead, as Brzezinski limited his public exposure, the Carter White House took steps to underscore Vance's preeminence. The Secretary spoke out on Africa policy, with Carter's approval, in ways that suggested that he had scored a clear political victory.

But Carter also reaffirmed, that June, Brzezinski's role as close personal adviser. And he did nothing to change foreign-policy procedures—Brzezinski retained the SCC chair and the staff prerogative of overseeing Presidential foreign-policy paper. And Carter reportedly assured him after that meeting that "we are going to continue running things as before." So Brzezinski kept the personal and procedural base to retain substantial influence and to rise again when circumstances were propitious.

At the Camp David peace talks of September, Vance was the central Carter adviser, with his Assistant Secretary, Harold Saunders, the prime workhorse and draftsman, and Brzezinski curiously on the sidelines. In fact, the very capable NSC Middle East aide, William Quandt, was working basically for Vance, as a member of the State-led team. The agreement brought Carter a dramatic if temporary political resurrection in the United States, and Vance's central role in it seemed to confirm a new preeminence.

But things changed rapidly in the final months of 1978. The Administration was moving simultaneously toward three major agreements: SALT II, the Egyptian-Israeli peace treaty outlined at Camp David, and normalization of relations with China. Vance was lead negotiator for the first two. Brzezinski was entrepreneur for the third; and to maintain secrecy, communications to Ambassador Leonard Woodcock in Peking went directly from the White House, with Vance's knowledge. There was hope that December would bring completion of all three negotiations, a remarkable policy and political coup. But only China met the timetable. Vance was in the Middle East when Carter gave the final go-ahead on normalization and moved the announcement date forward from January 1 to December 15. This decision—announced only six days before what was hoped to be Vance's climactic mission to Geneva on SALT II—may have caused the Russians to harden their position so as to delay an agreement.

And then there was the unraveling of the Shah's regime in Iran. Brzezinski was a strong advocate of reinforcing the ailing monarch, after others—including Ambassador William Sullivan—found the cause hopeless. Early in that same December, with Vance in the Middle East, Brzezinski was communicating directly with Sullivan and with the Shah's close adviser, Ambassador to the United States

Ardeshir Zahedi. George Ball, working briefly out of White House national-security-staff offices to prepare for Carter an independent assessment of the Shah's prospects, concluded not only that the Shah was "on the verge of collapse" (a judgment that Carter and Brzezinski rejected), but that there was "a shockingly unhealthful situation in the National Security Council, with Brzezinski doing everything possible to exclude the State Department." When Ball reported this view to Vance, stressing the Assistant's use of back-channel communications, the Secretary protested to Carter, and the Assistant countered with a claim that no one had produced a cable that had not been cleared by a senior State official. This "painful" debate before the President "was the last I heard of the matter," Vance recalled in his memoirs, "but the back-channel communication stopped."

With Vance regularly overseas, Brzezinski's room for maneuver increased, and he concluded 1978 far stronger than he began it. Nor, it appears, did the January 1979 fall of the Shah and the subsequent chaos in Teheran diminish his standing with the one constituent who most mattered, James Earl Carter, III. For if Ball or Sullivan saw the Iran policy-making problem as an erratic Presidential aide out of control, trying to manipulate what he did not comprehend, Carter saw it as the result of leaks, even sabotage, from the Department of State, people undercutting his policy of supporting the Shah. So, he summoned Iran desk officers and senior sub-Cabinet State Department officials from that department to a White House meeting and declared coldly that *their* leaking was disloyalty. They would have to stop it or leave the government. Then he "got up and left the room," giving no one a chance to answer the charges. He had assembled, and then humiliated, precisely those people in the State Department who were most loyal to him and whose allegiance he most needed. They could only conclude that it was his courtier Brzezinski, not his baron Vance, to whom he now looked for primary support.

On SALT also, the tide of influence was not in State's favor. In the fall of 1978, Paul Warnke—a strong Vance ally—resigned as SALT II negotiator. In the final negotiating phase before the June 1979 Vienna summit, it was Brzezinski who was most influential. When the treaty came to Capitol Hill in July, it was not Vance but Defense Secretary Harold Brown and JCS Chairman David Jones who were its strongest advocates. By contrast, during 1979 the number of State-chaired PRC meetings declined. Vance's standing was further weakened by his unwise statement that he would not stay beyond Carter's first term, which rendered him a "lame duck."

Throughout 1979, Carter grew weaker and weaker politically. His personal shuttle diplomacy extracted Israeli-Egyptian agreement on a peace treaty in March, but while this method demonstrated commitment, the fact that he had to go to such lengths suggested weakness as well. And that summer Camp David would take on a new meaning, as the embattled chief executive summoned prominent countrymen to the mountain to advise him on what had gone wrong with his Presidency, then returned to declare a national "malaise" and to require public resignations of all his top aides.

In 1979 also, conservative criticism of Carter's foreign and defense policies grew progressively stronger, further advantaging Brzezinski over Vance (and threatening the SALT II treaty to which both were now committed). Then, with the Iranian hostage seizure in November and the Soviet invasion of Afghanistan in December, the assistant emerged again, more than ever before, as a public policy spokesman while Vance receded from public view.

The post-Afghanistan climate created an exceptionally favorable market for Brzezinski's policy views, his penchant for crises, and his bureaucratic maneuvering. The deeper the crises, the more they fell into his SCC orbit. Carter declared his eyes opened on the Soviet Union, announced a new doctrine on the Persian Gulf, and expedited development of a Rapid Deployment Force for crisis contingencies. But like his boss, the assistant was strikingly alone at the pinnacle of power. He got little of the admiration and acclaim that had come to Kissinger. His style offended many who stood with him on substance. Responsibility for policy fiascos was placed eagerly at Brzezinski's doorstep, as when Carter embarrassed German Chancellor Helmut Schmidt by announcing the United States boycott of the Moscow Olympics at the end of a week during which no less than three senior American officials had assured Schmidt that no such step was imminent. And the President, whose approval ratings soared in the wake of the Iran hostage taking, found them down sharply again by March 1980. The *New York Times*–CBS News Poll cited as the primary reason "growing disapproval of Carter's handling of foreign policy."

In April he sent American rescue helicopters to their debacle in the Iran desert. Brzezinski had promoted and nurtured this venture. Vance, alone among Carter's advisers in opposing it, resigned in protest against the decision to undertake the operation. Carter quickly named to succeed him the widely respected senior senator from Maine, Edmund Muskie. Pressure mounted again for the President to establish guidelines, to curb the courtier's power—no speeches and public appearances for the national-security assistant, no negotiation with foreign governments. But at a weekend Camp David conference, Carter refused. True, he wished to exploit Muskie's standing and public articulateness. And Brzezinski did refuse cooperation on a projected *Time* cover story on him the week after Muskie's swearing in. But at the meeting the President made it clear that he identified himself with his assistant, not the new Secretary. "Zbig," he would say, "we won't let the State Department push us around."

Muskie was an established Senate baron, a man used to the spotlight and accustomed to insisting on his prerogatives. His movement across town brought speculation that he might be both willing and able to reverse the trend toward White House dominance. But he did not press Carter on procedures when his leverage was greatest—that is, *before* he accepted the job. And he started forty months behind Brzezinski in his knowledge of Administration policy and process. He never caught up. His brief flirtation with the idea that he might emerge as a compromise Democratic Presidential candidate cost him dearly with the President. By summer he was protesting exclusion from Carter's decision to declare a new policy on nuclear targeting, an exclusion due partly to Brzezinski-Brown mismanagement and partly to the assistant's determination that State officials be kept out of the details. By early fall Muskie was speaking out openly against Carter Administration procedures in a way that Secretary Vance never did. He "let it be known that he wants major changes in the way foreign policy is managed if he stays on in a second Carter Administration." And for direct quotation: "If I were President, I would appoint somebody as Secretary of State and make sure that the NSC role is that of coordinating and not anything else."

Muskie's disenchantment with Carter's policy making was broadly shared. Thus Ronald Reagan could only gain politically when, in a conciliatory October campaign speech, he made "reorganizing the policymaking structure" the first of "nine specific steps that I will take to put America on a sound, secure footing in the international arena."

> The present Administration has been unable to speak with one voice in foreign policy. This must change. My administration will restore leadership to U.S. foreign policy by organizing it in a more coherent way.
>
> An early priority will be to make structural changes in the foreign policymaking machinery so that the Secretary of State will be the President's principal spokesman and adviser. The National Security Council will once again be the coordinator of the policy process. Its mission will be to assure that the President receives an orderly, balanced flow of information and analysis. The National Security Adviser will work closely in teamwork with the Secretary of State and the other members of the Council.

Reagan: Politics over Policy

Alexander Haig sought to turn this campaign rhetoric into reality. Having followed up his service in Nixon's White House with a successful tour as NATO commander, having flirted with his own 1980 Presidential candidacy, having impressed Ronald Reagan in two preelection conversations, he had Richard Nixon's vintage endorsement: "The meanest, toughest s.o.b. I ever knew, but he'll be a helluva Secretary of State." He also looked conservative enough to be Jesse Helms's candidate to head off George Shultz. So when Reagan named him Secretary, the Washington betting was that here, at long last, was a baron who could really prevail.

The new national-security assistant, Richard Allen, was not much of a threat. Like Brzezinski, he had "earned" the job through service as Reagan's chief campaign adviser for foreign policy; unlike him, Allen was quickly revealed as a junior member of the Reagan team. Long-time California intimate Edwin Meese seized the prestigious West Wing corner office, dispatched Allen to the basement from which Kissinger had emerged, and put out White House organization charts making himself, not Reagan, Allen's direct supervisor.

To consolidate his position, Secretary-designate Haig drafted an organizational memo for Presidential signature, as had Kissinger and Brzezinski before him. Like them, he proposed a foreign-policy-making system that would put him in a key position: the State Department would direct, for the President, the national-security work of Defense, CIA, and the other foreign-affairs agencies.

Unfortunately for Haig, he did not know Ronald Reagan very well. And in contrast to Nixon and Carter, Reagan had neither commissioned the memo nor contributed much to its basic design. And Reagan was a President who *really* liked to operate collegially. So when Haig delivered the memo on Inauguration Day, it went to senior aides Meese and James Baker. When Meese consulted senior national-security officials like Defense Secretary Caspar Weinberger, the negative reaction was inevitable, as were the press leaks. By February, Meese had put Haig firmly in his place by brokering a jerry-built compromise. There would be three major coordinating committees—for foreign, defense and intelligence policy—chaired respectively by State, Defense, and CIA. There would be no formal process for coordinating these committees. Then in March Meese won Presidential endorsement of an even odder arrangement, placing Vice-President George Bush, not a day-to-day foreign-policy player, in charge of crisis management.

Having initiated in January a game he could not win, Haig raised the stakes in March, by publicly criticizing the new arrangement just as Reagan was about to announce it. The President responded with a terse formal statement which lacked even the customary obeisance to the Secretary of State's formal role: "Management of crises," it said, "has traditionally—and appropriately—been done within the White House." Just six days later, on the afternoon of the attempted Reagan assassination, Haig dug his hole still deeper by nervously declaring from the White House, on national television, "I am in control here."

Haig had come on strong, calling himself Reagan's foreign-policy "vicar," a phrase he had found in Paul Nitze's testimony before the Jackson subcommittee in 1960. Now the vicar was vanquished. Or, more precisely, the baron seemed to have "self-destructed" in his first seventy days.

Yet no courtier moved to fill the foreign-policy vacuum. Allen remained a second-rank player with weak White House ties; neither

Haig nor Weinberger was compelled to pay him much heed. His staff was the weakest the NSC had seen in many, many years. Meese, Baker, and Michael Deaver were very strong, and very close to Reagan, but their priority was the President's economic program. They got into international issues only when the domestic political implications were obvious.

Meese, remembering Reagan's Detroit promise to "try to convince the Japanese" to slow auto imports, made sure that Administration free-traders did not block Congressional efforts to pressure Tokyo: the result was a "voluntary" ceiling on the number of Toyotas, Datsuns, Hondas, et cetera, sold in the American market. So it was also with grain sales to the Soviet Union. Haig and Weinberger worried about sending a soft signal, but there was that Reagan campaign promise to lift Jimmy Carter's embargo. So, lift it Reagan did. And there was the proposed sale of advanced radar warning aircraft (AWACS) to Saudi Arabia. The national-security people, Weinberger in particular, had messed this up so badly that Reagan was threatened with a first-ever Congressional veto of an arms sale. So to the rescue came James Baker, organizing an October campaign of Presidential persuasion that got no fewer than ten Senators to buck pro-Israel pressure and publicly change their positions.

It was suggested to Meese in October that agency officials found the Reagan White House like a "black hole." When an issue entered it, no one outside could see what was happening until a decision emerged. Meese responded, "Exactly. That's the way we like it."

Few shared Meese's satisfaction. But on foreign policy many issues didn't really reach the White House, even though Reagan was convening the National Security Council more frequently than any President since Eisenhower. He and his aides had made economic policy their first priority—and their second priority, and their third priority. They were on a political roll, winning grand Congressional victories on omnibus bills to cut taxes and spending (except for the military). At Defense, Weinberger—an old California intimate—had carte blanche from Reagan, and the Secretary was equally accommodating to the military services. And on foreign policy Haig, for all his troubles, was the Administration's sole experienced senior international hand. So on the fairly large range of issues he could keep within State's domain, he generally got his way.

Policy making was further complicated by Reaganite ideology.

The White House might be downplaying foreign policy in 1981, but it had been central to the Reagan platform in 1980—a prime concern of the Reagan movement. The President had campaigned eloquently not just against the "vacillation, appeasement, and aimlessness" of Jimmy Carter, but against failed Establishment policies of at least two decades. Reagan was deeply anti-Soviet and anti-Communist. He had declared Soviet machinations to be the prime cause of the world's troubles, and he saw American arms buildup as the prime cure. To Reagan, the Panama Canal treaties had been a "giveaway," Vietnam a "noble cause," détente an "illusion," and the SALT II treaty (negotiated under his three predecessors) "fatally flawed." He brought into office a number of sub-Cabinet officials who identified with such views, especially at Defense. He also helped to bring into office a Republican Senate. So, if Haig showed a tendency to choose his assistant secretaries from the Kissinger wing of the foreign-policy elite, there was always Jesse Helms to raise hell with the White House, interrogate the nominees on Capitol Hill, and put legislative "holds" on their confirmation.

In its public face, then, Ronald Reagan's first year was history repeating itself as farce. Predecessors had seen bitter inner disputes, courtiers and barons fighting over serious policy stakes. But now a President who had denounced the infighting under Jimmy Carter found himself, within a year of the election, on the telephone with columnist Jack Anderson about whether there really was a "guerrilla" in the White House out to get the Secretary of State. The charge had been Haig's. So Reagan called the Secretary and *Allen* into the Oval Office to get them to stop, though it was widely known that Haig's guerrilla was really one of the senior trio, James Baker.

Still, the President usually deferred to Haig on policy, impressed by the substance of his arguments if not his labored, combative style of argumentation. So Haig could lead on most issues most of the time, unless and until it hurt politically. On Central America the Secretary went too far very fast. His rhetoric about "drawing the line" and "going to the source" provoked a public outcry that threatened Reagan's popularity and undercut attention to his economic program. So the White House told him to cool it. But on issues affecting China and Western Europe—even the Soviet Union—Haig generally prevailed.

In these issues Haig was aided no little by the uproar that careless Reaganite rhetoric had generated—especially over nuclear weapons. The Administration consensus had been to press military buildup first and arms control later, if at all. But this policy and its loose explication had swelled the ranks of antinuclear demonstrators in Europe, forcing the Administration into a commitment to begin talks on Intermediate (Europe-based) Nuclear Forces (INF) before the end of 1981. On East-West trade, where Weinberger and others wanted a virtual declaration of economic warfare, Haig managed to win shaky acquiescence in the Soviet natural-gas pipeline, which Reaganites abhorred but Europeans—left and right—were determined to complete. Even the Administration's response to Soviet-supported repression in Poland proved moderate enough to win plaudits from Anthony Lewis, and denunciation (for its softness) by Haig's onetime boss, Henry Kissinger.

Haig was emerging, as disgruntled hard-liners put it, as the Administration's "sheep in wolf's clothing." With his European connections, he was the man who insisted that continental politics had to be taken into account, and he used NATO pressure—which Reagan could hardly dismiss—to win his way in Washington.

As 1982 began, Reagan took a step which seemed to give Haig further strength. The Secretary had been vulnerable because he lacked an ally in Reagan's inner circle. Now the President fired Allen as national-security assistant and replaced him with William P. Clark. The pretext was a pseudo scandal involving a Japanese magazine interview with the First Lady, one thousand dollars and two Japanese watches. The reason was that Reagan—and his troika—wanted a senior national-security man in the White House whom they knew and trusted.

Judge Clark was such a man. He had preceded Meese as *Governor* Reagan's chief of staff, before his patron elevated him to the California bench. In 1981 Reagan called him again; the White House needed someone reliable—personally and politically—to serve as Haig's number-two man. The General was hardly overjoyed at being assigned a White House spy, but as things turned out Haig and Clark—two Catholic hard-liners—got on famously on the State Department seventh floor. The Secretary found Clark invaluable in his knowledge of Reagan and his trio; the Deputy Secretary developed enormous respect for Haig's policy judgment. In January 1982, Haig still lacked easy relations with Reagan. Clark's move gave the Secretary a White House man, close to the President, with whom he could deal, a Presidential connection once removed. And in his new job Clark did help Haig—for a while. He had the added advantage of long-standing ties with Weinberger and Meese.

The only problem was that Clark didn't know much about foreign policy. If he was unique among national-security advisers in the breadth of his prior Presidential relationship, he was unique also in the depth of his policy ignorance. To the Senate Foreign Relations Committee, he had revealed in his 1981 confirmation hearings what *Newsweek* labeled "a completely open mind," displaying no foreign-policy knowledge, either factual or conceptual. As a result, he amassed twenty-five votes against his confirmation as deputy secretary of state.

By the time of his White House move, Clark's Washington reputation was much improved. He had not transformed himself substantively, but he had shown an ability to get things done in the Reagan government. Once ensconced in the White House basement, he strengthened the top layer of the NSC staff by bringing Robert "Bud" McFarlane over from State as his deputy and engaging a fellow Californian, former Secretary of the Air Force Thomas Reed, as a senior consultant. The rest of the staff grew in size if not in quality, reaching the upper forties in substantive staff aides, the highest number since Henry Kissinger's heyday.

Still, what Clark did best was to connect with the other senior people, Ronald Reagan above all. And not only did he bring the NSC back into the general foreign-policy game; he began to bring the President in too. This was bound to mean trouble for Haig, whose approach to policy had been to reach for personal power and not always take Reagan's gut inclinations too seriously. Clark took them very seriously. He saw his job, above all, as "the conversion of [Reagan's] philosophy to policy," as he expressed it in a rare public speech in May 1982. Since the Assistant lacked comparable knowledge of foreign governments and leaders, and since he also had no prior exposure to the Washington political scene, Clark could not always be counted on to warn the President on those occasions where the market for Reagan ideology was unfavorable.

It certainly was unfavorable on East-West trade. Reagan wanted to squeeze the Soviet Union economically. But Europeans had economic and political interest in proceeding with the pipeline which would deliver them Soviet natural gas. American firms—including hard-pressed Caterpillar Tractor—wanted to share in the contracts.

The issue came to a head at the June 1982, seven-nation economic-summit conference at Versailles, Reagan's first European visit as President. The official American strategy was that proposed by Haig—offer reluctant United States acquiescence in the pipeline in exchange for agreement to toughen the credit terms offered the Soviet Union on trade in general, and to tighten in particular restrictions on selling goods with military applications. Reagan had never liked this strategy very much, and Haig was undercut when the Europeans offered little in broader trade restraint. The President's unhappiness became outrage when French President Mitterand said after the June summit that even the modest Soviet trade steps agreed to by the seven leaders were meaningless. So Reagan and Clark called an NSC meeting a week later, on a date when Haig was meeting Soviet Foreign Minister Andrei Gromyko in New York. There they rammed through a Presidential decision to apply economic sanctions against European-based firms that were using American technology to participate in the pipeline project.

Now it was Haig's turn to be outraged. The White House had by this single act blown his European accommodation campaign right out of the water. More than that, it had been done in a way that seemed almost designed to inflict maximum humiliation on him personally. Nor were things going well for him on another key policy front—the Middle East. He had been successful in winning a restrained American response to the Israeli invasion of Lebanon, but unsuccessful in seeking a mandate to fly to the area and mediate. So Haig threatened resignation—as he had done several times before. This time Reagan accepted, perhaps to Haig's surprise. A key reason was that Clark now agreed with other White House aides that Haig was too volatile, too much a solo operator, for the Reagan team. The date was June 25, 1982.

Yet another baron had fallen. Alexander Haig might have become the best hope in the Administration for Europeans and for moderates on Capitol Hill. But he could never work out a solid relationship with the President—personally, politically, or substantively. So when the crunch came and he had to call once again on his White House capital, he found that his account had run dry.

Haig's successor, George P. Shultz, seemed as suited to the Reagan style as Haig was unsuited. Both were pragmatic conservatives, men of the moderate right (who therefore represented the "left wing" of the Reagan Administration). But there the similarity ended. If the general's strategy had been what worked in the Nixon Administration—grab personal power for yourself, fend others off, operate on directly delegated authority from the President—Shultz was the ultimate team player. As Secretary of the Treasury in 1972–74 he had impressed his colleagues—though not always Nixon—with his capacity to move issues forward without cutting people down, with his ability to build consensus within government, while maintaining influence over policy's pace and direction.

Once he was confirmed, unanimously, in his new position, Shultz demonstrated this talent anew. He pulled together key people from within and without the Administration, engaged the President, and developed a comprehensive Mideast peace initiative that Reagan could unveil on September 1, 1982. This proposal was hailed as the most timely and professional foreign-policy initiative the Reagan regime had yet produced. And having accomplished this move *for* the President, Shultz gained some running room to repair some of the damage Reagan's instincts had wrought. He negotiated in November a face-saving allied arrangement to study a joint toughening of East-bloc credits. This gave Reagan at least a pretext for abandoning the pipeline sanctions he had so unwisely and unilaterally imposed in the previous June.

As 1982 drew to a close, then, Reagan Administration foreign-policy making seemed transformed. In 1981, the "system" was politics on top and chaos below, unregulated baronial conflict on those issues that lacked the political urgency to make it into Meese's "black hole." But Reagan had now done, willy-nilly, what no President since Truman had been willing to do. He had replaced two senior foreign-policy players. He had gotten himself a national-security assistant and a Secretary of State he could work with, and the two seemed compatible with each other. They had brought him personally into the foreign-policy making game on a regular basis. More than that, the new Reagan team seemed to reflect a balance between courtiers and barons often advocated but seldom accomplished: a strong Presidential national-security assistant who eschewed publicity, who saw his job as connecting his boss with the other senior players, and a Secretary of State who commanded broad respect, who had demonstrated a capacity to lead, but who also remembered, to return to the Acheson phrase, "which is the President."

Unfortunately for this balance, 1983 brought a series of challenges on just those issues where Shultz felt weakest—defense, arms control, and revolutionary war in Central America. Domestically and internationally, the Administration was under strong pressure to adjust, to move toward the center, on all of these issues. And on these issues Clark came into his own, as a major substantive influence on policy. But he sought not to adjust and accommodate, but rather to enforce what he termed the Reagan "philosophy." The President might talk, increasingly, about the need for bipartisanship, but what he meant was that Democrats should support him and his hard-line policies. This was a recipe, at minimum, for continued domestic conflict. And as foreign and national-security policy suddenly became, in 1983, the central preoccupation of the Reagan White House, the Secretary of State began looking like the man who wasn't quite there on the issues that mattered the most to the Reagan Presidency.

Central America had been a relatively low priority issue for the President personally—until UN Ambassador Jeane Kirkpatrick, a hard-liner and a Clark ally, returned from a trip there in February 1983 to report that the Salvadoran government that we backed was doing poorly in its civil war. As a result, Ronald Reagan got himself seriously into the issue for the first time. He called for an increase in United States military aid. He came close to endorsing, in public, the overthrow of the leftist Sandinista government of Nicaragua. He even got Senate and House leaders to convene a rare joint session of Congress, so he could speak on Central America and seek "bipartisan" support.

Some of the rhetoric was conciliatory. But it was also politically threatening; "Who among us would wish to bear responsibility," he asked, if a new leftist regime came to power in the region? And the policies themselves did not change. Reagan might accede to Congressional wishes that he designate a special ambassador to seek negotiations, but the man whom he chose—conservative Florida Democrat Richard Stone—made it perfectly clear that he wasn't going to put a lot of heat on our fractious regional friends. A still better signal was the replacement of Assistant Secretary Thomas Enders, who had called for a two-track strategy of fighting *and* negotiating.

Another central question was the defense budget. All the Congressional signals called for compromise: Reagan had won significant budget increases for two years, but with projected budget deficits of $200 million, public support had eroded. Congress had decisively rejected, in December, the Weinberger proposal to deploy the MX missile in the controversial "dense-pack" mode. As 1983 began, Virginia conservative Senator John Warner, himself a former Secretary of the Navy, said on February 1, "Nothing is certain but death, taxes and a cut by Congress in defense spending." But Weinberger was rigid. Clark aligned with him in resisting calls for compromise by pragmatic aides like James Baker. So Ronald Reagan would yield only very little, very late.

Most important, there was arms control. For the most part, the Administration stand through 1982 had been dominated by the Department of Defense. While the official United States strategic-arms-reduction (START) proposal did not contain everything that Pentagon leaders might have wanted, it was generally regarded as totally nonnegotiable since it required basic restructuring of Soviet strategic forces while meshing perfectly with Reagan modernization plans. Thus there was no risk that an arms-control agreement, real or prospective, would undercut Americans' support for "rearming America." But just to make sure Defense aides, led by Assistant Secretary Richard Perle, succeeded in hardening this position still further in the fall.

As 1983 began, the Administration was busy reassuring moderates by emphasizing how central an arms-control role would be played by George Shultz, who seemed really to want an agreement. But when conservative Democrat Eugene Rostow was fired as arms-control director, it was Clark, not Shultz, who picked his successor, an upwardly mobile conservative polemicist, Kenneth Adelman, from Kirkpatrick's UN delegation. (Adelman soon got himself and the Administration in hot water by his weak performance in confirmation hearings, where previous anti-arms-control statements were used against him. But Reagan stuck by him, spending valuable Presidential leverage with moderate Republicans to get him confirmed, 57–42.)

Nor was Shultz much in evidence when spring brought another arms-control opening. Reagan had responded to his defeat on MX-dense-pack by reaching toward the center, appointing a bipartisan Commission on Strategic Forces composed of barons and courtiers from previous administrations. Its members and "senior counselors" included Harold Brown, Melvin Laird, Henry Kissinger, and Jimmy Carter's SALT II counsel, Lloyd Cutler. Its chairman was Brent Scowcroft, Ford's national-security adviser. Together with its proposal that the MX be deployed without an expensive "basing mode" to protect it, the commission made several related recommendations. One was that Reagan's START proposal be "reassessed." Liberal and moderate Congressmen and Senators sought to use this language, and the balance of Congressional power they held on the MX, as a lever for prying significant policy changes from Ronald Reagan.

In July, they got some positive-sounding language in two Presidential letters. In October, they got more—a new administration START position that was more forthcoming, including a Senate-proposed "mutual build-down" of nuclear weapons. But to go this far, the President had to overrule his principal arms-control advisers and negotiators, raising doubts as to how aggressively his administration would pursue the new approach. And by this time, United States–Soviet relations had been further poisoned by the Russian shoot-down of a Korean passenger jet.

Judge Clark's fingerprints were on all these moves. He had clearly emerged, by the summer of 1983, as Reagan's most influential foreign-policy adviser. He even took control of Middle East policy, after Syria rebuffed the Israeli-Lebanese troop-withdrawal agreement that Shultz had negotiated. Then suddenly, in October, Clark walked off the foreign-policy stage, as he became the President's surprise choice to succeed James Watt as Secretary of the Interior.

In choosing Clark's White House successor, Reagan opted for conservative professionalism. Rejecting right-wing entreaties on behalf of United Nations Ambassador Jeane Kirkpatrick, and reversing, reportedly, an initial decision to give the job to White House chief of staff James Baker, he named instead Clark's former deputy, Robert

McFarlane, who had won broad respect in Washington for his brokering on arms-control issues.

So once again, Reagan's courtiers and barons had to sort out new relationships, as his third national-security assistant worked and jousted with his original Secretary of Defense and second Secretary of State. McFarlane, a former Marine officer with substantial executive branch and Congressional staff experience, proved himself an effective insider manager. He upgraded the quality of the NSC staff and the professionalism of its management of routine issues. The new national-security assistant also possessed a sensitivity to Capitol Hill nuances that had been lacking in most of his predecessors.

Unlike Judge Clark, McFarlane was not a Reagan courtier of long standing. So while Clark had been able to force decisions on issues, or even make them himself in Reagan's name, McFarlane had to operate more cautiously, especially in his first year. Unlike Richard Allen, he was clearly the focal point for White House foreign policy coordination: he briefed the President; he managed the process; he was involved in the major decisions. He kept to the staff role, less visible than the departmental barons, George Shultz and Caspar Weinberger. And on most issues, he was aligned with—and working closely with—the Secretary of State. But by early 1985, McFarlane was clearly emerging as a substantial force in Reagan foreign policy making: asserting himself more individually, conducting regular background briefings for the press, appearing regularly on network talk shows.

The departure of Clark gave the Secretary of State a new opening, a chance to establish the primacy that had seemed within his grasp in 1982. Shultz did not waste this opportunity. Identifying himself increasingly with the use of military force in the Middle East and the Caribbean, Shultz strengthened his ties with Reagan. His main governmental adversary on troop deployment issues was Defense Secretary Weinberger, buttressed by the Joint Chiefs of Staff—who were reluctant to fight anywhere unless a military action was popular and/or could be quickly concluded. On Lebanon, the military finally prevailed: with the situation deteriorating and the Presidential campaign approaching, Reagan announced a withdrawal (thinly disguised as a redeployment) of the Marine peacekeeping force. But on arms control and Soviet relations, the Secretary of State established a clear lead.

Opportunity came from transition in Moscow and election-year vulnerability on the issue in Washington. Reagan needed to neutralize the charge of his Democratic opponent, Walter Mondale, that he was the first President since Herbert Hoover not to have met with his Soviet counterpart. So Reagan invited Soviet Foreign Minister Andrei Gromyko to the White House in September 1984, and preparations to resume arms talks began shortly thereafter. By holding a series of arms control policy meetings at Cabinet—and Presidential—level, Shultz and McFarlane managed to avoid the sort of interagency wrangling which previously had led to extreme negotiating positions; they also limited, through this device, the impact of that formidable arms control adversary, Assistant Secretary of Defense Richard Perle. Shultz also struck an alliance with veteran arms control expert Paul Nitze, who as negotiator on Europe-based strategic forces had developed the only initiative of Reagan's first term that offered any promise of serious progress. Nitze accepted what was, in form, a demotion: from Presidential negotiator to "special adviser to the President and the Secretary of State on arms control matters." But his influence grew, for Nitze was the one arms control expert who was senior enough to participate effectively in Cabinet and Presidential-level deliberations. Finally, Shultz played a central role in the designation of a new U.S. arms control negotiating team in January 1985. This offered a sharp contrast to his lack of influence over the switch at ACDA two years before.

Still, as the talks resumed in March, the administration's negotiating posture was very general. Defense had not had to yield very much of substance, and the President himself seemed more committed than ever to his Strategic Defense Initiative, popularly known as "Star Wars." The Soviets were particularly anxious about the threat this might pose to their deterrent, and unless Reagan proved willing to limit SDI, Moscow seemed most unlikely to accept substantial cuts in the offensive forces which it would need to counter it.

Ronald Reagan had entered 1985 with enormous foreign policy opportunity: a resounding electoral victory, a chance to begin again at Geneva. No President since Dwight Eisenhower had been as well positioned, in American politics, to sustain support for agreements on intractable issues like arms control and Central America. Improvements since 1983 in policy processes and baron–courtier relationships could facilitate such achievements. But major compromises on policy substance would be required also, compromises well beyond what Reagan had shown himself willing to make in his first four and one-half years.

The Triumph of the Courtiers

Over the forty years since World War II, power has moved back and forth among courtiers and barons, not always predictably. Presidents have shown little capacity to predict how people and relationships would develop. Few are as purposive as Nixon in establishing how and where they want policy made; few seem able to make timely shifts of people or processes.

Nonetheless, there has been a strong trend toward concentration of power in the primary Presidential foreign-policy courtier, the national-security assistant. The main loser has been the prime baron, the Secretary of State. James Forrestal, who proposed the National Security Council in the forties as a super-Cabinet committee to constrain the President, would not be pleased.

A principal cause of this power shift has been the triumph of politics and ideology over foreign policy. Presidents use foreign policy more frequently for political reasons; Presidents increasingly head political factions committed to distinct, even ideological, policy positions, which they seek to implement once they are in office. This increases their distrust of the career bureaucracy and drives them to pull policy control into their own White House.

Another factor has been, inevitably, the personal ambitions of the national-security assistants themselves. With the White House job come powerful temptations to seize the brass-ring opportunity, to break out of the Goodpaster-Scowcroft mold, to breach the self-denying commandment of Truman's Admiral Souers to "forego publicity and personal aggrandizement."

In principle, most holders of the office might agree with McGeorge Bundy, who wrote in November 1980 that the White House national-security job was "one place where less would be more." In practice, few of them prove able to hold to a true staff role, to be more important on the inside than is known on the outside, to nurture and reinforce the ties between the President and his Cabinet aides. There have been exceptions: Brent Scowcroft in 1975–76; Robert McFarlane, at least through early 1985. But as a general rule, national-security assistants have moved into public prominence, and into conflict with those they are supposed to bring together. More often than not, they have ended up winners in the competition.

None of this means that national-security assistants have become master political managers. In practice, none has been. Nor has any of them been effective in coalition-building to strengthen foreign policy's domestic base. To the contrary, their protected position has encouraged them to short-circuit the broader domestic-policy process, and Presidents have often encouraged them to do so. Partly for this reason, national-security assistants have themselves become the focus of controversy, semilegitimate figures whose role adds to policy conflict.

Increased reliance on White House courtiers has meant greater fluctuation in policy content. It has also made the policy process more personality-dependent, and thus more idiosyncratic, since staff aides are less constrained than Cabinet barons. It has, finally, both encouraged and enabled Presidents to seize personal control of current policy operations, with consequences spelled out in the chapter which follows.

V The Operational Presidency

ENTWINED with the story of the triumph of the courtiers is its corollary—the growing capacity and willingness of Presidents and their White House aides to be not only policy makers but dabblers in diplomacy. Their ability to do so has been enhanced by a revolution in communications technologies.

When one reads of extraordinary events—a famous trial, the crucial meeting of Presidential advisers in a crisis, a great battle—one pictures it, in the mind's eye, as larger than life. The colors are vivid, the scene is set in 70mm Vistavision, even the low voices of the decision makers are amplified in quadrophonic Dolby sound. Yet, for the participants, what is often striking is the prosaic quality of the proceedings. The trial room may be stuffy and small; in the battlefield, an ordinary tree or rock remains printed in the memory of a soldier seeking cover; the decision maker may be worried not only about the crisis but also by a cold he picked up over the weekend.

The White House Situation Room conjures up the grand visions—a setting out of *Dr. Strangelove*, perhaps, a room with huge maps of the world on the walls, little lights blinking to indicate the crisis spots, colonels with pointers poised to show the disposition of contending forces. But in fact, it is nothing of the kind. You will find it by entering a side door in the basement of the West Wing of the White House, proceeding past a security guard at a small desk in a narrow corridor, then making a right turn past the desks of some NSC typists, another door, and you are there. It is a modest room—perhaps twenty by forty feet—a conference room ostensibly like any other conference room. A table accommodates fourteen or so if they sit cheek by jowl. There is room for maybe twenty lesser officials seated around the wall, their knees almost touching the backs of the chairs of their superiors (in easy note-passing range). To leave the room, as officials at such meetings occasionally do (trying always to look as if they are going to see or call someone even more important), they must stumble and squeeze past the legs and backs of the others. The chairs are modern but comfortable. Tucked under the undistinguished table are telephones which are very seldom used. The colors of the room are ordinary, in the hues of early-period Holiday Inn.

It is disappointing stuff for the junior officer who gets to see, for the first time, this legendary inner sanctum of foreign-policy power.

Behind the walls of the room, however, and in the East Wing of the White House, are communications machines that have extraordinary importance. They allow a President and his staff to receive instantaneously the cable traffic coming into the government's foreign-affairs agencies and to communicate directly with foreign officials.

High-tech communications have been a blessing for Presidents trying to manage our increasingly complex foreign affairs. But the blessing has been mixed. Since World War II, as power has flowed toward the courtiers in their unequal struggle with the barons, technology has followed and reinforced their triumphs. The machines have made it easier for a President to be his own Secretary of State, not only chief executive but chief diplomat too. We now have not only a Presidency that sets policy, as it should. In foreign policy we have an operational Presidency, as well. This is sometimes a good thing, but not always. For it further politicizes our policies, and it can lead to pressures for quick foreign action or agreement, when a President has put his own prestige on the line. It thus leads the President away from reflection and consultation both with his own apolitical experts and with our allies abroad.

FDR, like Woodrow Wilson before him, had been drawn to such a role. To keep him up-to-date on the latest war news, and to help him keep in touch with foreign political leaders as well as his own government, Roosevelt had the Navy establish—in what is now the White House Mess—an intelligence communications center called the Map Room. According to George Elsey, then a junior naval officer assigned to the Map Room staff, the center was open only to White House military personnel, the President, and Harry Hopkins, Roosevelt's close friend, confidant, and sometime foreign emissary. Elsey and his fellow watch officers kept current maps showing the progress of the war and managed a classified communications system. In addition, they "served as the secretariat for the President's communications with Prime Minister Churchill, Stalin, Chiang Kai-shek and other leaders of the Allied war effort." The effect of communications technology on the patterns of managing our diplomacy became immediately obvious. The State Department, already cut out of important parts of the action, now also could be more easily denied full knowledge. The Map Room, according to Elsey, became "the only place in the . . . government which kept complete files, incoming and outgoing, of all communications between the President and these figures." Harry Truman maintained the system until VJ Day, "at which point . . . the Map Room was rather rapidly dismantled."

Truman, and then Eisenhower, returned to what seemed at the time to be the normal ways of managing communications inside government and with the outside world. Eisenhower had a naval aide who handled the nuclear-communications "satchel," and there were White House communications facilities available for other emergencies, as well. But the White House did not regularly receive the cable traffic of the agencies, and did not have the staff or technical capacity to involve the President in day-to-day details. The White House staff had an understanding with Defense and the CIA that if they came across raw data that seemed vital to United States security, they would pass it along. It took an argument in front of Eisenhower between Allen Dulles and Eisenhower's staff secretary, Andrew Goodpaster, before Dulles' people at the CIA did even that to Goodpaster's satisfaction. The President's pictures of the world were painted largely by State, Defense and the CIA in daily summaries of their own traffic and analyses.

This would not do for John F. Kennedy; he was interested in reaching for the specifics, the details. And unlike Eisenhower, who preferred oral briefings, Kennedy the speed-reader was bored by them. It was the task of his National Security Assistant to feed his voracious appetite for current paper. Soon after the Bay of Pigs, a debacle in the policy-making system as well as in Cuba, it fell to Bromley Smith, the Eisenhower NSC holdover, to construct an information system that would serve the new Presidential appetite.

There was an old World War II bomb shelter under the White House mansion; the nuclear era had rendered it obsolete. It then housed some communications equipment under the control of the Army. Smith worked with military aide Chester "Ted" Clifton to put this equipment into twenty-four-hour use, for simultaneous receipt of incoming and outgoing cable messages to and from State and other agencies. The cables were then sent, initially by pneumatic tube, to Bundy's West Wing basement area, where clerks could sort them and make them available to Bundy, his staff, and Kennedy himself. Later, an automated message-handling system allowed the staff of the Situation Room to use computers to sort the messages before printing them up.

Setting up the system presented a string of operational problems. One was how to select the foreign-policy traffic that the White House wanted. For example, the total volume of cable traffic between Washington and our missions abroad was many times what the small White House communications staff could handle; some basis for screening them was necessary so that the Bundy people could be reasonably confident of getting the messages they wanted. This matter defied perfect resolution. At first, Smith tried to negotiate a list of subjects on which cables would be automatically relayed. This proved too complicated. So he fell back on a more primitive distinction: all communications marked with an urgency indicator of "priority" or above would go automatically to the White House. This worked better, since any smart bureaucrat or diplomat will label his or her own messages as urgent in order to do justice to their obvious importance. Indeed, this system soon generated more traffic than the White House wanted. In succeeding years, a flexible system evolved in which the Situation Room staff, in consultation with the NSC staff, programmed its computers and levied its requests of the bureaucracy according to a shifting set of substantive and other categories. While Henry Kissinger was the Assistant for National Security Affairs, White House demands for such traffic increased. When he became Secretary of State, the department's secrets were held more tightly. A month into the Carter Administration, State agreed to increase the flow to the White House again.

A harder potential problem facing Smith as he established the system was getting the cooperation of the agencies whose mail was to be read. The most crucial, State, proved surprisingly easy, because Rusk acquiesced, despite occasional doubts of Under Secretary George Ball about the bureaucratic implications of the new system. It proved unnecessary for Bundy to go to the President for his help in gaining the Department's cooperation, although he was prepared to do so. This did not mean that State had no ways of keeping private those communications it wanted to protect from White House eyes. Special "slugs" or code words could be used to tell State's communications people not to distribute those messages beyond the building. The word "STADIS" at the beginning of a cable from the field would presumably keep it within the family. "CHEROKEE," the name of Dean Rusk's home county in Georgia, became and was to remain the code for the Secretary's private channel; distribution of CHEROKEE messages was to be held to his office and the recipient. In practice, of course, even specifically restricted messages have a way of getting around the bureaucracy.

Defense was more complicated, and one problem never perfectly resolved was how to get a handle on the "back-channel" (undistributed) traffic from the military chiefs to field commanders. Clifton's recent Pentagon staff experience was helpful here.

The Pentagon supplied funds for the project. NSC money was limited, and it was only by "piggybacking" on Defense and CIA funding and staff that the system could be established without encountering laborious budgetary and bureaucratic opposition.

As time passed, new processes were established and new equipment was installed. Under Johnson LDX (long-distance Xerox) was developed; it allowed the transmission of classified documents, so that draft cables, memos and speeches could be transmitted more quickly to the NSC staff from the agencies. On this, as on other matters, one big impediment was winning the reluctant agreement of security personnel, who had to be shown that such a system would not encourage security leaks.

At the other end of these lines, centralized operations had been established at State (the Operations Center) and Defense (the NMCC, or National Military Communications Center). The introduction of computers at State also made a big difference in the ability of the government to recall its own diplomatic record. In 1967, when war threatened between Israel and her neighbors, the Department's old-fashioned filing system was consulted as officials attempted to put together a simple listing of all previous United States commitments to Israeli security, especially at the time of the 1956 Suez crisis. It turned out, according to Lucius Battle, then the Assistant Secretary for that region, that it would take days to discover these essential facts. The relevant files had been sent, for safekeeping, to storage facilities far from Washington. An Israeli delegation arrived in Washington before the American files were found—and the Israelis were armed, of course, with their own history of the American obligations. When finally found, after the war was over, the American records were the same. But it was not a model of preparation for important negotiations. (Years later, when the State Department had just computerized key records, Battle was invited by Secretary of State William P. Rogers to a ribbon-cutting ceremony for the new information system. Rogers asked if anyone wished to test the computer with a question. Battle raised his hand and asked, "What are our commitments to Israel?" They promptly appeared on the display board for all to see. Battle presumably slept better that night knowing that the State Department computer was awake.)

The Situation Room system allowed the White House necessary control over the diplomatic and military communications of the nation. The NSC staff and the President had to be in the position of knowing that his instructions were being faithfully implemented. And White House communications as a whole had to be tied together better, as they were—under the White House Communications Agency, the WHCA, pronounced "Wacka." (There is a story that in the early Eisenhower days, the Joint Chiefs were carrying out a communications exercise and sought to reach the President at night through military channels. The phone rang and rang, before finally being answered by someone, who said, "I'm just a cleaning man" and replaced the receiver to return to his more important duties.)

The growing sophistication of White House communications also offered the NSC staff some powerful advantages in the daily guerrilla warfare between State and White House functionaries. With instantaneous transmittal of messages, and a smaller and thus more efficient internal distribution system, NSC staffers could often read State's messages minutes before interested State officials had received them. Some former State officers still blanch as they remember calls from Robert Komer (to be nicknamed "Blowtorch"), who handled first the Middle East and then the Vietnam pacification program for the White House under Johnson. Komer would revel in asking his victim to discuss the meaning of cable 2056 from Tel Aviv or

42896 from Saigon, when there had not yet been a chance to read the hot new item. It certainly helped to promote faster paper shuffles in the State Department. It also helped to promote Komer's dominance of his colleagues.

The Situation Room and its communications system thus helped Presidents to seize control of the foreign-policy system. It helped the NSC staff to serve the President as he must be served, even if it offered also unfair advantages in the bureaucratic competition. But established initially to bring Kennedy and his staff more fully into the policy game, it would be employed by subsequent Presidential aides—especially Kissinger and Brzezinski—to keep out State and Defense, sometimes even their Secretaries. The new communications networks allowed both Presidents and White House staffers to get more deeply into the daily business of diplomacy, sometimes acting without the knowledge of the officials actually charged with those responsibilities. The machines have allowed the growth of the operational Presidency.

There is nothing new in Presidents taking personal, operational control of the big issues. Summit diplomacy has an ancient history, dating back at least to the visit by the Queen of Sheba to Solomon's Jerusalem, where "she communed with him of all that was in her heart"—an open style of diplomacy of which Roosevelt was later to be accused in his dealings with Stalin. And, of course, summits were an accepted instrument in the age of classical European diplomacy, as at the 1815 Congress of Vienna. No nineteenth-century American President ever traveled abroad, but Teddy Roosevelt broke the rule by visiting Panama. Woodrow Wilson's extended and ultimately fruitless presence at the Versailles Peace Conference to end World War I served to warn his successors about the dangers of such personal diplomacy. Still, the fact remains that every one save Harding has met personally with foreign leaders, either at home or abroad.

Franklin D. Roosevelt disregarded Wilson's experience in undertaking his own World War II summits. Especially at the Yalta Conference of February 1945—or so it seemed to many contemporary and later critics—Mr. Roosevelt went too far in acknowledging Soviet control over Eastern Europe. According to the accounts of the time and soon thereafter, he was tired, dying, and too eager to make a peace with Moscow. He played up to Stalin by poking fun at

Churchill. Too many deals were cut right at the table. And Truman, despite his more feisty behavior with Stalin, came under the same attacks for weakness after the Potsdam summit. No matter that neither gave away anything that Stalin was not already in a position to take or hold by force of arms. In sound foreign-policy circles, the rule was set—summits create overwhelming pressures for leaders, particularly leaders of democratic countries, to reach agreement. Presidents become preoccupied with whether they will be seen personally as succeeding or failing, so they become too willing to make concessions of national interest in order to avoid a stalemate.

Eisenhower played by that rule of caution in his first years, especially since Senator Joseph McCarthy was strenuously against the summits with the Soviets that our European friends were urging. It was not until after 1955, when the Democrats began to run with the issue, that Eisenhower shifted his view and agreed to meet with Soviet leaders.

In April 1960, in the only major article Dean Rusk allowed himself to write before becoming Secretary of State, he warned the next President, whoever he might be, of the perils of summitry. A President engaging in personal diplomacy, he argued, loses the time necessary to feel out the situation and probe for concessions; allows personality to intrude; comes under political pressure to create at least the pretense of accomplishment; loses control of other issues while concentrating on the negotiation; and gives adversaries an opportunity to try to affect our own elections. "I conclude," he wrote, "that summit diplomacy is to be approached with a wariness with which a prudent physician prescribes a habit-forming drug."

But by then, Presidents were turning a deaf ear to this conventional wisdom of the foreign-policy establishment. Eisenhower was committed to his doomed Paris summit in May 1960, and President Kennedy rushed to Vienna during his first summer in office, with disastrous results. His successors would make summits a regular feature. Just as war had become too important to be left to the generals, foreign policy was now too important to be left to the diplomats. And too glamorous. And too popular.

The coming of international jet travel has meant that statesmen can circle the globe more and more, relying on formal diplomatic channels and ambassadors less and less. Things move very slowly in these traditional channels. Summit meetings, with the attendant media attention, can help break issues loose from national bureaucracies. The bureaucracies have a deadline for action as they prepare for the summits; Presidents may make decisions at them. At some risk, Presidents can actually accomplish something.

Certainly, summits can be occasionally silly or frightening in the quality of the discussions. Sir Harold Nicolson, in his diaries of the 1919 peace conference, recalls discovering that the British Prime Minister Lloyd George was using a *topographical* map in trying to convince the Italians that a territorial claim was *ethnographically* unsound. At a still sillier level, Roosevelt included his son Elliott in obnoxious bantering with Stalin about the desirability of the Allies' summarily executing German officers by the thousands after victory in World War II. But especially if they are well prepared in advance, and a President takes the time to learn the issues with care, summits can make the crucial difference—as Jimmy Carter demonstrated at Camp David with Anwar Sadat and Menachem Begin.

The problem is that the impulse toward summitry is but a part of a more general trend toward deep White House involvement in all the details of our diplomacy, complicating lines of authority and action, and allowing the NSC staff to cut out other officials with a need to know what is being said to foreign governments.

Almost inevitably, the White House staff takes over the duties of coordinating a President's communications with foreign leaders, as the Map Room did for Roosevelt. Over the years, for example, Presidents have developed a pen-pal relationship with dozens of leaders around the world. The letters are, of course, coordinated by the NSC staff. The rather desultory exchanges with leaders of smaller nations are usually handled in close cooperation with the State Department; the hot stuff, or the letters to our closest allies or to Soviet leaders, have sometimes not been shared. State usually has seen a draft of these messages, although sometimes for the eyes only of the Secretary and not his experts. Final versions of the President's letters have not always found their way to State's files.

Even more secretive have been the increasingly frequent telephone or teletype conversations between Presidents and foreign chiefs of state. For many years, the special lines that had been established to London, Paris, and elsewhere were so difficult to use that

Presidents simply picked up the telephone and called their foreign peers on commercial lines. In the Carter Administration, teletype machines that could carry encoded messages were set up with a number of our major allies. Transcripts of communications between the President and other leaders on these devices were usually shown to Secretaries Vance and Muskie, but others at State were rarely included. According to James Reston, President Carter also tried to use the hot line for noncrisis exchanges with the Soviets, but the scheme failed; the line was not, ironically, considered by Brzezinski to be private enough.

It is not overly cautious to suggest that a tendency for Presidents to communicate instantaneously with foreign leaders, without time for careful consideration during the course of the exchanges, is at best disadvantageous in a serious negotiation—and at worst, dangerous. The exclusion of the career experts also means that the officials most involved—White House staffers—are those whose interests include the President's political image. There is always the temptation to try to achieve an immediate gain at the possible expense of an enduring accomplishment. Richard Nixon's SALT I offensive-arms agreement was a tragic example, a genuine breakthrough tarnished by sloppiness on specifics as Kissinger struggled to meet the President's political timetable.

The corollary to increased Presidential involvement in operational detail and personal diplomacy is a tendency for the White House staff itself to get involved in dealings with foreign governments. This has been the pattern surrounding the economic summits that have become a regular event since the initial get-together at Rambouillet in 1975. Most of the meetings have been rather general in nature, with the assembled leaders comparing notes on their respective economic and political situations and prospects and agreeing to the broad generalities of the communiqués. There is an occasional spat on substance, the most visible being the 1982 disagreements between Reagan and his colleagues over East-West trade. But only rarely, as in the early Carter years, are leaders pressed to make concrete commitments to which they can later be held.

It is within participating governments, however, that summits make the biggest difference in how international economic policy is made and negotiated. The "Sherpas"—the aides appointed to ease the way to the summit—not only gain great influence on policy within the government but also themselves get together five or six times a year. Some of the Sherpas are drawn from foreign ministries—for example, in the case of the Japanese and Italians. But this has not usually been so for the Americans. In the Carter Administration, summit preparations were put in the capable hands of Henry Owen, who used his position and his access to the President to become perhaps the most important governmental figure in broad international economic policy, and one of those from whom the foreign officials were most interested in hearing.

Brzezinski began pushing hard for establishing an analogue on the political side. The economic summits should have a political dimension as well, he and his staff argued, or there should be scheduled political summits beyond the regular NATO get-togethers (whose preparations were largely in the hands of the NATO officers in the foreign ministries). The NSC argument was always couched in terms of national and Presidential interest, of course. But there was no doubt about who would be the political Sherpas and the effect that that would have on the relative roles of the NSC staff and State when it came to communications with our allies. State officials couched their objections in equally elevated substantive terms, but the root of their budding concern was clearly bureaucratic. While an allied summit meeting in Martinique, at which State and other foreign-ministry representatives were excluded, was a victory for the Brzezinski position, the proceeding was not to be repeated on a regular basis—in part, perhaps, because of the State Department objections, and in greater part because of difficulties in getting the allies to agree.

But the failure of this effort at making Sherpary political as well as economic was unusual for the years since 1969, when most efforts by the NSC staff at becoming diplomats as well as policy coordinators have been all too easily crowned with success. While the courtiers made headway in the internal game during the 1960s, Henry Kissinger was the first to muscle his way into a significant piece of the foreign action. At the very start of the Nixon administration, he set out to establish a negotiating track that might bring about an end to the war in Vietnam. As chronicled in his memoirs and elsewhere, his talks with the North Vietnamese were conducted in the greatest secrecy; while the world thought the negotiations were being conducted in the formal talks between American and North Vietnamese representatives in Paris, the real work was being managed by Kissinger and the Vietnamese during his secret visits to a different part of that city. For many months, not only were the bureaucrats at State excluded from the knowledge of his efforts; the Secretary of State and the Asian experts on the NSC staff too were left in the dark. Even when the circle of knowledge was slightly widened to include a few at State, the memoranda describing the secret track in the negotiation were occasionally edited to remove the most sensitive points before they were allowed to escape Kissinger's office.

Not surprisingly, it was in the secret, rather than the formal, Vietnam negotiations that the Vietnamese were willing to do their business. The pattern was thus to be repeated in the negotiations on SALT II, with somewhat less secrecy (but a continued reliance on "back channel" messages about which our formal negotiators knew little).

There is no doubt that Kissinger was a brilliant negotiator, and that the system of double tracks, of secret maneuver behind the screen of public charade, particularly suited his style of diplomacy. It was efficient. It reduced the possibility of leaks. Perhaps not coincidentally, it also offered tremendous bureaucratic advantage.

But there were costs as well. When the National Security Assistant, on these and other issues, begins to do State's business and doesn't inform the Department of what has been said, everyone—including our foreign interlocutors—can become confused. And as the practice has continued, many State officials have found themselves, when meeting with foreign diplomats, in the embarrassing position of guessing about their own government's position on serious issues. When they guess wrong, or stand mute and fearful of guessing at all, confidence in American diplomacy is diminished. Nor are the procedures for ensuring popular and Congressional control of our foreign policy anything but damaged. In addition, when only a few select officials in the White House know what is being told to foreign governments, the press is more vulnerable to manipulation. There is no way for reporters to check the accuracy of what is being said in the White House backgrounders. The Congress, which has assured access only to State officials, may be as misled as the foreign diplomats who rely on the incompletely knowledgeable department for information. When Gerard Smith, the chief American negotiator in the formal SALT I negotiation, tried to gain support for the treaty in testimony during the last days of its negotiation, he only generated suspicion about it since he was unable to answer Congressional questions on some of the details. They were being handled secretly by Kissinger.

When State Department experts are excluded, the benefits of their knowledge is lost; an apolitical voice is not heard; policy continuity beyond the current administration and institutional memory are endangered; the morale and therefore loyalty of the bureaucracy suffers; and foreign officials can play State off against the NSC staff.

Kissinger took the action with him when he went to State, and Brent Scowcroft at the White House was content to manage coordination of policy affairs, which he did very well. But Brzezinski seemed determined to recapture Kissinger's White House role and public glory. Posing on the Great Wall in China, or brandishing a rifle near the Khyber Pass, he seemed to wish reporters to perceive him as the central figure not only in policy but also in practice. On a number of occasions, he pressed for authorization of personal missions abroad—to Moscow, for example, or to Tehran. These capitals he was denied. Other trips were not. On one occasion, he is said to have gained the President's agreement to a trip before informing Secretary of State Vance that he had such an intention, thus giving Vance no chance to argue against it. On a visit to Algiers in late October 1979, Brzezinski happened to run into two moderate Iranian leaders when such an encounter had not been planned as a part of American diplomacy nor desired as a part of American strategy. Iranian militants used the meeting to discredit the two moderates in Tehran, and their authority was "greatly weakened" at the very time the 444-day hostage crisis was beginning.

Brzezinski's personal management of the final stages of the China normalization negotiation allowed the kind of secrecy that Presidents cherish. On the final day before it was announced, the Assistant Secretary of State for Asian Affairs, Richard C. Holbrooke, was called to the White House to help work on the preparations for the announcement. He was not allowed to call and tell his office at State what he was up to. (His absence led immediately, of course, to widespread and highly accurate speculation at State about what was going on.) One result of all the secrecy was that the White House was able to avoid giving the Congress much warning of normalization. Congressional irritation then complicated the risk of gaining support for the move; the Senate had specifically called for consultation on such a move.

The ability of the Situation Room to use back channels—to pass messages to our embassies or foreign officials through secret CIA or Defense channels—also allows the White House to instruct our representatives abroad without the knowledge of the State Department. Both Kissinger and Brzezinski used these channels to set up their own meetings with foreign officials. Their use also for dealing on substantive matters directly with American representatives abroad can lead to real confusion. This was evident in the last days of the Shah, when no one knew whether our special representative to the Iranian military, General Huyser, or our Ambassador, William Sullivan, really spoke for America—and who in Washington was instructing each. It can also make life difficult for our ambassadors. One ambassador at a particularly sensitive post during the Carter Administration handled the embarrassment by calling the Assistant Secretary for that region and suggesting that the State official ask him questions about what was going on. He could then respond in ways that conveyed the substance of his latest private message from the White House without having "volunteered" the information. Thus did the official in Washington with primary responsibility for implementing policy learn what the full nature of the policy was. Even with Amtrak, the engineers of the trains are supposed to have some knowledge of where all the tracks are leading.

When Edmund S. Muskie became Secretary of State in 1980, he apparently thought at first that he could dominate the NSC under the same ground rules that had so frustrated his predecessor. He soon discovered otherwise, and he had his staff prepare a draft treaty with the White House. Under its terms the NSC staff would continue to coordinate the making of policy, but with a more open handling of the minutes of interagency meetings. The National Security Assistant and his staff would, however, meet with foreign officials only rarely, and then in the presence of State officials. Solo foreign missions by the NSC staff would be forbidden. Meetings with the press would be limited, and there would be an end to the unilateral background briefings at which the "real" American policy was explained. But by the summer of 1980 it was too late to gain such an understanding. Most senior officials were more interested in whether there would be a second term for the Administration than in how to organize themselves for foreign policy.

The Reagan Administration began its operation in ways that suggested *it* might act in the ways recommended by Muskie's staff. Control of negotiations returned promptly to departmental hands. The President showed little personal interest in direct involvement, beyond the obligatory meetings with foreign counterparts on state visits. His first National Security Assistant, Richard Allen, had no mandate to negotiate with foreign officials. Indeed, Allen even yielded an important staff prerogative, that of clearing major State and Defense messages.

Allen's successor William Clark was no more inclined to make himself a direct foreign-policy negotiator. He saw his job as coordination—above all, making sure that the agencies understood what Ronald Reagan wanted and that they acted on this understanding. He worked to influence what State and Defense leaders did, but not to take their place and do it himself. Until the end of his tenure, he seems to have eschewed the personal, back-channel diplomacy that was Kissinger's forte. He dealt substantially with the press, but less than Brzezinski had done and almost never for attribution. He remained at his desk in the White House, and traveled mainly when and where Ronald Reagan traveled.

Still, Clark found ways of taking effective command. One was by firing and hiring senior aides. His efforts went beyond expanding the NSC staff to nearly fifty policy professionals, a number reminiscent of Henry Kissinger, and getting nine senior aides designated "Special Assistant to the President" to enhance their status and power. By early 1983 Clark seemed, more than any of his predecessors, to be orchestrating key foreign-affairs personnel changes outside the White House. It was he who forced the controversial January firing of arms-control Director Eugene Rostow and his replacement by Kenneth Adelman. It was Clark who worked with UN Ambassador Jeane Kirkpatrick to seize the policy initiative in Central America, and then insisted on the reassignment (to Madrid) of Assistant Secretary of State Thomas Enders, who had been Shultz's—and before him, Haig's—point man for the region. And it was Clark who helped to do in the U.S. Ambassador to El Salvador, Deane Hinton.

It was also the National Security Assistant and his top aides who, in order to save the MX missile from Congressional demolition, organized the President's Commission on Strategic Forces. Clark's Deputy, Robert McFarlane, served as the point man in negotiations among the Administration, the Commission, and the Congress to save the missile. And Clark got military manuevers going in Central America as a show of United States strength in the summer of 1983. He did this without consulting or even informing the State Department, at least up to the time the story began to hit the newspapers.

On the Middle East, Clark insisted that McFarlane be named to succeed State's Philip Habib as the President's Special Envoy, in preference to Shultz's candidate, Donald Rumsfeld. (Rumsfeld was later to get the job, when McFarlane moved on to bigger things.) A senior White House official gave two reasons for this choice. One was that State had "let the ball slip away," had lost the initiative as Lebanon plunged ever deeper into disaster. The second was that "White House connections and clout" were necessary to achieve maximum United States influence.

Clark's predecessors had grabbed specific operational roles; Clark preferred to exercise control through personnel. This meant that, even in an administration not engaged in much serious negotiation, Presidential or otherwise, operational power moved toward the White House. For State officials concerned about the operational Presidency, this was a new refinement on the same old threatening trend.

When Clark then left the White House for Interior and his protégé became his successor, McFarlane inherited the electronic levers of power. His good working relationship with Secretary Shultz was not apparently strained by any bold use of those levers—in part because of McFarlane's careful definition of his own role, in part because, during at least the first year and more of McFarlane's tenure, this was not an administration which pursued a very active diplomacy, whether from the State Department or the White House. But when the Reagan Administration or its successor might show greater interest in reaching actual international agreements, there remained that communications capacity to exploit for the President's personal benefit.

The growing sophistication of communications technology has been the handmaiden of the operational Presidency. The Presidential push for control produced the gadgetry for control, and the gadgetry whetted the appetite for more control, in turn. But technology has produced only the temptations and possibilities, not the motives for increased White House involvement in the details of carrying out our foreign policies. As Presidents have been held more and more accountable for success or failure abroad, as they have trapped themselves with their own rhetoric and been abused by the rhetoric of their opponents, they have thought it useful to be seen as being in charge. It must be made clear to the press and to the public that it is the President who is making the decisions, that he is up front, that he is to get the credit. And he does get public applause when it works.

But there is a price to be paid.

Within the government, the operational Presidency has cut deeply into State Department influence. Much of State's business involves the manipulation of words, the definition of the American stance on international issues in the ways most comprehensible to foreign governments. This is easy for a White House information operation to preempt—far easier, say, than decisions about complex and technical Pentagon programs. Another prime source of State power in Washington has been its role at the center of communications with foreign governments, and its primary position in receiving and analyzing information about them. If the White House can reach selectively into this State-managed system—or, worse yet, circumvent it entirely—the credibility of our representatives abroad is badly undercut. And sometimes, no one will know who is supposed to be saying what to whom.

This is not to say that State can or should make foreign policy on its own. But it can and should play a strong role in that process, and it must be able to represent the nation effectively abroad.

Moreover, when the President gets caught up in details, the traditional prescription for sensible policy making gets stood on its head. He is supposed to set policy and make the big decisions. When trapped by time-consuming operations, when plunging into a few key enterprises, he becomes like an orchestra conductor who grabs the first violin and plays it vigorously, perhaps even brilliantly. The violin may sound terrific. But the other instruments are left without clear direction. And the conductor-turned-violinist becomes so absorbed in his personal performance that he loses his sensitivity to what the other instruments are doing. The President thus loses his capacity to see things whole.

Summitry and communication with other foreign leaders most certainly can be useful. But they should remain the servant of a coherent diplomacy, rather than part of a process that twists diplomacy out of shape. No symphony can play as it should when the violinist suddenly sounds too loud.

There are also personal and political costs for the operational President. In his press conferences, he is expected to know all the facts, on the spot, in a way that Franklin Roosevelt or even Dwight Eisenhower never were. He loses something more important when he is expected to know the capital of every nation in Africa: he loses political insulation. Not all foreign-policy engagement brings public success. Most immediate efforts on international issues end in ambiguity; there may be as many losses as wins. And Eisenhower, recognizing this, could push Dulles out front to take the heat and deflect criticisms that would otherwise land in the Oval Office. Similarly, it may be that President Reagan benefited from the same pattern in his 1984 re-election campaign. His obvious and embarrassing lack of mastery of the details of his own Administration's actions abroad never seemed to hurt him with the voters. Indeed, it may have helped insulate him personally from the damage of a setback such as the Lebanon debacle. By contrast, Kennedy, Nixon and Carter were directly exposed.

A Presidency that becomes trapped by details and the drama of personal engagement, politically opportunistic, is a Presidency unable to exercise broad leadership and mobilize widespread support. In the long run, the operational Presidency threatens both the diplomacy and the domestic political fortunes it is designed to serve.

Conclusions

THE making of American foreign policy is in a perpetual state of crisis. Hardly a practitioner or commentator or scholar would quarrel with this judgment. The argument is over why and what should be done about it.

But the debate gets nowhere. In fact, the debate itself has become part of the crisis. Liberals and conservatives mostly shout at each other, with each side seeking our salvation largely through the elimination of the other. Those more or less in the center try to escape the fray by focusing on technical solutions, such as working out the proper bureaucratic balance between the Secretary of State and the President's national-security adviser. But these proposals cannot reach the larger sources of our discontent.

Some of the futility of foreign-policy debates is inherent in the subject. So much is open to reasonable argument. Current catastrophes sometimes reappear in history as occasions of farsighted courage. Or time can uncover the flimsy foundations of contemporary successes.

Yet, the evidence is powerful that a good part of what administrations have done during the last two decades has not been reasonable, even by broad standards. Too many of their actions could not be justified on the substantive merits without severe intellectual contortions.

The record suggests that the crisis or breakdown in the way we make foreign policy is a systemic one.

Our Presidents have trapped themselves in webs mostly of their own making—in basing policies on ideologies that bore little resemblance to foreign realities, and in shaping much of their action for the sake of short-term political advantages. This web has been tightened by changes in our political subculture—by the increasing power of ideological purists within the Democratic and Republican parties and by the emergence of a new Professional Elite that, unlike its Establishment predecessor, deepens rather than bridges divisions.

Congress and the news media, no longer silent partners to an imperial Presidency, have made debates still more noisy, partisan and doctrinaire. Both institutions have asserted more power without accepting more responsibility. Other divisions have become institutionalized in the clash between the enduring professional and bureaucratic perspectives of the State Department, which emphasizes long-term relations with foreign powers, and the President's White House team, whose concerns are at once more narrowly political and more broadly national. In the struggle with the Department, White House and National Security Council aides have used their access to the President and the technology of modern communications to grab control of the issues they wish to dominate. The result of all these changes has been an American incapacity to conduct a steady and sensible foreign policy.

More than a century ago, Lord Palmerston set forth his famous dictum that Britain had no permanent allies or enemies, only permanent interests. Any country's definition of its interests will evolve, of course, as domestic values change and as the world takes on new forms and problems. But serious nations do not redefine their national interests every few years, as we have been doing for most of the last two decades.

They do not suddenly make human rights a keystone of policy, only to relegate human-rights considerations to the dust bin in the next administration. They do not condemn arms sales as evil only to turn around and declare four years later that it is the world which is evil and that arms sales are therefore necessary. They do not rush headlong for détente with the Soviet Union only to return to a new kind of cold war when unrealistic hopes about future Soviet behavior go unfulfilled. They do not inaugurate a process for peace in the Middle East, as Presidents Richard Nixon and Jimmy Carter did, and then pursue a new "strategic consensus" against Moscow while neglecting Arab-Israeli negotiation, then condemn Israel for its attack on Palestine forces in Lebanon, and finally make Israel into the centerpiece of Middle East policy, as President Reagan has done. With such wild swings in policy, we cannot hope to make much headway on any of these hard international issues.

On the contrary, foreign accomplishments generally come because a nation has been able to sustain a course of action over a long period of time. To be sure, a great man like President Anwar Sadat of Egypt may seize a moment and change the course of history. But the bulk of international issues must be fought out in the trenches year after year, often after the great man has departed. Even the smallest nations such as Nicaragua or Afghanistan have been able to resist superpowers simply by refusing to do their bidding. Many international problems have their roots in centuries long past. To affect these situations, powerful nations must be able to lean on them with full weight over time.

If the Soviet Union enjoys any real advantage over the United States, it is not that its leaders are more clever and tougher than our own. It is that Soviet leaders can pursue a line of action steadily until they wear down the opposition, or until an opportunity arises. There is an old Spanish proverb: "The Devil gets his way not because he is smarter than we are, but because he has been around longer."

The costs of our inconsistency, of our systemic breakdown, have been staggering.

1. A Wounded Leadership

The costs begin at the top, with our badly wounded political leadership. Deep ideological cleavages on foreign policy were a driving force behind an unprecedented series of primary challenges to sitting Presidents—Eugene McCarthy and Robert Kennedy attacking Lyndon B. Johnson in 1968; Ronald Reagan challenging Gerald R. Ford in 1976; and Edward Kennedy taking on Jimmy Carter in 1980. By contrast, even the controversial Harry Truman had little trouble getting his party's support for another term in 1948.

Turnover has been even greater among these Presidents' senior advisers. In the last thirteen years, our four Presidents have had six Secretaries of State, five Secretaries of Defense, and six national-security advisers. Over this same period, and for fifteen years before that, the Soviet Union has had one Foreign Minister, Andrei Gromyko.

Repeatedly, party activists try to kill off ideologically offending

Presidents. And as Presidents grow weaker, they put more and more political distance between themselves and those carriers of unwelcome foreign problems, their Secretaries of State. Ford may have admired Secretary of State Henry Kissinger immensely, but he ended up disinviting the former Harvard professor from the 1976 Republican Party Convention and ostentatiously abandoning use of the word "détente," which had become synonymous with Kissinger's policies. Similar political gaps developed for Kissinger's successors: in the course of time between Carter and Cyrus Vance; almost instantly between Reagan and Alexander Haig. It is hardly coincidence that the Secretaries since 1960 with the longest tenures—Dean Rusk for eight years and William P. Rogers for nearly five—were men who not only deferred to their bosses but essentially acquiesced in major power gains by White House courtiers, McGeorge Bundy and Henry Kissinger.

2. *Organizational Disarray*

Every newly elected President since Kennedy has compounded the leadership problem by making a promise that he would not keep—that his Secretary of State would be his principal foreign-policy adviser and spokesman, and that the State Department would be the lead agency in the formulation of policy. Each stated that the national-security adviser would be primarily a "coordinator." But in practice, as Kissinger wrote in his memoirs, "every President since Kennedy seems to have trusted the White House aides more than his Cabinet."

In making such pledges, these Presidents have echoed the recommendations of virtually every public commission, organizational expert and foreign-policy commentator who has addressed the subject. To these experts, primacy for the State Department meant order and coherence; it would mitigate the growing confusion over who really spoke for the President and stress the continuity of American interests. Thus, policy might be less "political" and less oriented toward the short run.

Why did none of these Presidents deliver? One reason was that they came to see Foreign Service personnel as more interested in getting along with their foreign clients than in pressing American interests as these Presidents defined them. But another reason, increasingly important, was that an aide in the White House could better serve their political objectives. Kissinger helped Nixon stage foreign spectaculars that meshed with his 1972 election timetable. Carter, turning back broadly supported pleas to muzzle his national-security assistant, Zbigniew Brzezinski, reportedly told his second Secretary of State, Edmund S. Muskie, "I need Zbig to speak out publicly. He can go after my enemies. He can protect my flanks."

Under Reagan, the political connection has grown stronger. His first national-security assistant, Richard Allen, worked for Presidential Counselor Edwin Meese III, who, unlike Allen, knew nothing about foreign policy. And when Allen departed, he was replaced by William P. Clark, another California crony of Reagan's with a noticeably limited background in the business. Meese and Clark were political men, pure and simple. They knew the President's needs and beliefs and little more. And when Clark moved to the Interior Department, who should seek to succeed him in October 1983 but White House Chief of Staff James Baker III. In this case, the political man lost out—to a conservative national-security professional, Robert McFarlane. But the fact that Baker could come so close—even be offered the position in principle, according to White House aides—showed how far we had moved from Truman's scrupulously nonpolitical Sidney Souers, or Eisenhower's Andrew Goodpaster.

3. Widening Gap Between the President and the Bureaucracy

Dominance by White House aides has meant exclusion of the bureaucracy from much of the serious, Presidential foreign-policy business. The gap was not always so wide. Under Truman and Eisenhower, professionals were important participants in foreign-policy making. These Presidents brought only a thin layer of people from outside the professional bureaucracy into key foreign and defense positions. Under Kennedy and Johnson the number of outside experts increased, as did suspicion of career professionals. To Nixon and Kissinger, the bureaucracy was largely a gaggle of liberals and Democrats often conspiring with allies in Congress and the press against the Administration. The Carter White House seemed to consider professional civil servants and Foreign Service officers and military officers as representing only their own institutional interests, which often conflicted with the President's.

At the NSC staff, the shift began when Kennedy and Bundy moved out most of Eisenhower's career staff and gave the primary senior jobs to persons identified with their Administration. Kissinger removed almost all of Johnson's NSC aides, but most of their replacements were people already in the government. Under Carter and Reagan, there was a sizable jump in noncareer appointments. The Reagan team, the most suspicious of all about career officers, went furthest of all in applying a political and ideological test to candidates for NSC staff slots and middle-level positions in the agencies as well. Many moderate and conservative Republicans who had served under Kissinger were excluded.

The result has been a squandering of mainstream talent, and the substitution of elite professionals sometimes skilled more at making waves than at making government work. Ideological "trustworthiness" has been purchased at the price of experience and expertise. In most other countries, a change in political leadership might bring a handful of trusted outsiders into key positions. In the United States, the number reaches into the hundreds.

The influx of true believers has not ameliorated the normal competition between the White House and the State Department, State and Defense, and the like. Rather, it has added a new ideological dimension cutting across the institutional rivalries and made it far harder to resolve differences in pragmatic ways. And by weakening the bureaucracy, it has imposed on our government a painful loss of continuity.

4. The Policy Pendulum

With the bureaucracy largely cut out of the action, displaced by an ideologically polarized Professional Elite flowing in and out of government, the predictable result has been sharp swings in the content of American foreign policy. Polar views do not always prevail, but they come to have enormous impact, because they are held by many conservative and liberal activists to whom Presidents respond. So as administration succeeds administration, policy is jerked back and forth on key issues such as human rights, nuclear proliferation, and, above all, arms control.

Both Carter and Reagan were responding to ideological views prevalent among their supporters on arms control. The left wanted to go beyond "controlling" arms to real disarmament. Yet, there was nothing to show that Moscow—or Washington—was prepared for such a step. The right tended to regard arms-control talks as a Soviet device to lull the American people into a false sense of security and weaken support for higher military spending to offset alleged Soviet military superiority. With such views pulling Presidents one way and the other, it is hardly a surprise that no United States-Soviet arms-control agreement has been ratified since 1972. Ideologues are not satisfied with modest results, with taking necessary steps rather than great leaps forward.

And as Presidents swung in one direction, Congress went the other way. In 1979, the Senate made it clear that it would not approve SALT II without more spending on arms. Beginning in 1982, Congress has made its support for the Reagan buildup in strategic forces contingent upon serious efforts at arms control. Thus, we went from no arms control without arms to no arms without arms control in the space of three years. There was no change in Soviet behavior during these years; only in ourselves. In 1979, public support for arms control was marginal at best. Now heavy majorities are backing a nuclear freeze. A consensus behind sensible and effective arms-control measures cannot be created while the public and political pendulum swings so quickly.

5. *Credibility Gaps*

When Presidents are, in time, pulled toward the center, they lack credibility, for the maladies of their pasts linger on. Carter's conversion to power politics never rang quite true after his initial defense cuts and his speech about abandoning the "inordinate fear of communism." Reagan's metamorphosis on arms control is doubted today, for how could he bargain seriously with leaders who, in his words, "reserve the right to commit any crime, to lie, to cheat." Indeed, the doubt became so prevalent that many Democrats, and a number of Republicans, specifically tied their support of the new MX missile in

1983 to changes in the Administration's negotiating position vis-à-vis Moscow.

All this adds up to a permanent credibility crisis. Even if Presidents make a sincere transition from a campaign perspective to a governing one, they are unlikely to be believed if they begin from so far out in left or right field. It will seem as if they are only playing politics. And their leadership cannot be effective if Presidents are always in the position of having to prove that they mean what they say.

6. *The Narrowing Basis of Support*

Lacking broad public trust in their measured judgments, Presidents have had to struggle for majorities on most important issues. Everything is up for grabs, and Presidents are embroiled in constant fights. At best, from Nixon on, Presidents have had to put together tentative and undependable majorities that risk coming apart as soon as trouble rears its head.

To maintain their shaky support, Presidents have had to weigh in personally on almost every issue. From an arms sale to a base agreement to a vote on a weapons system, Administrations have not been able to carry their positions without the active involvement of the top man. This not only drains Presidential energy and capital, but also enhances the political content of every question. Battle lines are drawn, as the opposition smells an opportunity to hand the President a political defeat. No President can carry out foreign policy under such conditions.

7. *The Quick Fix and Political Theater*

Because administrations have not been able to count on the necessary support, they have resorted increasingly to Band-Aids and gamesmanship. When Henry Kissinger could not get Congressional support for more standard military and economic aid for South Vietnam, he called in Senator Hubert H. Humphrey and arranged to have more food aid under Public Law 480 (a position that Humphrey later reversed). Kissinger was also legendary for political theater—dramatizing his personal shuttle diplomacy, managing to have agreements that had been virtually prearranged portrayed as major breakthroughs. But after a while, ingeniousness and deviousness become fused in the public mind. In the short run, such tactics inflate reputations and help in getting through the day or the week. But they smack of manipulation, and after a while, those being manipulated tire of it.

A classic case of a quick policy fix was the decision in the Carter Administration to go ahead with the deployment of medium-range missiles in Europe. The President had seriously fractured European confidence in him by his handling of the neutron bomb and by a seeming overeagerness for arms control. It became something he had to make up for. So, when West German Chancellor Helmut Schmidt and other European leaders started applying pressure on him to respond to new Soviet missiles in the European theater, Carter and his team decided quickly and resolutely to deploy new American medium-range missiles. This, it was felt in the Administration, would turn European attitudes toward Carter around and gain needed European backing for the SALT II Treaty, and play well with domestic audiences skeptical of the President's toughness. Not nearly enough thought was given to the political problem this created for Western European governments—whether they could deliver public support for deployment, and what would be the broader effect on the tissue of European societies. But once the deployment decision was made it became necessary to the credibility of NATO to follow through.

8. The Narrow "Political Window" for Serious Diplomacy

With all the political and ideological baggage brought into the White House, and with the next election always so near, Presidents are left with a year—two at most—to conduct serious diplomacy. It takes the first twelve or eighteen months for an administration to climb down from campaign rhetoric into even modest pragmatism. The last twelve to eighteen months are consumed by the ever-expanding Presidential election season.

Presidents seeking reelection can sometimes use foreign policy to take advantage of their internal opponents, but external adversaries can take advantage of Presidents who need a political boost in their reelection drive. Richard Nixon managed to outfox Hanoi in 1972, getting a provisional peace agreement in time to help in the voting booths, then disavowing it shortly thereafter and bombing North Vietnam as a signal of future toughness. His leverage that October derived from Hanoi's apparent belief that Nixon was certain to be reelected and strengthened by a new four-year mandate. Had the race been closer, Hanoi could have exploited his need and pried more favorable terms from the United States. Jimmy Carter was highly vulnerable to the machinations of Iranian leaders during the hostage drama eight years later. Hawks in Ronald Reagan's Administration feared he would be driven to make sudden arms concessions in 1984, in order to conclude an arms pact he could use against his Democratic opponent. There was the precedent of Nixon's sloppiness on SALT I twelve years before, when—in order to enjoy a triumphant departure from Moscow—he signed an agreement with ambiguities that would plague his successors.

9. Politics and Ideology

Finally, Presidential policy often ends up reflecting a tug of war between ideological commitment and political expediency. An all-too-clear example was the Reagan Administration's Lebanon fiasco. Initially, U.S. Marines were dispatched there in the late summer of 1982 as part of a broad multilateral effort to stabilize Lebanese politics and negotiate removal of foreign armed forces. Experts knew that long-standing religious and factional rivalries might cause the newly formed Lebanese government and its reconstituted army to unravel. And as this in fact came about, it could have been presented to the American people as a regrettable local development: we had tried, but the Lebanese had been unable to get their political act together.

Instead, President Reagan fixed on the aspect of the problem that meshed with his ideology, the East-West angle. A resurgent Syria, buttressed by large Soviet arms shipments, was threatening Washington's designs and seeking to regain influence it had lost when Israel invaded Lebanon in 1982. To the President, this made everything clear: Lebanon became a test case of responding firmly to Soviet-backed military threats. But in practice this meant choosing sides in the Lebanese civil war, and thereby abandoning the neutrality necessary to sustain the role of peacekeeper.

Ideology said stand fast and respond with growing American force. But electoral politics dictated the opposite, for once 241 United States Marines were killed by an October 1983 terrorist attack and their mission was bypassed by events, Congressional and public sentiment turned sharply in favor of withdrawal. Reagan's political advisers felt the Marines had to be removed to defuse the issue in the 1984 Presidential campaign. So the President responded by moving in both directions at once. He attacked Democrats for their alleged willingness to "surrender," even after he had secretly approved, in February 1984, a plan to remove the Marines. And when he announced his decision to withdraw them, he also ordered a massive bombardment of areas around Beirut controlled by Syrian-backed Moslem forces. This could not much impede their drive toward humiliating the U.S.-backed government. But it was a way of being ideologically "tough" and politically expedient at the same time.

This was not good policy for the United States, but it was all too typical of how our government has come to perform on key international issues.

This does not mean, of course, that recent years have brought *no* constructive foreign policy accomplishments, or that politics and ideology have dominated every case, but the trend has been clear. And even were this not so, the United States can afford such behavior far less now, in the eighties, than in the days when our world power was overwhelming.

What is to be done?

The beginning of wisdom is to understand what has not worked and why, and what likely will not work and why. For until we cease chasing a legion of phantoms, fads and gimmicks, solutions will continue to elude us.

We cannot go back to the "good old days" of consensus, the Establishment, and the imperial Presidency.

Henry Kissinger, at a time when his policies were under attack, expressed a hope shared by many foreign-affairs experts: "The present ordeal of the whole nation is too obvious to require commentary. The consensus that sustained our international participation is in danger of being exhausted. It must be restored." It seems a laudable objective, the whole nation pulling together once again, but is it feasible? And apart from feasibility, did the kind of consensus Kissinger longed to recapture serve us well?

Irving Kristol may have overstated matters somewhat when he wrote that "one cannot imagine any crisis in world affairs, short of an overt military attack upon American territory, to which the American government could respond with the assurance of enthusiastic congressional and popular support." But the fact is that the United States faces policy challenges that are far more complicated than in the decade following World War II. Their very breadth and complexity mean that no single, overarching principle or doctrine can guide our response. With all of his brilliance and wiliness, Kissinger came close to harnessing the conflicting strains. But he did so mainly with mirrors—by giving each side to believe that he was doing its bidding—and not through forging agreement on basic beliefs.

Even if some overall consensus on a single policy or doctrine could be fashioned, it would not serve us well. Such a consensus inhibits needed debate and diminishes our sense of how different the problems and regions are from one another. Facts are made to fit the preordained theory, and all the facts begin to look alike. Vietnam is made into an Asian Berlin. Central America is transformed into Vietnam.

Consensus in the form of another Truman Doctrine stifles debate, creates policy paranoia, and denies the essential ingredient of policy—choice. Each Presidential act becomes "necessary." As William Graham Sumner wrote in "War," "If you want war, nourish a doctrine. Doctrines are the most frightful tyrants to which men ever are subject, because doctrines get inside of a man's own reason and betray him against himself." Doctrines may be convenient devices for manipulating public opinion and isolating political enemies, but in the end they undo and trap the authors themselves.

Without consensus on doctrine, apparent consistency may be lost, but discrimination is gained. On any specific policy issue or area, broad agreement can and should still be reached, after debate has illuminated the issues involved. Such a specific consensus could turn out to be wrong, or grow outdated, but there is a better chance of recognizing this and changing it if it is not encased in a larger, almost religious whole.

Again, Kristol saw the issue. "Consensus is what sustains an ideological foreign policy, and no great power—not the United States, not Russia, not China—can have a foreign policy that fits neatly into an ideological *Weltanschauung.*" In fact, much of our bitter current dissensus comes from activists on the right and the left seeking to impose their ideologies in a world that stubbornly proves more complicated. The problem is how to restore confidence in leaders who resist such ideologies, not how to define a new doctrine that bestows assent in advance of explanation.

Nor can the old Establishment be resurrected. The country is too diverse now even to imagine its being led by a small group of men meeting in cozy Harvard and Yale club rooms or the board rooms of Wall Street. Besides, it is clear that the Professional Elite serves a special and needed purpose in a complex modern world, that of supplying expertise.

What we need is not to long for a group and time that is irrevocably gone, but to seek to recapture the good that the old Establishment represented—namely, a centrist political force that can help the country stay on a steadier and publicly supportable policy course.

Nor need such a center force always support middle-course policies. There are occasions when steering the straight and narrow is merely a recipe for prolonging difficulties. Such was the case, we believe, in Vietnam, where our leaders could not bring themselves either to attempt a more decisive use of force or to carry out a policy of extrication. Similarly, some argue more decisive action might fit the present situation in Central America. By neither cracking down hard on abuses by the Salvadoran right nor making an all-out effort at a negotiated settlement, the Reagan Administration may well be pursuing the path of losing slowly and painfully for all. Alternatively, the United States might step back from the quagmire of internal Central American politics, and declare we could live with whatever regimes came to power in the region, so long as they did not align themselves with the Soviet Union (or Cuba). A strong center provides the fulcrum for being able to move toward more decisive action when necessary. For the most part, however, it would insist on balanced policies taking account of the full range of interests involved. Arms control, for example, would be incorporated within our broader national-security policies, but as a critical element of these policies.

As for the new Professional Elite, its strengths should be drawn upon while its excesses contained. Its expertise is needed, and the "think tanks" that it populates produce policy analyses that can be of enormous value. But increasingly, the elite seems to produce more political warfare than serious scholarship. Those who exercise political power should be more aware that extremist elements in the Professional Elite will cause them mainly political harm. For a while, their presence in Congress and the Administration will please the party faithful, but before very long, they come to discredit their bosses with their inexperience and dogmatism.

One indirect way to control their numbers and effects might be simply to reduce the flow of the elite into government, particularly those without experience and particularly at high levels. The Reagan Administration, for example, was very much better served by Under Secretary of State Lawrence Eagleburger—a veteran Foreign Service officer of conservative views—than by ideologues. In general, we believe that Presidents and senior Cabinet officers should limit sharply the number of outside experts in their administrations and rely more on career civil servants, diplomats and military officers. New ideas and fresh blood need not be excluded. But beyond the small number of veterans who fill Cabinet and senior sub-Cabinet posts, outside experts are better placed in analytical and functional jobs than in operating positions.

There is a similar case for moderation on Capitol Hill, for cutting back on personal foreign-policy aides. The size of Congressional staffs has begun to level off, as their patrons recognize the costs of having too many ambitious aides pressing them to stretch their policy time thinner and thinner. Senators and Representatives who do not plan to concentrate personally on foreign policy might eschew full-time personal-staff aides in this field. Committee staffs could then be made the prime repositories of expertise, as they once were. And most committee staff members could be pooled, once again, into a nonpartisan whole instead of reinforcing the trend toward separate Democratic and Republican staffs.

We recognize that there will likely be a world series between the Chicago Cubs and the Cleveland Indians before we witness such a transformation—or a full reversal of the flood of political appointees into government. But its unlikelihood does not render it any less desirable.

Concerning the imperial Presidency, we should not seek its return any more than that of the Establishment. Presidents are indeed better situated to represent the national interest and lead than the multiheaded institution of Congress. At the same time, Presidents have no monopoly of wisdom or fact. Now that legislators have had the opportunity to pursue so many Executive Branch secrets, there is a general realization that they contain no magic and that legislators themselves possess the essential information for major policy choices.

When Congress is serious about influencing matters, that will inevitably make the President's job more complicated. It may hinder persistent and effective action, and confuse other nations. We will pay this kind of price for having our particular Constitutional system. But there are better and worse ways for the two branches to behave within this system, and, all too often, Congress has been plainly irresponsible.

During most of the Vietnam War, Congress criticized the President, but essentially played the game of "the President knows best." Only at the very end did Congress legislate and take responsibility for preventing further American military involvement. In 1979 and 1980, Congress flayed the SALT II Treaty, but did not reject it. It was left in political limbo. In 1981, Congress required the President to certify human-rights progress in El Salvador as a condition for further aid, but then did not hold him to the terms, half expecting and half forcing him to lie about the progress in order to get the money. Congress has extolled the War Powers Resolution, which demands notification when American troops are about to enter combat, then failed to hold Presidents strictly to the law.

What this adds up to is a form of fake activism, playing to the media and public grandstanding, complicating Presidential action without offering alternatives, and avoiding responsibility.

One partial remedy is some de-reform and recentralization of power and responsibility in Congress. Scholars who have looked at the problem have proposed such sensible steps as realigning committee jurisdictions and enhancing the powers of the leadership. For example, the Senate's Foreign Relations and Armed Services committees could be merged into a Committee on National Security, at least for the purpose of dealing with issues like arms control and overseas-base rights. But given continuing claims to political turf, the prospects are very dim.

A broader approach would be to seek general agreement on the proper roles of the two branches. Warren Christopher, Deputy Secretary of State under Carter, suggests a "new 'compact' between the Executive and the Congress on foreign-policy decision making based on mutually reinforcing commitments and mutually accepted restraints." Congress "would affirm the President's basic authority to articulate and manage our foreign policy." The Executive would "cooperate fully with the Congress" in helping it fulfill its role, obedient to the laws, in a "renewed spirit of bipartisanship." Former Senator J. William Fulbright has offered a slightly different formulation of "leaving to the executive the necessary flexibility to conduct policy within the broad parameters approved by the legislature." These are sensible and worthy constructions, but without teeth and dependent on larger changes in attitudes that we discuss below.

Nor can we draw much hope from a whole second range of prescriptions, from constitutional revolution to bureaucratic engineering.

A number of groups and individuals, seeing how politics has fed the breakdown of our foreign-policy system, have proposed a variety of Constitutional changes—to reduce political pressures on our leaders, or to bridge the gap between branches by electing Presidents and legislators on the same timetable. One hardy perennial is the idea of extending terms for Congressmen from two to four years. Quite apart from foreign-policy concerns, this seems to strike many observers as a good idea, but few are prepared to invest the time necessary to gain passage.

Of greater potential interest is the suggestion for changing the Presidential term from four to six years with no right to run again. This goes directly to the point that recent Presidents seem to have spent more of their first term with their eye on the second than has been sound for either domestic or foreign matters. The interest in reelection may, of course, dampen the impact of ideology as the President reaches for broad voter support. Nonetheless, Presidential exploitation of foreign policy for short-term political gain has been sufficiently flagrant to make it unwise to dismiss this proposal out of hand. The longer term would certainly eliminate the problem of Presidents compromising the national interest to promote their own reelection.

But the prospect of suffering through six years of an inadequate President is a major drawback. The six-year term thus becomes an idea that cures one malady at the risk of possibly precipitating greater ones. The interest in it is, however, a good sign, a sign that people are beginning to appreciate that partisan politics has intruded too far into our foreign policies.

Organizational and international experts have sought smaller solutions in the form of rejiggering the balance of forces within the Executive Branch. They have argued, and with some wisdom, that Constitutional and basic institutional reforms are beyond our practical grasp, that major difficulties lie within the Executive Branch, and that the best way to deal with them is to strengthen the hand of the Secretary of State against the encroachments of White House advisers in general and the national-security adviser in particular. One rationale is that the State Department somehow represents enduring and long-range American interests, while the White House personnel, the courtiers, take a more narrow political view of things. Again, there is considerable power to this argument, but attempts to implement the prescription have failed repeatedly.

Henry Kissinger wrote in his recent memoir: "Though I did not think so at the time [when I was national security adviser], I have become convinced that a President should make the Secretary of State his principal adviser and use the national security adviser primarily as a senior administrator and coordinator to make certain that each point of view is heard." Yet he wrote also: "For reasons that must be left to students of psychology, every President since Kennedy" has leaned the other way. Seen from the White House, the departments represent parochial rather than national interests. Also, what counts is "propinquity," or "the opportunity to confer with the

President several times a day." Thus Kissinger explained why his retrospective recommendation stood little chance. The reason, not at all mysterious, lies not in Freud, not in "psychology." Rather, it can be found in the good and bad reasons of domestic and bureaucratic politics.

Egged on by White House aides, our recent Presidents have come to see the State Department as almost the enemy. To them, the department thinks only of relations with country X and not with the political lumps the President will have to take in helping country X. It lacks the broader view to make tradeoffs with economic and military concerns, and with legitimate domestic interests. Also, professional diplomats tend to stress flexibility as opposed to policy or purposeful behavior. They tend to roll with the tide rather than seek specific accomplishments or solve problems, things Presidents like to do and legitimately get credit for. All these things are true, though all are only part of the larger political explanation for Presidential behavior.

But State and its officials also have much to offer—expertise on international realities; a needed brake on the White House proclivity to seek political spectaculars; an important institutional memory. Moreover, a Secretary who gives priority to his Presidential connection can make the department work for him—and the President—and not the other way around.

In practice, a case can be made for making either the Secretary or the national-security assistant the President's primary adviser. And it is unrealistic to try to structure in advance how any President will run his own show. Usually the President himself will not know what he wants, what arrangements and which people he feels comfortable with, until he has been in office for some months. And however the system is constructed, power will flow to those whose style and views are most compatible with the President's own.

That said, there are several points a President should bear in mind, whatever bureaucratic wiring diagram he prefers or promulgates:

> The personalities of his three top advisers—the Secretaries of State and Defense and the National Security Assistant—will be central in setting the tone and public perception of his Adminis-

tration. And the personality of the NSC adviser matters most, given his propinquity to the Oval Office. The President should therefore choose his lieutenants not only for their separate talents, but with an eye to how they will work together.

If the Assistant is to be the director of policy formation, he should be strictly an inside operator. To avoid the massive confusion of the last decade and more, the adviser should not speak publicly, engage in diplomacy, nor undermine the Secretary with Congress and the news media. A President who cannot demand that of the adviser and an adviser who cannot so forbear are simply asking for catastrophe for their Administration. But while enforcing these constraints, the President must also make it clear that the Assistant is the person in charge.

If the Secretary, as senior Cabinet member and head of the agency with expertise, is to be the leader, the President must go out of his way to help the Secretary sustain such a role. And he must insist that the national-security adviser not undercut this effort. Given the political advantages of the adviser, the Secretary needs all the help he can get.

Since it is likely that the President will not know his own mind or really grasp the abilities and chemistry of his big three for several months, he might consider avoiding instant reorganization plans. Just take the existing mechanism, use it for a while, see how things really work, and then formalize the relationships he finds effective. There would be some embarrassment, to be sure, but far less than the silliness and personal ugliness that arise from situations where the formal structure is at variance with the real one.

Presidents should also give serious thought to the idea of a stronger career component of the National Security Council staff. The penalty for amateurism in this key operation has been high.

It is time to recognize that the dimensions and depths of our problem go well beyond bureaucratic plans and personalities. We must reexamine our fundamental attitudes and ways of thinking about foreign-policy making. We are only fooling ourselves if we believe that anything less will do.

We are not speaking here of seeking an end to politics or a transformation of human nature. Rather, we are in search of an awareness of what we have been doing to ourselves so that we can bend toward moderation and civility. Our nation is not so weak, as we face the world, that we must deny ourselves these virtues. Nor are we so strong that we can afford to be without them. This is what is needed: some intellectual honesty; a return to common sense in thinking about foreign policy; some reflection about personal self-interests; and a reassertion of national interests.

Intellectual Honesty

If there is any one truth to policy debates, it is that there is no one truth. Truth or good sense or a reasonable course of action, whatever it is to be called, runs over a spectrum of possibilities. Within this range, there is room for legitimate debate, given uncertainties of judgment and fact. There are few who have participated in the political or scholarly arenas who would venture to deny this. And yet, debates are conducted in the Administration, Congress, the media, and even scholarly journals as if the right course was plain, unseen only by fools and knaves. Such debate rewards those with the verbal precocity to demolish opposing arguments without ever addressing them.

Our system presses politicians to pretend, perhaps even believe, that they have answers for all the questions. It surrounds them with expert and polemical aides and intellectuals whose profession it is to supply these answers. It connects them to ideological factions which insist that they deliver on the "mandate" once the election is won. It provides them with forums such as Congress and the media, not to grapple with the difficulties of the real world, but to score points over political adversaries without having to accept responsibility themselves.

But in the real world, policy making is very different. It is a process of knowing generally where you want to go and then making endless mistakes in getting there. The honesty is in recognizing when a mistake is made; courage lies in altering action accordingly. To think one possesses a monopoly on the knowledge of the right course is to blind oneself to mistakes and to forbid oneself to cooperate with those who think somewhat differently. On so many issues, we have reached the point where participants in the policy process will not support anyone who varies from the right course by more than a fraction. That meant that liberals were even unable to work with liberals in the Carter administration, and conservatives with other conservatives in the Reagan administration.

There can be no serious debate of policy toward El Salvador, for example, until there is honest recognition that the causes of revolution there are internal and, to some extent, external. A history of poverty and repression are mixed together with Cuban, Nicaraguan and Russian backing in an inseparable mass. Each has to be dealt with. To deny either the internal or external elements is to distort the debate, warp policy, and weaken grounds for solid domestic backing. But a debate focusing on facts can shed light on the relative importance of the various causes and force proponents of particular solutions to explain how they would accommodate these facts or alter them.

Our policy toward the Soviet Union will never mature until the debate embraces the assumption that Soviet leaders can make and keep a deal *and* that they are tough and ambitious wielders of power whose values differ profoundly from our own. Both factors have to be taken into account, not just in words to appease critics, but in deeds. Nor can the Soviet Union be at once "the evil empire" to be isolated and checked by military force alone, and the recipient of virtually unilateral American concessions. For example, President Reagan cannot say the Soviets are behind all our problems in Central America and Lebanon, and at the same time grant them sweeping assurances that we will not embargo grain sales for foreign-policy reasons. Perhaps if his condemnations were less absolute and his concessions less sweeping, this would suggest a new pragmatism and sophistication. But the extreme nature of both sets of actions points toward other explanations—an excess of politics and ideology. It is not the kind of coherent behavior that inspires trust and support.

By 1983, the normal policy-making system had so broken down that Reagan had to establish outside commissions to find supportable approaches on both Central American policy and arms control with Moscow. These Kissinger and Scowcroft commissions, for all the sense they might try to inject into our debate, show not so much the adaptability of our system as its bankruptcy. Patchwork emergency operations are needed because the participants in the process cannot even talk reasonably to each other.

But precisely because our divisions are so deep, and our debates so ideological and unreal, such commissions can't solve our problems either—at least not for long. The Scowcroft Commission on Strategic Forces triggered reformulation of Reagan's arms control position and saved the MX missile from a 1983 death on Capitol Hill. But in 1984 and 1985, MX was again on the chopping block amidst continuing debate on strategy and arms control. As for Kissinger's National Bipartisan Commission on Central America, the "consensus" it generated scarcely outlasted the report's January publication.

To go beyond such emergency patchwork operations, what we badly need is honest debate on facts and goals, conducted with both civility and frankness. The question is not whether to debate, but how.

Common Sense on Policy

Ambiguity is in the nature of power and political relationships. Our allies, let alone the Soviets, will never be what we want them to be. They have their own power, values and interests that must be accommodated and checked. Every political relationship requires duality and suppleness. None can be reduced to either-or and succeed.

In one of those rare moments of official self-revelation, Edward J. Derwinski, the State Department Counselor under Shultz and a former Congressman, displayed the rigidity of mind that can condemn us to failure at home and abroad. In a newspaper interview, he said that one of the biggest surprises in making the transition was that Congress and the State Department still resembled a couple on their first date, with "a lack of familiarity" about each other. "Congressmen," he continued, "tend to approach issues that fall into black and white categories. The approach of the State Department is to look at all sides, study all options, try for compromise. Well, when you're in the political world, you approach things in a more precise and hard-nosed fashion. You either come down for or against aid to Turkey or Greece, for or against a base agreement with the Philippines."

It is not just Congressmen who have come to see things in either-

or, or for-and-against terms. That attitude predominates among the Professional Elites and the media as well. There is an unwillingness to allow Presidents to pursue goals with seemingly conflicting means—to confront and cooperate with the Soviet Union; to have contacts with, and provide aid to, countries such as Angola and Nicaragua, yet bargain hard and employ threats if necessary; to push allies toward a coherent trade policy with Moscow, without banging them over the head.

But effective foreign policy requires, in Thomas Hughes's words, "functioning despite ambivalence." It requires persisting in involvements that serve our interests, while we remain aware of their drawbacks and costs. It requires that we abandon illusions of easy victories or magical doctrines.

In short, we need a more common-sensical and realistic conception of foreign policy, of the limits of American and any other nation's power, of how real accomplishments require persistence, slogging in the trenches year after year, adjusting our initiatives so that other nations can, in their own interests, accept and support them. To this end, Presidents and their principal aides should give the highest priority to public foreign-policy education—to spelling out the difficulties, describing the sources and limits of our influence, laying out realistic and not phony alternatives, and then explaining the policies they have chosen to pursue.

New Awareness of Real Political Self-Interests

Perhaps the hardest choir to preach to is the one manned by politicians, elites and the media. Who is to tell them what their self-interests are in getting reelected, or positioning themselves for high office, or entertaining and making money? As long as their behavior brings immediate rewards, why should they change, or worry about the longer-term effects on our policy-making system?

The nightly newscasts of the major television networks continue to devote large chunks of time to feature stories or "soft news" at the expense of hard news and explanations of problems. But revenues also continue to go up. Legislators continue to get reelected, most of the time. Members of Professional Elites continue to claim top positions for the advocacy services they render.

But, for Presidents, recent history offers a more ambiguous message, one that should cause aspirants and those in office to ponder their self-interests again. Presidents Johnson, Ford and Carter all jeopardized reelection prospects through mishandling of foreign affairs. And as White House aides pointed toward the 1984 campaign, they feared Ronald Reagan's shaky record as world leader would emerge as his greatest political weakness. For while Congress and the media have not earned good grades for remedying their own shortcomings, they have not hesitated to highlight and harass Presidents who have misused American foreign policy for ideological and political ends. This, in turn, has damaged Presidential standing with the public at large, though Reagan escaped retribution at the polls.

Presidents have made and reinforced their own traps. In gaining office and in beating back opponents, they have continued to speak and act on the basis of both the Munich and Vietnam analogies—Don't lose and don't intervene. They pretend that we can be number-one militarily and not raise taxes, that their efforts will produce success if only their domestic critics leave them alone. The public, then, holds them to standards they cannot meet.

No matter how debased now the coin of our political rhetoric, words still have meaning and consequences. If Presidents promote illusions of easy and quick success, if they suggest new magic formulas, they risk not only later disillusion and defeat, but a deeper public cynicism about leadership in general. And as they exaggerate the differences between their own approach and the "fundamentally flawed," if not *wicked*, views of their opponents, they create discontinuities and uncertainties that harm us abroad.

Responsible foreign policy may be the most powerful potential political weapon for Presidents. It is the one area where they are clearly looked to above all and by all. To the extent that they are seen to be acting sensibly and in the national interest, they can in fact strengthen their political power and standing. That Presidents may look back on the records of their predecessors and see their self-interest in statesmanship—that remains our best hope for changing attitudes and thinking.

There is a moral here for would-be Presidents. What they say in pursuit of the White House *will* be held against them, should they get there. None of their recent predecessors was able to cast aside easily or inexpensively his extreme campaign rhetoric after inauguration.

Yet, in their bitter primary battles, we found Walter Mondale and Gary Hart trading foreign policy charges of the most primitive sort: Mondale accusing Hart of indifference to Communism in Central America; Hart implying that his adversary would make El Salvador another Vietnam. As each tried to skewer the other on one horn of the peace-containment dilemma, he laid the political trap in which he himself would have become ensnared had he reached the White House. For he too would have been blamed for failing to live up to the rhetoric that came before responsibility.

Adlai Stevenson, in accepting his party's nomination for President in 1952, dwelled on just this point. "What does concern me in common with thinking partisans of both parties," he said, "is not just winning this election, but how it is won, how well we can take advantage of this great quadrennial opportunity to debate issues sensibly and soberly." And "even more important than winning the election is governing the nation." Then: "Let's talk sense to the American people. Let's tell them the truth, that there are no gains without pains, that we are now on the eve of great decisions, not easy decisions . . ."

The Public and a Return to Responsibility

What happens in the world today has more impact on Americans than did events at any time in our history. Issues of war and peace, trade and finance affect our lives intimately and directly. Yet, public ignorance and indifference remain appalling. Recent polls show that vast majorities have no idea what is going on in Central America, whose side we are on, or what is happening in the arms talks with Moscow. We believe this results, at least in part, from an all-too-justified public cynicism—a belief that few of their leaders are making much sense, that most of their leaders are simply playing politics, and that there is not much that can be done about any of it. Yet, for better or worse, the affairs of our democracy will be settled by the people. And they should be, for the common sense of the general public is a better guide than others yet devised. It is the public, moreover, which ultimately reaps the benefits of our policies, or pays the price.

How can the public contribution to our policies be more informed, more constructive? There is no way to educate everyone, or to halt the special-interest, oft-ideological advocacy that floods corridors on Capitol Hill and mailboxes throughout the land. But there is a special mediating and moderating role to be played by those three to ten million Americans who hold the trust of their communities by virtue of their leadership positions in business, educational and civic organizations, and in state or local politics. This group does have the background, education, access to power, and above all, the responsibility to inform itself and act.

These are neither the few thousand members of elites and Washington politicians nor the multitudinous silent majority. They are people with the practical wisdom born of success in working with others, in leading cooperative enterprises. It is they who benefit most from the democracy that has enabled them to flourish. And it is they, more than any other group of Americans, who can insist on a middle course, practical programs for living with and in the world, and an end to the twisting in the winds of our own making.

This leadership stratum is out there, in communities across the nation, waiting to be energized by national political leaders and would-be Presidents who are prepared to talk sense. They know that something is wrong, but they are not quite sure what it is. When they hear common sense, they will respond and recognize the leaders who have the courage to voice it. They have it in their power to become guardians of the national interest.

These community leaders can be the core of a new and very broad American center, a new political culture that will demand and allow Presidents, working with the Congress, to formulate and conduct a serious foreign policy. There are no ready miracles and recipes for doing this. It requires an alteration of attitudes, a new civility, and a return to some old principles.

> We must understand once again that democracy and partisan politics are symbiotic but not synonymous. Our policies must be arrived at by democratic means; this does not mean that every issue must be joined for political advantage.
>
> We must remind ourselves that there is a difference between a leader and a politician. Leaders require political skills and

must be political animals, but they also must serve purposes larger than the pursuit of power and survival. To act politically on behalf of a policy is necessary in a democracy; to use a policy for the sake of politics is mere destructiveness.

We have to learn anew the difference between policy debates and ideological warfare. Neither the Congress nor the people will follow a President for long unless they understand the sense of what he is doing and why he is not doing other things. It is easy to make prudence appear like appeasement or Cold War hysteria; far too often, that is what ideologues of the right and left who dominate our public debates have done.

Finally, we must appreciate the distinction between confidence and consensus. It may be impossible for us to reestablish the kind of foreign-policy consensus we had years ago. We are too diverse and the world is too complex. And even if we could achieve a new consensus, we might end up once again entrapping ourselves in its "self-evident" truths, once again disregarding realities abroad and holding our Presidents to impossible doctrinal standards. But confidence is certainly something we can choose to repose in leaders who show, through their steady and sensible policy approach, that they merit it. And confidence is something we can show in each other, as we debate issues with the aim not of generating heat but of shedding light.

It is a matter of self-interest for our political leaders and our political institutions. In the long run Congress has gained little or nothing from playing the role of spoiler, from living by the light of being able to say, "I told you so." The burgeoning Congressional foreign-policy staff has not only been a thorn in the side of the Executive Branch, but a growing burden for legislators as well. Presidents have complicated their own (and others') lives by putting forward organizational designs that they and their aides proceed to ignore. None of them seems to have profited by playing the game of balancing the Secretary of State against the Secretary of Defense against the National Security Assistant. And organization charts cannot substitute for a process which enables the key players and institutions to gain confidence in the policies of the President.

Most of all, it is not in the interest of our future Presidents to continue transforming so much of their foreign policy into the world of domestic politics. In the end, every last one of them in the last twenty years has been damaged by the reality and the perception that they were using foreign policy for their own partisan purposes. Only Presidents can lead foreign-policy making. Only they can get issues resolved in ways that endure in the bureaucracy and in the Congress. But they can do this only if they restore the conviction that in matters of foreign policy, they can set aside partisan politics and really represent the national interest. They, together with other American leaders, must return to responsibility. Otherwise, we will continue to be, as we face the world, our own worst enemy.

Notes

Introduction: Foreign Policy Breakdown

PAGE

13 "As Chancellor I worked . . ." *Washington Post,* May 5, 1983.

13 "the impulse to view . . ." *Time,* April 9, 1984, p. 67.

20 "Counter-elites emerged . . ." William Schneider, "Public Opinion," in Joseph S. Nye, Jr., ed., *The Making of America's Soviet Policy* (New Haven: Yale University Press [for the Council on Foreign Relations], 1984).

24 "when repeated failures . . ." Thomas L. Hughes, "The Crack-Up: The Price of Collective Irresponsibility," *Foreign Policy,* No. 40 (Fall 1980), p. 35.

I. Presidents: the Triumph of Politics

PAGE

33 "We're not going to talk . . ." Glenn D. Paige, *The Korean Decision* (New York: Free Press, 1968), p. 141.

34 Foreign policy in prewar elections. Robert A. Divine, *Foreign Policy and U.S. Presidential Elections* (New York: New Viewpoints, 1974).

36 "violated the rules . . ." George W. Ball, *The Past Has Another Pattern: Memoirs* (New York: Norton, 1982), p. 145.

36 "No one expects . . ." *Ibid.,* p. 446.

37 Kissinger's advice to Ford. Gerald R. Ford, *A Time to Heal* (New York: Harper & Row, 1979), pp. 373–74.

37 "political balance of power . . ." *Facts on File,* July 16, 1980, p. 534.

38 On public opinion and Presidential decisions, see, for example, S. Verba et al., "Public Opinion and the War in Vietnam," *American Political Science Review,* June 1967.

40 "like an investment prospectus . . ." Harry S. Truman, *Memoirs,* Vol. II, *Years of Trial and Hope* (Garden City, N.Y.: Doubleday, 1956).

40 The conservatives needed . . . See Dean G. Acheson, *Present at the Creation, My Years in the State Department* (New York: Norton, 1969), pp. 219–25. In Acheson's account, the State Department draft was not revised by Truman, but was brokered within the government by Acheson himself.

40 "I believe . . ." Truman, *Memoirs,* Vol. II, p. 106.

40 "We must take a positive stand . . ." *Ibid.,* pp. 107–8.

41 "After I delivered my speech . . ." *Ibid.,* p. 106.

41 "the congenital aversion of Americans . . ." George F. Kennan, *Memoirs 1925–1950* (Boston: Little, Brown, 1967), p. 322.

41 "requests of foreign countries . . ." *Ibid.*, pp. 321–22.
42 "I do not want and will not accept . . ." Robert A. Divine, *Foreign Policy and U.S. Presidential Elections 1940–1948*, pp. 171–283.
42 "Free men in every land . . ." Truman, *Memoirs*, Vol. II, pp. 242–43.
44 "pro-Communist group . . ." See Richard M. Freeland, *The Truman Doctrine and the Origins of McCarthyism* (New York: Knopf, 1971), p. 347.
44 War fears and losing the Cold War. See Paige, *Korean Decision*, pp. 45–48.
44 McCarthy and the "Commicrats." Robert Griffith, *The Politics of Fear, Joseph R. McCarthy and the Senate* (Lexington, Ky.: University of Kentucky Press, 1970), p. 123.
45 "This was a time when . . ." Louis Halle, *The Cold War as History* (New York: Harper & Row, 1967), pp. 219–20.
45 "growing unpopularity paralleled . . ." Kenneth N. Waltz, "Electoral Punishment and Policy Crises," in *Domestic Sources of Foreign Policy*, ed. James N. Rosenau (New York: Free Press, 1967), p. 273.
45 "[Truman] was not able to make . . ." Walter Lippmann, *New York Herald Tribune*, August 24, 1956, quoted in John Spanier, *The Truman-MacArthur Controversy* (New York: W. W. Norton, 1965), p. 270.
46 "the negative, futile and immoral policy . . ." Robert A. Divine, *Foreign Policy 1952–1960*, p. 135.
46 "We must tell the Kremlin . . ." *Ibid.*, p. 51.
47 A few days later, Dulles . . . elaborated. *Ibid.*
47 Polish-American voters . . . *Ibid.*, pp. 55, 84.
47 Eisenhower explained . . . "falling dominoes." "The President's News Conference of April 7, 1954," *Public Papers of the Presidents: Dwight D. Eisenhower, 1954* (Washington, D.C.: Government Printing Office, 1960), p. 383.
47 Despite having thus dramatized . . . See Leslie H. Gelb with Richard K. Betts, *The Irony of Vietnam: The System Worked* (Washington: Brookings Institution, 1979), pp. 51–60.
48 Eisenhower himself seems . . . Divine, *Foreign Policy . . . 1952–1960*, pp. 35–36.
48 As Samuel F. Wells argues . . . Samuel F. Wells, Jr., "The Origins of Massive Retaliation," *Political Science Quarterly*, Vol. 96, No. 1 (Spring 1981), p. 34.
49 "If a President wants to leave . . ." John E. Mueller, *War Presidents and Public Opinion* (New York: John Wiley, 1973), p. 233.
50 When Adlai Stevenson and Chester Bowles . . . Divine, *Foreign Policy . . . 1952–1960*, p. 233.
50 "Astonishingly [Robert Divine writes]" . . . *Ibid.*, p. 235.
50 "Twenty-three years ago . . ." Michael Roskin, "From Pearl Harbor to Vietnam: Shifting Generational Paradigms and Foreign Policy," *Political Science Quarterly*, Vol. 89, No. 3 (Fall 1974), p. 572.
51 "But the voters weren't willing . . ." Samuel Lubell, "Personalities vs. Issues," in Sidney Kraus, *The Great Debate* (Bloomington, Ind.: Indiana University Press, 1962), pp. 160–161.
51 Playing on these post-Sputnik fears . . . See Warren E. Miller, "Voting and

Foreign Policy," in *Domestic Sources of Foreign Policy,* ed. James N. Rosenau (New York: Free Press, 1967), p. 217.

51 The promise of a new . . . R. A. Divine, *Foreign Policy . . . 1952–1960,* p. 282.

52 The new President . . . Peter Wyden, *Bay of Pigs: The Untold Story* (New York: Simon and Schuster, 1979), pp. 65–67.

52 It was not only that . . . *Ibid.,* p. 100.

52 When one of Kennedy's closest . . . *Ibid.,* p. 165.

53 Walt W. Rostow recalls . . . Rostow, *The Diffusion of Power—An Essay in Recent History* (New York: Macmillan, 1972), p. 270.

53 "Kennedy told Rostow that . . ." Arthur M. Schlesinger, Jr., *A Thousand Days—John F. Kennedy in the White House* (Boston: Houghton Mifflin, 1965), p. 339.

54 Kennedy's White House Chief of Staff . . . Kenneth O'Donnell, "LBJ and the Kennedys," *Life,* Vol. 69, Aug. 7, 1970.

54 "symbol of the tragic irresolution . . ." Morton Berkowitz, P. G. Bock and Vincent J. Fuccillo, *The Politics of American Foreign Policy* (Englewood Cliffs, N.J.: Prentice-Hall, 1977), p. 137.

54 "If at any time . . ." Elie Abel, *The Missile Crisis* (New York: Bantam Books, 1966), pp. 11–12.

54 Senator Richard Russell . . . *Ibid.,* p. 102.

58 By 1951 . . . polls showed . . . George Belknap and Angus Campbell, "Political Party Identification and Attitudes Toward Foreign Policy," *Public Opinion Quarterly,* Fall 1951.

58 By 1964, voters were moving away . . . See Norman H. Nie, Sidney Verba and John R. Petrocik, *The Changing American Voter* (Cambridge, Mass.: Harvard University Press, 1976).

60 In 1963, for the first time . . . *Public Opinion,* August/September 1979, pp. 30–31, and Lawrence W. Lichty, "Video vs. Print," *The Wilson Quarterly,* Special Issue 1982, p. 54. (Respondents were permitted to name more than one source.)

61 "If I don't go in now . . ." David Halberstam, *The Best and the Brightest* (Greenwich, Conn.: Fawcett, 1972), p. 643.

62 "Frank, the next time you want . . ." Ronald Steel, *Walter Lippmann and the American Century* (Boston: Little, Brown, 1970), p. 559.

62 "I knew that if we let Communist . . ." Doris Kearns, *Lyndon Johnson and the American Dream* (New York: Harper & Row, 1976), pp. 252–53.

64 Later analysis revealed . . . Milton J. Rosenberg, Sidney Verba and Phillip Converse, *Vietnam and the Silent Majority: The Dove's Guide* (New York: Harper & Row, 1970), p. 49.

64 Nixon's campaign theme on Vietnam . . . Rowland Evans, Jr., and Robert D. Novak, *Nixon in the White House—The Frustration of Power* (New York: Random House, 1971), pp. 76–77.

66 "American cannot—and will not—conceive . . ." Richard Nixon, "U.S. Foreign Policy for the 1970's," A Report to the Congress by President Richard Nixon, Feb. 18, 1970, p. 6.

67 On Vietnam, he used . . . Marvin Kalb and Bernard Kalb, *Kissinger* (Boston: Little, Brown, 1974), pp. 384–85.

68 All this helped Nixon take . . . *New York Times*, May 23 and June 2, 1972.

70 "Every four years, the United States . . ." *New York Times*, May 14, 1976.

70 a "morality in foreign policy" plank . . . Gerald R. Ford, *A Time to Heal*, p. 398.

71 "What if," he asked, "we had been able to . . ." *Ibid.*, p. 437.

71 Carter "did much to help Americans . . ." Stanley Hoffmann, "Requiem," *Foreign Policy*, Spring 1981, p. 3.

72 And while there was public . . . See John Rielly, "The American Mood: A Foreign Policy of Self-Interest," *Foreign Policy*, Spring 1979.

73 Polls in mid-1978 showed . . . *Public Opinion*, July/August 1978, pp. 24–25.

75 "Were Mr. Carter's advisers . . ." *New York Times*, July 11, 1978.

79 "foreign policy of self-interest . . ." John E. Rielly, "The American Mood."

81 If we could not "defend ourselves . . ." Ronald Reagan, "Central America: Defending Our Vital Interests," Address to the Congress, April 17, 1983.

81 The push of the Munich analogy . . . For a more detailed history of the development of the Munich and Vietnam paradigms and their political force, see Michael Roskin, "From Pearl Harbor to Vietnam: Shifting Generational Paradigms and Foreign Policy," *Political Science Quarterly*, Vol. 89, No. 3 (Fall 1974). As Ole R. Holsti and James N. Rosenau show, the relative weight given these two viewpoints has never been dependent on generational differences, as one might suppose. Indeed, differing attitudes on foreign policy show a much better correlation with occupation than with age. See their "Does Where You Stand Depend on When You Were Born?," *Public Opinion Quarterly*, Vol. 44, No. 1 (Spring 1980).

82 By the second year of Reagan's Presidency . . . See Bruce Russett and Miroslav Nincic, "American Opinion on the Use of Military Force Abroad," *Political Science Quarterly*, Vol. 91 (1976); Russett and Donald R. Deluca, " 'Don't Tread On Me': Public Opinion and Foreign Policy in the Eighties," *Political Science Quarterly*, Vol. 96, No. 3 (Fall 1981); and Alvin Richman, "Public Attitudes on Military Power, 1981," *Public Opinion*, December/January 1981–82.

82 And by February 1983 . . . *New York Times*, Feb. 6, 1983. See also John E. Rielly, ed., *American Public Opinion and U.S. Foreign Policy 1983* (Chicago: Chicago Council of Foreign Relations, 1983), for similar data.

83 And our elites . . . See, for example, Verba et al., "Public Opinion and the War in Vietnam."

83 As Kenneth Waltz has pointed out . . . Kenneth N. Waltz, "Electoral Punishment and Foreign Policy Crises," p. 291.

84 Harris polls show . . . James L. Sundquist, *The Decline and Resurgence of Congress* (Washington, D.C.: Brookings Institution, 1981), pp. 352–53.

84 While polls show continued . . . "Opinion Roundup," *Public Opinion*, October/November 1979, p. 35.

84 Anthony Downs has argued . . . Anthony Downs, *An Economic Theory of Democracy* (New York: Harper & Row, 1957).

85 "the more hostile or cynical . . ." Samuel P. Huntington, *American Politics: The Promise of Disharmony* (Cambridge, Mass.: Belknap Press, 1981), p. 4.

85 For our institutions . . . *Ibid.*, pp. 16–18.
85 Both liberal and conservative Americans . . . Louis Hartz, *The Liberal Tradition in America* (New York: Harcourt, Brace, 1955), p. 286.

II. From "Establishment" to "Professional Elite"

PAGE
92 "Few men in the State Department . . ." Don Kurzman, *Genesis 1948: The First Arab-Israeli War* (New York: New American Library, 1970), p. 216.
103 "I would add that . . ." Godfrey Hodgson, "The Establishment," *Foreign Policy*, Spring 1973, p. 13.
106 "a sort of Praesidium . . ." Richard Rovere, *The American Establishment and Other Reports, Opinions and Speculations* (New York: Harcourt and World, 1962), p. 8.
106 For critical accounts of Council history, see Leonard and Mark Silk, *The American Establishment*, (New York: Basic Books, 1980), Chapter 6; John Franklin Campbell, "The Death Rattle of the Eastern Establishment," *New York* magazine, Sept. 20, 1971; and Robert D. Schulzinger, "Whatever Happened to the Council on Foreign Relations?," *Diplomatic History*, Fall 1981.
107 "The Council plays a special part . . ." Joseph Kraft, "School for Statesmen," *Harper's*, July 1958, p. 68.
109 "No, but I have a well-known brother . . ." Unpublished transcript of Senate Foreign Relations Committee hearing of Feb. 12, 1981, U.S. National Archives, p. 71.
122 As has been noted . . . Nelson Polsby, *Consequences of Party Reform* (New York: Oxford University Press, 1983).

III. Congress and Press

PAGE
130 "In 1954 he consulted . . ." See Richard H. Immerman, "The Anatomy of the Decision Not to Fight: Multiple Advocacy or Presidential Choice?" Paper presented to Presidency Research Group, 1982 Annual Meeting of American Political Science Association, Denver, Colorado.
130 "lacked constitutional authority to act . . ." Dwight D. Eisenhower, *Mandate for Change* (Garden City, N.Y.: Doubleday, 1963), pp. 468–69. See also James L. Sundquist, *The Decline and Resurgence of Congress* (Washington, D.C.: Brookings Institution, 1981), pp. 114 ff.
131 "The U.S. position," *Congressional Record*, Sept. 26, 1963, p. 18205.
132 "highly unlikely . . ." J. William Fulbright, "American Foreign Policy in the Twentieth Century Under an Eighteenth Century Constitution," *Cornell Law Quarterly*, Vol. 47 (Fall 1961), p. 7.
133 "no longer prepared . . ." Henry A. Kissinger, *Years of Upheaval* (Boston: Little, Brown, 1982), p. 357.
133 For broad analysis of the Congressional revolution, see Thomas E. Mann

and Norman J. Ornstein, eds., *The New Congress* (Washington, D.C.: American Enterprise Institute, 1981) and Lawrence C. Dodd and Bruce I. Oppenheimer, eds., *Congress Reconsidered,* second edition (Washington, D.C.: Congressional Quarterly Press, 1981).

136 "lived all their lives ... citizens." U.S. Senate, Special Committee on the Termination of the National Emergency, "Emergency Powers Statutes: Provisions of Federal Law Now in Effect Delegating to the Executive Extraordinary Authority in Time of National Emergency," Nov. 19, 1973, pp. 111, 1.

137 ... from 2030 to 10,190." Harrison W. Fox, Jr., and Susan Webb Hammond, *Congressional Staffs: The Invisible Force in American Lawmaking* (New York: The Free Press, 1977), p. 171. For committee staff numbers, see Norman J. Ornstein et al., *Vital Statistics on Congress, 1982* (Washington, D.C.: American Enterprise Institute 1982), pp. 114–15. For a broader analysis, see Michael J. Malbin, *Unelected Representatives: Congressional Staff and the Future of Representative Government* (New York: Basic Books, 1980).

139 "Maybe if you ..." Peter Wyden, *Bay of Pigs: The Untold Story* (New York: Simon and Schuster, 1979), p. 155.

140 "the only known vessel ..." James Reston, *The Artillery of the Press: Its Influence on American Foreign Policy* (New York: Harper & Row [for the Council on Foreign Relations] 1967), p. 66.

140 "a perceptively growing," Chalmers M. Roberts, *The Washington Post: The First 100 Years* (Boston: Houghton Mifflin, 1977), p. 384.

140 "Our job in this age ..." Reston, *Artillery of the Press,* pp. vii–viii.

141 "It seems now more ..." Cronkite quoted in Peter Braestrup, *Big Story,* 2 vols. (Boulder, Col.: Westview Press, 1977), p. 134.

141 ... the *Post*'s "coming of age" ... David Halberstam, *The Powers That Be* (New York: Alfred A. Knopf, 1979), p. 578.

141 ... the "cooperative, competitive ... most important," *New York Times,* June 19, 1971.

147 "potential for electoral damage." Charles W. Whalen, Jr., *The House and Foreign Policy: The Irony of Congressional Reform* (Chapel Hill, N.C.: University of North Carolina Press, 1982), p. 148.

148 On Turkey, see the case study by Ellen B. Laipson, "Congressional-Executive Relations and the Turkish Arms Embargo," Congressional Research Service for the House Foreign Affairs Committee, Congress and Foreign Policy Series, No. 3, June 1981.

151 our "collective irresponsibility," ... Thomas L. Hughes, "The Crack-Up: The Price of Collective Irresponsibility," *Foreign Policy,* Fall 1980, pp. 33–60.

151 "an American newspaper correspondent ..." *The Twenty Years Crisis, 1919–1939: An Introduction to the Study of International Relations* (New York: Harper Torchbooks, 1939; reprinted 1964), p. 164.

152 And one scholar ... Lawrence Lichty, "Video vs. Print," *The Wilson Quarterly,* Special Issue 1982, pp. 53–55.

152 "... only 60 percent ..." Richard L. Rubin, *Press, Party, and Presidency* (New York: Norton, 1981), p. 154.

153 ... a "redefinition of what is 'news' ..." *Artillery of the Press,* p. viii.

154 On television reinforcing skepticism, see William Schneider, "Public Opinion," in Joseph S. Nye, Jr., ed., *The Making of America's Soviet Policy* (New Haven: Yale University Press [for the Council on Foreign Relations], 1984).

156 "a return to the situation . . ." John G. Tower, "Congress Versus the President," *Foreign Affairs*, Winter 1981/82, p. 243.

156 "It is the responsibility . . ." Edwin Meese in *Washington Post*, April 15, 1983.

156 "decision, activity, secrecy, and . . ." *The Federalist* (New York: Random House, Modern Library), p. 454.

156 "an invitation to struggle . . ." Edwin S. Corwin, *The President: Office and Powers* (New York: New York University Press, 1940), p. 200.

156 "separated institutions . . ." Richard E. Neustadt, *Presidential Power: The Politics of Leadership* (New York: Signet, 1964), p. 42.

IV. Courtiers and Barons

PAGE

166 "an integral part . . ." and "further enlargement"—see Anna Kasten Nelson, "National Security I: Inventing a Process (1945–1960)" in Hugh Heclo and Lester M. Salamon, eds., *The Illusion of Presidential Government* (Boulder, Col.: Westview Press, for the National Academy of Public Administration, 1981), pp. 234–35.

167 "writing caustic . . ." Daniel M. Smith, "Robert Lansing," in Norman A. Graebner, ed. *An Uncertain Tradition: American Secretaries of State in the Twentieth Century* (New York: McGraw-Hill, 1961), p. 121.

169 "that from first to last . . ." Dean Acheson, "The President and the Secretary," in Don. K. Price, ed. *The Secretary of State* (New York: Prentice-Hall, for the American Assembly, 1960), p. 33.

169 "I can't trust . . ." Robert J. Donovan, *Conflict and Crisis: The Presidency of Harry S. Truman, 1945–48* (New York: Norton, 1977), p. 157.

169 "long cable reports . . ." Harry S. Truman, *Memoirs*, Vol. II, *Years of Trial and Hope* (Garden City, N.Y.: Doubleday, 1956), p. 75.

170 On Truman and the NSC, see also Anna Kasten Nelson, "Inventing a Process," pp. 235–45.

170 "serve as a continuing organization . . ." Truman, *Memoirs*, Vol. II, *Years of Trial and Hope*, p. 60.

170 "non-political confidant . . ." Untitled description of role of NSC Executive Secretary, n.d., Truman Library, Sidney Souers Papers, Box 1.

171 "The gap between . . ." Neustadt in Francis H. Heller, ed. *The Truman White House: The Administration of the Presidency 1945–1953* (Lawrence, Kan.: Regents Press of Kansas, for the Harry S. Truman Library Institute, 1980), p. 112.

172 The NSC data is drawn from Eisenhower Library, Index to NSC Series, Ann Whitman File; letter from Gordon Gray to President Eisenhower, January 13, 1961; and George Weber to McGeorge Bundy and Walt W. Rostow, "The Output of the NSC in the Eight Years of the Eisenhower Administration," Jan. 27, 1961, Kennedy Library, National Security Files, Box 283.

172 "Assume that . . ." Robert Cutler, "The Development of the National Security Council," *Foreign Affairs,* April 1956, pp. 448–49.
173 On Eisenhower-Dulles relations, see Richard H. Immerman, "Eisenhower and Dulles: Who Made the Decisions?" *Political Psychology,* Autumn 1979, pp. 3–20; and Fred I. Greenstein, *The Hidden-Hand Presidency: Eisenhower as Leader* (New York: Basic Books, 1982).
174 "led to showdowns . . ." Townsend Hoopes, *The Devil and John Foster Dulles* (Boston: Atlantic, Little-Brown, 1973), p. 140.
174 had failed "to meet the standard . . ." and ". . . disregard of proper forbearance . . ." Hoopes, p. 155.
175 "President in Council" . . . Gordon Gray, Group Oral History Interview on Eisenhower Administration policy making, June 11, 1980, National Academy of Public Administration (NAPA), p. 67. For more on how the Eisenhower system operated, see I. M. Destler, "A Lost Legacy? The Presidency and National Security Organization, 1945–60," paper presented to United States Military Academy History Symposium, West Point, New York, April 1982.
175 "expressed a strong preference . . ." Cutler, "Guidance from President on Conduct of Council Meetings," April 2, 1958, Eisenhower Library, Whitman File, Administration Series.
175 "the process of coordination . . ." Robert H. Johnson, "The National Security Council: The Relevance of Its Past to Its Future," *Orbis,* Fall 1969, p. 715.
176 "when some paperwork . . ." and ". . . staff secretary now." Oral History of Andrew J. Goodpaster, Columbia Oral History Collection, quoted with permission; and confirmed by personal interview with Goodpaster, Jan. 18, 1982.
177 ". . . the political side of things." Goodpaster, Columbia Oral History.
177 "Tending the door . . ." Bundy to Kennedy, "The Use of the National Security Council," Jan. 24, 1961, Kennedy Library, National Security Files, Box 183.
177 "began monitoring all meetings . . ." John S. D. Eisenhower, *Strictly Personal* (Garden City, N.Y.: Doubleday, 1974), p. 234.
178 "hidden hand" . . . Fred I. Greenstein, *The Hidden-Hand Presidency: Eisenhower as Leader* (New York: Basic Books, 1982).
178 "Andy, our policy is clear . . ." to ". . . I've lost my last friend." Interview and Correspondence with Goodpaster, Jan. 18, 1982, and Oct. 3, 1983.
179 "a nonpartisan study . . ." U.S. Senate, Committee on Government Operations, Subcommittee on National Policy Machinery, *Organizing for National Security,* Vol. I, Foreword, p. iii.
180 "losing the cold war" . . . *Ibid.,* Vol. II, pp. 267, 272, 273.
180 "The authority of the individual . . ." *Ibid.,* Vol. I, p. 16.
180 "the President may—and does . . ." Statement of May 24, 1960, *Ibid.,* Vol. I, p. 579.
181 'supported the conclusions . . ." Nelson, "Inventing a Process," p. 256.
181 Gordon Gray letter of resignation. Letter is in Eisenhower Library.
182 "dangerous influence" . . . Personal interview with Richard E. Neustadt, Feb. 28, 1982.

183 "should be avoided by all means . . . by General Goodpaster," Neustadt, "Memorandum on Staffing the President-Elect," Oct. 20, 1960, Transition Papers, John F. Kennedy Library, pp. 7–8, 20.

183 "Introducing McGeorge Bundy . . ." Neustadt to Clifford, Jan. 3, 1961, JFK Transition Papers.

185 Bissell to succeed Dulles . . . Peter Wyden, *Bay of Pigs: The Untold Story* (New York: Simon and Schuster, 1979), p. 96.

186 "you ought to have in hand . . ." Bundy to JFK, n.d., Kennedy Library, Presidential Office files, Box 62.

187 "The President called it . . ." Bundy to Kenneth O'Donnell, Jan. 5, 1962, Kennedy Library, National Security files, Box 283/18.

188 "a memorandum on the present . . ." Kennedy to Rusk, Aug. 16, 1961, Kennedy Library, Presidential Office files, Box 68a.

189 "JFK agrees . . ." Handwritten note on Lois G. Moock to Bromley Smith, June 22, 1962, Kennedy Library, National Security Files, Box 290.

190 "The manner and style . . . give it another prod." Oral History Interview with Robert W. Komer, Kennedy Library, Part 4, Oct. 31, 1964, pp. 20–22, quoted with permission.

191 "*not*—though this is . . ." "Memorandum for the President: Current Organization of the White House and National Security Council for Dealing with International Matters," June 22, 1961, Kennedy Library, National Security Files, Box 283/15, unsigned.

191 "A quick look . . ." Bundy to President, March 24, 1961, Presidential Office File, Box 62, Kennedy Library.

192 "Clearance of the Bowles Cuba speech . . ." Bundy to the President, Sept. 17, 1962, Presidential Office files, Box 62a, Kennedy Library.

192 "It is true that . . ." Oral History Interview with Bromley Smith, Tape #1, July 29, 1969, Johnson Library, p. 18.

193 "1. What progress are we making . . ." Kennedy to Bundy, May 15, 1963, Kennedy Library, Presidential Office files, Box 62a.

197 "not been consulted . . ." Harriman to LBJ, November 9, 1964, Johnson Library, National Security Aides file: Bundy, 73c.

199 "work principally, but not necessarily . . ." Johnson Press Conference of March 31, 1966, in *Public Papers of the Presidents,* 1966, pp. 385, 388.

201 "Neither the formal arrangements of the 1950s . . ." "Organization for the Management and Coordination of Foreign Affairs," a final report of the President's Task Force on Government Organization, Oct. 1, 1967.

202 "The reaction to the war . . ." Bill D. Moyers, "One Thing We Learned," *Foreign Affairs,* July 1968, p. 664.

202 "From the outset . . . as crucial." *RN: The Memoirs of Richard Nixon* (New York: Grosset & Dunlap, 1978), p. 340.

203 "The security gap . . ." Radio address of October 24, 1968, portions reported in *New York Times,* Oct. 25, 1968.

204 "all Departments concerned . . ." Richard M. Nixon, "U.S. Foreign Policy for the 1970's: A New Strategy for Peace," Report to Congress, Feb. 18, 1970, p. 22.

204 "came to deal increasingly . . ." Henry Kissinger, *White House Years* (Boston: Little, Brown, 1979), p. 29.

208 "Given the improbable combination . . ." David K. Hall, "The National Security Assistant as Policy Spokeman, 1947–1981," paper prepared for delivery at the American Political Science Association Annual Convention, New York City, Sept. 3, 1981, p. 29.
212 "I had seen . . ." John Hersey, *Aspects of the Presidency* (New Haven: Tichnor and Fields, 1980), pp. 227–28.
212 "I think we worked together . . ." Gerald Ford, *A Time to Heal* (New York: Harper and Row, 1979), p. 29.
213 "wear only one hat." *Ibid.*, p. 325.
217 And according to Brzezinski. Zbigniew Brzezinski, *Power and Principle* (New York: Farrar, Straus, Giroux, 1983), p. 62.
219 "heading the operational staff . . ." Brzezinski quoted in *New York Times*, Dec. 17, 1976.
219 "Next to members of my family . . ." Jimmy Carter, *Keeping Faith* (New York: Bantam Books, 1982), p. 54.
222 "a shockingly unhealthful situation . . ." George Ball, *The Past Has Another Pattern* (New York: Norton, 1982), p. 462.
222 "painful" debate . . . Cyrus Vance, *Hard Choices* (New York: Simon and Schuster, 1983), p. 328.
222 Then he "got up and left." Jimmy Carter, *Keeping Faith*, p. 450.
224 He "let it be known . . . and not anything else." *New York Times*, Oct. 6, 1980.
225 "The present Administration . . ." Address of Oct. 19, 1980, reprinted in *New York Times*, Oct. 20, 1980.
237 the only initiative of Reagan's first term . . . For detail, see Strobe Talbott, *Deadly Gambits: The Reagan Administration and the Stalemate in Nuclear Arms Control* (New York: Alfred A. Knopf, 1983), ch. 6.
238 "one place where less would be more.' McGeorge Bundy, "Mr. Reagan's Security Aide," *New York Times*, Nov. 16, 1980.

V. The Operational Presidency

PAGE
244 The Map Room in the White House. Oral History interview with George M. Elsey, The Harry S. Truman Library, May 1974.
245 "the only place . . . rapidly dismantled." Elsey interview.
249 "she communed with him . . ." I Kings 10:2.
250 Eisenhower played by that rule . . . For the history of this and earlier periods of summit diplomacy, see Elmer Plischke, *Summit Diplomacy* (College Park, Md.: University of Maryland Press, 1958), and Keith Eubank, *The Summit Conferences 1919–1960* (Norman, Okla.: University of Oklahoma Press, 1966).
250 "I conclude," he wrote . . . Dean Rusk, "The President," *Foreign Affairs*. April 1960, p. 361.
250 And too popular. . . . Throughout the 1950s, despite the Cold War sentiment, polls showed support by a majority of Americans for summit meetings with Soviet leaders. See Hazel Gaudet Erskine, "The Cold War: Report from the Polls," *Public Opinion Quarterly*, Summer 1961, pp. 303–6.

251 Lloyd George was using a topographical map . . . Sir Harold Nicolson, *Peacemaking 1919* (London: Constable, 1933), p. 333.
251 Roosevelt included his son Elliott . . . Eubank, *Summit Conferences*, p. 67.
252 the line was not, ironically . . . *New York Times*, April 5, 1983.
255 Iranian militants used the meeting . . . Cyrus Vance, *Hard Choices* (New York: Simon and Schuster, 1983), p. 373.

Conclusions

PAGE
272 "one cannot imagine any crisis . . ." Irving Kristol, "Consensus and Dissent in U.S. Foreign Policy," in *The Legacy of Vietnam*, Anthony Lake, ed. (New York: New York University Press, 1976), p. 91.
273 "Consensus is what sustains . . ." *Ibid.*, p. 100.
276 "a new 'compact' between . . ." Warren Christopher, "Ceasefire Between the Branches," *Foreign Affairs*, Summer 1982, p. 998.
276 "leaving to the executive . . ." J. William Fulbright, "The Legislator as Educator," *Foreign Affairs*, Spring 1979, p. 726.
276 variety of Constitutional changes . . . Lloyd N. Cutler, "To Form a Government," *Foreign Affairs*, Fall 1980, pp. 126–43.
277 "Though I did not think so . . ." Henry A. Kissinger, *White House Years* (Boston: Little, Brown, 1979), pp. 30ff.
282 "Congressmen," he continued . . . *New York Times*, July 1, 1983.
283 "functioning despite ambivalence." Thomas L. Hughes, "The Crack-Up," *Foreign Policy*, Fall 1980, p. 49.

Index

ABOUT THE AUTHORS

I. M. DESTLER is a Senior Fellow at the Institute for International Economics, Washington, D.C. His previous positions include Senior Associate at the Carnegie Endowment for International Peace (where he directed the project on executive-congressional relations) and at the Brookings Institution, Staff Associate to the President's Task Force on Government Organization, and staff assistant on Capitol Hill. He is the author of ***Presidents, Bureaucrats, and Foreign Policy*** and *Making Foreign Economic Policy.*

LESLIE H. GELB is the National Security Correspondent of *The New York Times.* He has served as Director of Politico-Military Affairs at the Department of State and Deputy Assistant Secretary of Defense for Policy Planning and Arms Control, and worked in the U.S. Senate. He was also a Senior Fellow at the Carnegie Endowment for International Peace and the Brookings Institution. His book, *The Irony of Vietnam,* won the 1980 Woodrow Wilson Award for the best book published on government, politics, or international affairs.

ANTHONY LAKE is a Five College Professor in International Relations at Mount Holyoke College. He was Director of Policy Planning for the U.S. State Department, in charge of the State Department transition for the President-elect (1976–77), Director of the International Voluntary Services, and a member of the National Security Council staff (1969–70). He served in Vietnam and Washington as a Foreign Service Officer in the 1960s. He is the author of *The "Tar Baby" Option: American Policy Toward Southern Rhodesia* and contributing editor of *The Legacy of Vietnam*.

Printed in the United States
By Bookmasters